The Heritage of the Reformation

The Phoenix Series

Edited by JAMES LUTHER ADAMS

I shall die with my nest, and I shall multiply my days as the Phoenix.
—Job

Similarly that precious bird the Phoenix manifestly teaches us the laws of resurrection....Not unwillingly nor unforseeing does it die....
Then after a space it rises up in the joyous mound, not a shadow but the truth, not an image but the very Phoenix, not another but, although better, yet the same bird as before.
—St. Zeno

For it dies that it may live.
—*The Phoenix*, attributed to Lactantius

The
Heritage
Of The
Reformation

By

WILHELM PAUCK

University of Chicago

Library Edition, THE FREE PRESS, *Glencoe, Illinois*

Trade Edition, BEACON PRESS, *Boston, Massachusetts*

1950

PRINTED IN THE UNITED STATES OF AMERICA

By The Modern Franklin Co. Chicago, Illinois

15535

Table of Contents

Part I

The Reformation

CHAPTER 1

Luther and the Reformation

T HE Reformation stands once more in the center of attention. Many of those who try to understand the troubles
of our civilization in terms of historical tradition feel compelled to assign to the Reformation a significant influence
upon the modern mind. There are some who are persuaded
that only a rediscovery of the faith of the Reformers will bring
about the renewal of Christianity which they believe to be a
pre-condition of the reconstruction of the common life. There
are others who make the Reformation responsible for many
of the ills of the present day. Many ascribe to Luther in particular the responsibility for the shaping of the German mind.
Some even go so far as to consider the German Reformer as
one of the spiritual ancestors of National Socialism. Much of
this is nothing but historical fantasy. It has arisen either from
ignorance or from the will to distort historical facts for purposes of propaganda. The power of such arbitrary opinions
could be discounted if the common conceptions of the major
tenets in the teachings of the Reformers were sounder than
they generally are.

It is instructive to examine some of these ideas. First of all,
I must note the interesting fact that the Reformation and particularly the work of Luther are generally seen as the seed-beds
of either authoritarianism or of individualism.

I

It is often said that Luther paved the way for modern
authoritarianism, particularly in the political sphere, by his
opposition to the radical political and economic movements of
his time and by his encouragement of political authority in
the new evangelical churches. This judgment is generally ap-

1

plied to the Lutherans also. As a matter of fact, this criticism
of Luther's Reformation is determined by a strange inter-
mingling of judgments concerning Luther and the Lutherans.
The development of Lutheranism, particularly in Germany,
is viewed in such a way that Luther himself is made responsible
for the development of Lutheran churches under the influence
of later historical conditions, and thus Luther appears as the
father of that political conservatism which was characteristic of
the majority of German Lutherans during the nineteenth
century.

Conversely, modern Lutheranism is identified with decisions which were imposed upon Luther and his immediate followers by the conditions and requirements of the sixteenth
century. It is strange that, in this connection, the historical
differences between the Lutheranism of Germany and that of
other, especially the Scandinavian, countries are almost entirely overlooked, so that what Lutheranism has become in
Germany is regarded as the representative expression of Luther's whole work.

Another, almost completely opposite, opinion views Luther's
Reformation as the main source of modern *individualism*. This
judgment is, of course, inspired by the work of the modern
historians who are wont to mark the beginning of modern civilization by the year 1517, when Luther began the attack upon
medieval Roman Catholicism which was to result in the movement of the Reformation. But while it is quite right to attribute decisive significance to Luther's deed which destroyed the
claims of papal supremacy over the whole of human life, it is
not permissible to interpret this deed as if it had been inspired
by a spirit akin either to the individualism of the Renaissance
or to the individualistic freedom of the eighteenth and nineteenth centuries. For Luther protested against papal authority
not because he desired to pit the authority of his own mind
against that of the papal church, but because he found it
irreconcilable with the Word of God which he had rediscovered
in the Bible. Luther can therefore hardly be regarded as the
pioneer of that secular individualism which found its most
definitely marked expression in political liberalism, nor can he
be considered as the pathfinder of that religious individualism
which is the attitude of so many modern men.

It is not surprising that Roman Catholics should be most prone to attribute to Luther an individualistic spirit and to make him then responsible for that divisiveness of modern civilization which has found expression in the modern cultural crises. They are inclined to idealize the unity of the cultural life which, under the leadership of the church, supposedly prevailed in the Middle Ages, and in consequence of this idealization to lay the responsibility for the disunity of modern life at the door of Luther and the Reformers, hoping in the meantime that modern men will see the errors of their ways and return to the obedience of the only institution of salvation.

Such is the view of the celebrated neo-Thomist Jacques Maritain. In one of his early books, entitled *Three Reformers* which, by the way, he has never repudiated, he makes a vicious attack upon Luther. He treats him, together with Descartes and Rousseau, as if there prevailed a continuity between the "revolutions" which are associated with these names. He suggests in particular that the religious subjectivism of Luther, the philosophical subjectivism of Descartes, and the social subjectivism of Rousseau were woven of one cloth. In his mind there is no fundamental difference between Luther's saying at Worms "Here I stand; I can do no other," and Descartes' slogan *Cogito, ergo sum*. In his judgment, both statements reflect a spirit of revolt against the religious-cultural unity represented by medieval Catholicism and its philosophy.

A similar, but much more guarded and cautious, appraisal of Luther is to be found in the most remarkable history of the German Reformation by a Roman Catholic. It was written by Joseph Lortz, Professor in the Roman Catholic Theological Faculty in the University of Münster, under the title, *Die Reformation in Deutschland*. (It was published in 1940 by Herder in Freiburg-Breisgau.) The very irenic, ecumenically-minded author concludes that Luther was not a good listener (*"Luther war kein Hörer"*). By this he means that the Reformer did not know how to obey, because he desired to identify his own self with the truth (or better: to inject himself into the truth) by which he was to live. In his opinion, Luther's trouble was that he was too much of a religious personalist who made personal commitment the essence of religion itself. Lortz considers this an attitude of mind which must inevitably lead to an heretical dissolution of the objective, super-personal authority of the Church. In other words, he too sees the main feature of the Reformation and of its spirit in an individualistic and, in the end, subjectivistic way of believing and thinking. In all this he has touched on the most important difference between Roman Catholicism and Protestantism. He observes correctly that Luther's conception of faith was that of a personal trusting relationship between man and God, but he fails to understand that while this faith is something utterly different from obedience to the authority of the Church, it is also not an individualistic religiousness. Throughout his life, Luther fought against two fronts: on the one hand, against the heteronomous religious tyranny of the Pope and, on the other hand, against the autonomous religious arbitrariness of the sectarians, whom he named *"Schwärmer."* His own position was that of a theonomous Biblicism, i.e., in the Bible he found the Word of God by faith in which God could become *his* God. Thus he overcame a heteronomous objectivism which excludes personal commitment, as well as an autonomous subjectivism which disregards super-personal authority.

It is understandable that Roman Catholics have difficulty in comprehending this teaching of Luther, particularly in view of the fact that Protestantism itself has moved away from it to such an extent that it has almost lost it. For Protestant Orthodoxy has exchanged the heteronomy of the papal tradition for the heteronomy of a wrong Biblicism and of creedalism, while Protestant Modernism has renewed the religious autonomy of the Reformation sectaries by regarding religious experience, psychologically, historically, and sociologically understood, as the only adequate source of the Christian life.

II

However one estimates the merits of the theology of Karl Barth (and I believe that serious questions must be raised concerning the adequacy of his interpretation of the Christian Gospel), it is impossible to deny that by setting his dogmatic theology in contrast both to Roman Catholic and "modern" Protestant teachings he has brought all theologians once more face to face with the main issue of Luther's thought. But Protestants, particularly those of America, are hardly able to tolerate this confrontation with Luther's teaching! They have lost the sense of the vitality of Luther's Reformation to such an extent that they continually misunderstand some of its most vital tenets. They commonly interpret Luther's fight against papal authority as a battle for the personal right of everyone to believe as he pleases. In harmony with this view, it is customary among them to understand the Lutheran doctrine of the universal priesthood of believers as if it asserted that everyone is to be his own priest. What Luther actually taught was that faith is indeed a very personal decision—a decision for God as he has disclosed himself in Jesus Christ and not for what anyone might choose to be his god—and that one who has been given by the Holy Spirit the power of this decision is henceforth related to his fellowmen in love and in unselfish service. No insistence recurs more frequently in Luther's sermons than this, that everyone must do his own believing just as everyone will have to do his own dying. But in thus impressing the very personal character of faith upon his hearers, Luther never was unmindful of the fact that in the Christian community no one is ever left alone. So he assured his congregation also of the comfort which would come to each one of them in his hour of death, for then, so he said, all the angels and the saints, yea, the whole Church would be with him. In this same spirit he proclaimed the glorious teaching that each believer, having become a son of God by virtue of his faith, must be a priest to his fellowmen, a mediator between God and man.

This shows that Luther had a deep sense of the fellowship-character of the Church and that when he preferred to describe the Church in the words of the Apostle's Creed as the *communio sanctorum* he desired to deny both an ecclesiastical institutionalism and a non-churchly atomism. In view of this, it is surprising to note that, in his book entitled *What is Christianity?*, the distinguished editor of the *Christian Century*, Dr. Charles Clayton Morrison, makes the Reformers, and particularly Luther, responsible for what he calls the "Protestant heresy," namely, the substitution of the concern for personal salvation for the community-character of the Christian faith. He attributes to the Reformers an attitude which has become general in modern Protestantism under the influence of Pietism and secular individualism, and he goes so far as to say that "the church which the Reformers had in mind was merely in their minds." He writes this in connection with his discussion of the Reformers' teaching on the invisibility of the Church. He overlooks the fact that Luther specifically asserted that by characterizing the true Church as invisible he meant to call attention to its spiritual nature without denying its concreteness as if it had to be viewed "Platonically," as he put it.

Dr. Morrison's major concern, namely, the affirmation of the "historical" community-character of Christianity (Augustine stated it in the sentence: "Christ and the Church belong together") is sound, but it is regrettable that due to his misconception of the faith of the Reformation he has failed to see that in attacking the individualistic perversion of Christianity by modern Protestants he might have claimed the authority of the Reformers as his allies.

Another misunderstanding of Luther's spirit, which is widespread among Protestants, is closely related to this erroneous view of the unsocial and un-churchly character of the Reformation. It concerns Luther's position in the Peasants' War. There is no need to defend Luther for the extreme harshness of his writings against the revolters. Even when one takes the crudeness of his age into account, his anger and demand for punishment appear as excessive. But the criticism commonly levelled against him in connection with his relation to the peasants is not primarily directed against his personal behavior but against the principles which guided him. It is said that he was unable to see the social responsibility imposed upon him as the leader of the Reformation and that he was a cultural defeatist. Yet the nature of the decision imposed upon him by the peasants' revolt was such that these general criticisms do not seem pertinent. Luther opposed the peasants not because he did not sympathize with their demands for social justice but because it seemed to him that, insofar as they identified their cause with his, they were using his religious demand for the universal freedom of the Word of God in order to bolster their own economic and political ends. When the revolt had broken out (even before the peasants had received Luther's reply to their communication to him), and when it proved to be a leaderless, plan-less, destructive revolution, Luther found himself face to face with a decision between anarchy and tyranny. He recognized both as evil. Yet he regarded anarchy as an evil greater than tyranny, and he called upon the princes ruthlessly to break the rebels. He never justified tyranny as such and by his words addressed to the princes, not only after the blood-bath of the Peasants' War but also throughout his life, he again and again condemned it. Luther was here confronted with a concrete historical situation of most fearful import. It is certainly superficial to say that what he did was inspired by a lack of Christian social responsibility. One wonders what his critics, had the same concrete choice been put before them, would have done.

III.

So far I have discussed certain pretty general misconceptions of Luther's teaching which clearly sap the vitality of the Reformation in our day. I now turn to the views recently expressed by two distinguished leaders of American Protestantism which, because they will find an echo in wide circles, are very important. These views concern the character of the Reformation.

I turn to an article by Professor William C. Bower, published in *Christendom* (Summer, 1944) under the title "Protestantism's Inner Conflict." Its main thesis is that contemporary Protestantism is faced by the dilemma of having either to choose between the Renaissance and the Reformation, its "two essentially different historical sources," or to decide for a synthesis between the two. Professor Bower characterizes the "two sources of Protestantism" as follows. The Reformation, he says, was "a reaction from orthodox Roman Catholicism." He wants it noted "that with the exception of certain important doctrines, such as that of salvation by faith, that of transubstantiation, and the authority of the Bible," this revolt against Catholicism "was chiefly in the realm of ecclesiastical practice." As a result, he believes, the theology of Protestantism has for the most part moved well within the orthodoxy of Catholicism. The Renaissance, on the other hand, was a "reaction from the whole intellectual, social and political system of the Middle Ages. As such it was a reaction against Catholicism as only one phase of medieval culture. . . . It focused attention upon the world of nature and of man as distinguished from the supernatural and otherworldly." By placing the emphasis upon inductive reason, inquiry and experimentation, it became "the fountainhead of liberalism"; in it "the structural foundations of the modern world" were laid.

Under the influence of these two sources, Professor Bower writes, the history of Protestantism must be seen as marked by two tendencies—"toward liberalism on the one hand, and toward a reaffirmation of a traditional medieval orthodoxy on the other." The choice of contemporary Protestantism, as he sees it, is either to return to the "orthodox Catholic origin of Protestantism," involving a renunciation of "the liberalism that derives from the Renaissance" together with "self-reliance, the social gospel, and rational religion," or "to go forward to an even more radical application of the methods of empirical and experimental thought to the problems of religion and life." Professor Bower advocates that the second alternative be chosen, but he also states that "it is devoutly to be hoped that [Protestantism] will not lose the fundamental and enduring values that it has inherited through its long and significant orthodox tradition."

This whole view is remarkable, so it seems to me, not on account of its plea for a certain kind of Protestant liberalism, but because of its rather unusual interpretation of Protestantism in general and of the Reformation in particular. It cannot be doubted that there exists in Protestantism the dilemma of which Dr. Bower speaks. However, when one searches for its historical roots, one is guided not to the Reformation and the Renaissance, but to the Reformation and the Enlightenment. Liberal Protestantism has arisen from the latter movement. The origins of this movement lay in part in the Renaissance insofar at least as it can be said that the culture that had been planted in the Renaissance came to full blossoming only in the Age of Reason. The full unfolding of the Renaissance had been retarded by the Reformation, as Troeltsch has pointed out in his analysis of modern civilization, but the Reformation and the cultural conditions which it produced made it possible for the intellectual culture of the Renaissance to flourish under new auspices in the so-called "modern" centuries. Only if one takes this rather complicated cultural process into account, is it permissible to say that Protestantism as we know it originated in the Reformation *and* in the Renaissance. But in such a case, it must be recognized that the dependence of Protestantism upon the Renaissance was indirect rather than direct. However, even with such qualification, this is a rather unfortunate characterization of Protestantism. A historically much more correct analysis would derive Protestantism from only one source, the Reformation, and attribute the rise of Protestant Liberalism to the transforming influence of the intellectual forces of the Enlightenment upon Reformation-Protestantism. That Professor Bower speaks of two sources of Protestantism, the Renaissance and the Reformation, is, I suspect, due not only to his rather simplified interpretation of the cultural beginnings of modern history (for the actual relations between the Renaissance and the Reformation were, except for Humanism, very slight), but also (and primarily) to his failure properly to understand the spiritual nature of the Reformation.

It is certainly astonishing that he can say that the Reformers' "revolt against Catholicism was chiefly in the realm of ecclesiastical practice." For as a matter of fact, ecclesiastical practices were of secondary significance to all Reformers, and particularly to Luther. Their opposition against the Papacy and their criticism of the Mass belong to the realm of practice, to be sure, but they were inspired, first and last, by religious and theological considerations for the proper understanding of the Gospel. In the light of this, it is surprising that Professor Bower can suggest that except for "certain important doctrines such as that of salvation by faith, transubstantiation, and the authority of the Bible," the theology of Protestantism, insofar as it was inspired by the Reformation, moved within the orthodoxy of Catholicism. For precisely the doctrines of salvation by faith and of the Bible made all the difference in the world in the contrast between the Reformation and Roman Catholicism.

Indeed, one must go so far as to say that wherever Protestantism ceases to derive its life from the faith in the forgiving grace of God as the Bible witnesses to it and as the Reformers rediscovered it, it is cut off from the sources of its spiritual life For the difference between Protestantism and Roman Catholicism does not lie in the field of world-views and philosophies, as Professor Bower seems to believe, but in the realm of the religious relation of men with God. If the difference were primarily philosophical and intellectual, Roman Catholicism

would not take Protestantism as seriously as it does. The Roman
Church has always known how to come to terms with changing
world-views. Its adoption of Aristotelianism in the Middle
Ages, its alliance with the Renaissance, and the growth of
Neo Thomism in our day prove this fact. Also in Protestantism
the concern with intellectual and secular world-views has been
of secondary importance. But what matters most decisively is
whether one understands Christian salvation as by grace and
faith or as by works, as an absolute reliance upon the divine
word of forgiveness or as confidence in the sufficiency of man.
With this issue, Professor Bower should have dealt more profoundly than he has done. That he did not do so, is, in my
opinion, due to the fact that he failed to see the real issue of
the Reformation.

IV

The other contemporary Protestant leader of whom I must
speak is Reinhold Niebuhr. Because of his sharp attacks upon
Liberalism, he is often characterized as a "neo-orthodox" theologian. In my opinion, this characterization of him is not fitting.
The only real neo-orthodox theologian of our time is Karl
Barth. But it must be acknowledged that Reinhold Niebuhr
has re-discovered a very important element of the Christian
faith which has been forgotten and neglected in modern Protestantism, although it lived in the very heart of the religion
of the Reformers. This element is the teaching on sin. Niebuhr's interpretation of sin as pride and un-faith, as an abuse
and misconception of man's finite freedom is a significant re-
affirmation of "biblical religion," as he himself sometimes puts
it, and of the faith of the Reformers. One may even go so far
as to say that insofar as Niebuhr's view of the "Nature and
Destiny of Man" is determined by the recognition that the believing man, the Christian man, is always *simul iustus ac
peccator* (simultaneously righteous and sinful), he is re-stating
one of the profoundest insights of Luther. Thus there seems to
be injected through him into contemporary American Protestantism a note of Reformation-faith which, as it becomes
stronger, may imbue it again with the power by which Christianity is distinguished from other religions and philosophies
of life.

However, precisely because Niebuhr is widely regarded as one who is bringing "classical Protestantism" to life among us, it is very important to recognize that he fails to understand the whole of the faith of the Reformers and particularly that of Luther. First of all, it is to be noted that his thinking appears to be conditioned by a strange animosity against Luther which is all the more surprising in view of the fact that he is more closely related to Luther's faith than to any other. He takes frequent occasions to suggest inadequacies in Luther's teachings, but these criticisms do not seem to be founded on a careful study of Luther's work. They also seem to arise from a disregard of modern Luther-research. It seems that Niebuhr's interpretation of Luther is still primarily determined by that of Ernst Troeltsch who made the mistake of seeing the Reformer too much in the light of the spirit of modern (nineteenth century) German Lutheranism. Thus it is understandable that he can attribute a "cultural defeatism" to Luther's Reformation as if it were true that Luther had failed to articulate the ethical, and particularly the social-ethical, implications of his faith. That this was not really the case is known to anybody who ever read Holl's very thorough essay included in his *Luther Aufsätze,* under the title "Der Neubau der Sittlichkeit." Here it is convincingly shown that Luther's faith involved clear ethical principles which were capable of a wide social and cultural application. These principles were personal freedom, grounded in faith, and social, communal responsibility, based on love. Holl has not only indicated how in Luther's own work and thought these principles were extended into the whole of human life, but he has also proved what a radical departure they represented from Roman Catholic ethics. In his essay "Die Kulturbedeutung der Reformation" he demonstrated their very concrete, in many respects revolutionary, historical significance. One who is acquainted with this Luther-interpretation (and it is only one, perhaps the best, among many others) cannot but be astonished at Niebuhr's charge of Luther's cultural defeatism. I say all this in full awareness of the fact that while this charge does not apply to Luther, it may justly be levelled against certain features of Lutheranism as they developed after the Reformation as a result of historical

conditions and in disregard of what could have been learned
from Luther himself.

With all this I have not yet mentioned Niebuhr's most significant failure to understand Luther properly. He is of the
opinion (and this opinion is very decisive for his own interpretation of the Christian Gospel, as I shall show) that the
faith of the Reformer was such that in it sanctification was so
subordinated to justification that redemption could never be
experienced as an actuality. Here he seems to me to commit the
error of following certain Lutheran interpretations of the for-
ensic character of justification in which sanctification as a divine
act and as a human experience has become detached from forgiveness. Thus it is possible for him to assert (and this is his
own view) that the Christian faith is that man is divinely redeemed "in principle," but never "in fact." Just what the relation between this "in principle" and this "in fact" is, he never
makes fully plain. This failure he has in common with certain
Lutherans. But not with Luther himself! Luther knew that the
whole life of a Christian must be a life of repentance, that
throughout his life in the body he is in process of being saved
(*"Wir sind's noch nicht, wir werden's aber!"*), that perfection
lies in the future. This knowledge was grounded in the assurance that God does not lie when he gives his promise of forgiveness, that the Holy Spirit that sanctifies the man of faith "is not
a sceptic." In other words, Luther's faith certainly was that in
Christ sinful man had not only the assurance but the actual gift
of forgiveness, sanctification, renewal. This confidence was the
citadel of the freedom of the Christian man, because it was the
trust that the Gospel really was good news.

Niebuhr seems to me to have fallen into the very error
which he attributes to the Lutheran Reformation. Had he
rightly understood Luther's interpretation of the Gospel, he
would have been compelled to stress its promise of the renewal
of life without having to lose the emphasis upon the power of
sin that pervades all human and also the Christian life. As his
teaching now stands, it is really not marked by the Gospel, but
by a faith that is much closer to that of the Hebrew prophets
than to that of the witnesses of Christ. God for him is not
primarily the Father of Jesus Christ who in justifying man also
redeems him thus reconciling himself with him, but the trans-

cendent Lord of history in whose presence all idols are shattered and all human absolutes which are conceived in pride and defiance are reduced to vanity.

As a result, Niebuhr's outlook is determined by a profound suspicion of the deceit that lives in all human self-sufficiency and self-perfection and of the demonic violence that is hidden in all absolutizations of human values. This scepticism is healthy insofar as it enables a realistic view of the human situation. It may be regarded as a pre-condition of the Christian life but it is not of the essence of the Christian faith itself.

If Reinhold Niebuhr had laid more emphasis on redemption, he would perhaps have found it impossible to suggest that the most significant task today is the achievement of a synthesis of the Reformation and the Renaissance. By this recommendation he means something else than Professor Bower does. For Niebuhr desires to secure an important place for all that the Reformation teaching on justification implies. In contrast to Bower he treats it not as a doctrine of secondary but as one of primary importance. He knows particularly that the Reformers' view of life in the light of the doctrine of justification was radically different from that of Roman Catholicism and that of the leaders and representatives of the Renaissance. When he, nevertheless, pleads for a synthesis between the Reformation and the Renaissance, he does so because his interpretation of justification prevents him from affirming the possibility of a Christian life of redemption, so that he is forced to seek the promise of a fulfillment of human life elsewhere. Therefore, he praises the Renaissance view of the "infinite possibilities" that inhere in human life, and hopes that what it represents will be developed in the cultural life, but at the same time he wants to adhere to the teaching on justification because if culturally applied it will prevent the rise of an absolute trust in human possibility and keep man humble before God. But it is very doubtful whether the synthesis thus conceived is really possible. Niebuhr himself is fully aware of the fundamental difference between the spirit of the Renaissance and the spirit of the Reformation, and he should have concluded that the essential secularism of the former cannot be blended with the conscientious religiousness of the latter. But he has been driven to embrace the "program" of this synthesis because he cannot see how on the basis of justification-faith a sanctificationist ethic, an ethic that envisions a fulfillment of life, can be constructed. Herein he has missed the true understanding of the Reformation. This failure is very regrettable because, among the modern American Christian thinkers, he has come nearer than anyone else to revive the faith of the Reformation.

V

Most of the misinterpretation of Luther's personality and work could be undone and rendered ineffective, if the results of the modern research in the Reformation were taken seriously. Ever since 1883, when the four hundredth anniversary of Luther's birth was celebrated, but particularly since 1917, when the beginning of the Reformation by the publication of the ninety-five theses on October 31, 1517, was commemorated all over Protestantism, several generations of scholars, especially of Germany and Sweden, have studied all phases of the Reformation. They have produced a veritable Luther Renaissance. Its effects have made themselves felt in Protestant thought and life all over the world. The Barthian theology has been its foremost carrier. Contemporary continental Protestantism is saturated with it. In this country, Protestantism has not let itself be touched by this revival of the spirit of the Reformation. Only a few individual scholars have concerned themselves with it. The Lutheran and Calvinist churches have preferred to stay within the channels of their confessional and ecclesiastical traditions. They are only now slowly beginning to realize that the fresh knowledge of the Reformation and particularly of Luther's work which modern historical scholarship has made available might become a source of a revival of the Protestant faith.

In all this, we are confronted by the general problem, how the Church is to use the results of the modern historical research of its traditions. Just as Biblical scholarship has not yet been absorbed by the mind of the American churches, so also the scholarly investigations of the critical periods of church history (especially the Reformation) have not yet really affected them. For this reason, wrong interpretations of major events and movements are permitted to guide Christian thinking. The Church must learn to keep pace with its scholarship.

CHAPTER 2

Luther's Faith

I N HIS SERMON on the occasion of Luther's burial on February 22, 1546, Bugenhagen characterized the reformer, his long-time friend and colleague, with the following words: ". . . . he was without doubt the angel of which the Apocalypse speaks in Chapter XIV: 'And I saw an angel flying through the midst of heaven, who had an eternal gospel to preach,' . . . . the angel who says: 'Fear God, and give glory to him!' These are the two articles of the teaching of Martin Luther, the law and the gospel, by which the whole Scripture is opened and Christ made known as our righteousness and eternal life."[1]

Luther—an angel of God! Such a description suggests that his contemporaries understood his person and work in a religious sense.

I

Luther himself thought of himself and of his work in the same way. He did not wish to be called a prophet (only once[2] he spoke of himself as "the prophet of the Germans") but he had the sense of a *divine mission*. In opposition to the defenders of the old faith who called him a heretic, he thought of himself as an *"ecclesiasticus* (churchman) by the grace of God."[3] God had called him, he felt, to use his office of "Doctor of the Holy Scripture" for the reformation of the church according to the gospel. So he wrote: "I have received my doctrine by the grace of God from heaven, and, what is more, I have kept it in the presence of one who can do more with his little finger than a thousand popes, kings, princes, and *doctores* could do."[4] In the same spirit, he once described his mission in the following Pauline way: "If I should want to boast, I should glory in God that I am one of the apostles and evangelists in German lands, even though the devil and all his bishops and tyrants do not want me to be such; for I know that by the grace of

15

God I have taught and still teach faith and truth."[5] Such high claims he justified with the certainty that he was speaking "Christ's word" and not his own. Therefore, he did not hesitate to conclude: "So my mouth must be his whose words it speaks."

Because he knew himself to be an instrument of God and because he felt "more acted upon than acting,"[6] he argued that the whole cause of the Reformation could not be measured by human norms. When in his old age he looked back upon the beginnings of the Reformation and contemplated "the very great, heavy care and trouble" which the work of the Reformation had cost him, he exclaimed: "Had I known all in advance, God would have been put to great trouble to bring me to it."[7] Remembering the days of the Diet of Worms, he pondered: "Truly God can drive one mad; I do not know whether now I could be so daring."[8] However, in the midst of the crisis of his trial, he had written: "The die was cast; and so I did not want to do anything else than what I did. I began to put all my trust upon the Spirit who does not carry on a lazy business."[9] Thus he explained that all that took place at the height of the Reformation, occurred not because he had planned it so but by "divine counsel."[10]

This feeling of being divinely led he expressed best in the following characteristic words: "God has led me on as if I were a horse and he put blinkers on me that I could not see who came running up upon me. . . . . A good deed rarely issues from planning wisdom and cleverness; it must all happen in the vagaries of ignorance."[11]

These descriptions of the feeling of being called to a work that he had not chosen for himself are all the more impressive because Luther did not derive any pretensions of personal authority from his sense of mission. He did not wish his own special gifts and abilities to be regarded as extraordinary or authoritative. He resented it that his opponents called his teaching "Lutheran," and he got no satisfaction from the fact that his followers called themselves by his name. "Who is this Luther?" he wrote. "My teaching is not my own, and I have not been crucified for the sake of anyone. . . . . Why should it happen to me, miserable, stinking bag of worms that I am, that the children of Christ should be called by my insignificant name? . . . . I am and will be nobody's master. With the one church I have in common the teaching of Christ who alone is our master."[12]

When, one one occasion, he wrote: "So say I, Dr. Martin Luther, the unworthy evangelist of our Lord Jesus,"[13] he desired to appeal to the authority of Christ who alone, according to his opinion, should be heard as a prophet.[14] But at the same time, he wished to be taken seriously in his judgment of himself as an unworthy servant of Christ. He dared to appeal with certainty to God's word, but he also confessed frankly that Christian obedience was a daily task for him and the cause of never-ending efforts. That is why he did not want to justify his right to speak in the name of God by his own Christian attainments. "Let everyone," he wrote, "be responsible for his own feelings. As for me, I regard myself as a Christian. Nevertheless, I know how difficult it has been for me, and still is, to apprehend and to keep this cornerstone (Christ). But they certainly do me wrong (who call me a Lutheran), for—God strengthen me!—I am a small, poor Lutheran."[15]

No one understands Luther who does not pay attention to the two aspects of his sense of calling; namely, on the one hand, the assertion of being held and supported by God, and, on the other hand, the rejection of any personal worth and authority.

II

His *faith* corresponded wholly to the spirit which guided him in his work.

His deepest convictions were determined by his conception of God. God, as he saw him, was the restlessly working, driving power in all that is, the ever-active, creative livingness which lets no creature rest still. God is at work everywhere and in all, also in the godless, even in the devil.[16] The whole universe is his "masquerade in which he hides himself while he rules the world so strangely by making a hubbub."[17] The almighty power of God is nowhere and yet everywhere. Because it moves everything, it is immanent in all; but because it creates everything, it transcends all.

It must be present at all places, even in the smallest leaf of a flower. The reason is this: "It is God who creates, works, and preserves all things by his almight power and by his right hand, as we confess in the creed. He sends out no delegates or angels when he creates and preserves, but everything is the working of his own divine power. But if he is the creator and preserver, he himself must be present, creating and preserving his creature in its most inward and most outward being. That is why he himself is in the very inwardness and in the very outwardness of every creature, from end to end, below and above it, before and behind it. Nothing can be more present and be more really within all creatures than God himself."[18]

"God is smaller than anything small, bigger than anything big, shorter than anything short, longer than anything long, broader than anything broad, slimmer than anything slim, and so on; he is an inexpressible being, above and beyond all that one can name or think."[19]

This all-comprehending, all-penetrating creativity is the fountain and spring of life and of all good. It is closer to every one of us than any of us are to each other.[20] As it is God's nature to create all from nothing, so he is able "to help the forsaken ones, to justify sinners, to resurrect the dead, and to save the damned."[21]

He is the life of every being. He determines everything. He is present everywhere. But he is impenetrable and inscrutable. In such a way Luther spoke of God—most articulately in his book against Erasmus, *Of the Bondage of the Will,* and in his treatises on the Lord's Supper, called forth by his controversy with Zwingli. There he disclosed his profoundest thoughts of the creative power by which he felt himself driven and overcome. But he had still more to say.

"It makes a difference whether you say that God is present or whether you say that he is present for you. But he is there for you, when he adds his word (to his presence) and binds himself, saying: Here you shall find me. When you have the word, you can grasp him and have him and say: Now I have thee, as thou sayest. So it is with the right hand of God; it is everywhere, as no one can deny; but it is also nowhere; therefore you cannot apprehend it anywhere unless it binds and confines itself for your benefit to one place. This happens when it moves and dwells in the humanity of Christ. There you will most certainly find it. Otherwise you must run through all creation from end to end, groping and fumbling about, here and there, without finding it. Although it is really there—it is not there for you."[22]

In Christ the mysterious, inscrutable Lord of everything has made himself accessible. In him he is made comprehensible, because he has revealed himself in him without abandoning his mystery. He is hidden in the humbleness of the child in the manger. In the cross he is not *directly* visible as the victor over hell, death, and the devil. He is abscondite in the message of Christ about the mercy that seeks the sinner. And yet— "Whosoever does not apprehend this man born of Mary, simply cannot apprehend God; even if they should say that they believe in God, creator of heaven and earth, they believe really only in the idol of their heart, for outside of Christ there is no true God."[23] In Christ men have the "mirror of God's paternal heart." In him God is a God for them, their God. In Christ he is really the ever-renewing fountain of all good.

But men do not want to accept this teaching of God, for, so Luther argued, "Man by nature does not want God to be God; he would much rather that he himself were God and that God were not God."[24] Because of his self-sufficiency and selfishness, he is God's enemy. Though, when relying upon himself, he is driven from presumptuous security to despair in himself without being able to extricate himself from this dilemma, he refuses to acknowledge that he is a created being responsible to his creator. This unfaith is his sin. It is incomprehensible to him that he is a creature of God (this is proved by the fact that when he engages in worship, he tends to fashion an idol for himself); but it is utterly unfathomable for him that God should be a Father of sinners. His moral sense rebels against such a thought. If there is a God at all, so he thinks, God is the Lord of the righteous in whose sight only the worthy ones are acceptable.

Such is man's natural religiousness, according to Luther's opinion. Faith is its opposite. It is the acknowledgment of God's sovereignty and the belief in his accessibility in Christ and his word. Faith meant to Luther simply to have God. "Having God," he wrote in the *Larger Catechism*, "is nothing else than heartily to believe and trust in him; .... this trusting and believing makes both, God and idol; for these two belong together, faith and God."[25]

This faith, Luther taught, must be seen as the personal act of the believer ("If you believe, you have,"[26] he repeated unceasingly), but he knew also that it is the work of the Holy Spirit and as such a gift of God. Faith can therefore be an event only if the Christian becomes a new person. It is Christ who forms this new person. "I do not live in my own person, but Christ lives within me. To be sure, I live as a person but not in myself or for my own person."[27] The person of the believer transcends itself, so to speak.[28] This was the experience of Luther's prophetic religion.

He tried to interpret this experience of faith in many ways, for all his thinking circled around it. "Faith," so he defined, "is the knowledge of things not seen; it is directed to things that are not apparent. In order that faith may occur, it is therefore necessary that all that is believed be hidden."[29]

Faith is a miracle that cannot be understood according to ordinary criteria. Particularly when one has found God merciful, such faith appears as a blindly trusting audacity. "For this is the nature of faith that it dares trust in God's grace . . . . Faith does not require information, knowledge, or security, but a free surrender and joyful daring upon an unfelt, untried, unknown goodness."[30] From here Luther came to the remarkable conclusion that all certainty must be founded not upon human experience but upon divine revelation. "Our theology is certain," he said, "because it places us outside of ourselves; I do not need to rely upon my conscience, my senses, and my doing, but I rely upon the divine promise and truth which never deceive."[31]

And yet—faith must be a personal experience in order to be valid. A Christian must have faith by virtue of a personal deed and decision. "You yourself must decide; your neck is at stake. Therefore unless God says to your own heart: This is God's word, you cannot comprehend it. . . . . If you do not feel it, you do not have faith, but the word merely hangs in your ears and floats on your tongue as foam lies on the waters."[32]

III

In what a terrific tension Luther held his faith! On the one hand, he viewed it with radical seriousness as the work and gift of God who acts upon man from without. On the other hand, he experienced it as a concrete personal decision and commitment. In contemplating this tension, one understands why religion was a perpetual crisis and an unceasing battle for Luther.

This is the meaning of the *tentationes,* the agonies of faith, in which he was drawn again and again.[31a] He experienced that the merciful God withdrew from him. He was overcome by doubts concerning his work, when he questioned whether he should have dared to upset age-old customs and traditions in the church.[32] He felt that, in the light of the human need for security, the ambiguity of divine grace was unbearable. He then sensed the nearness of God not as love and consolation but as wrath and damnation. When such thoughts beset him, he felt that he was being attacked by the devil and thrown into a battle for his faith. He attributed such agonies to his psychological propensity to melancholy, but he knew also that he did not understand their true significance by such a psychological interpretation. Indeed, he held these agonies of faith to be unavoidable because he was aware that, from the viewpoint of ordinary human experience, faith was an impossibility.

He overcame these *Anfechtungen* (assaults), as he called them in his own tongue, by appealing to Christ and by relying upon the First Commandment: I am the Lord, thy God; thou shalt have no other gods before me. When he was free again and restored in the faith, he knew more definitely than ever before, that the inborn and acquired human certainties and safeguards are nothing ultimately sure and that man deceives himself when he pretends to possess certainty in himself. Thus these agonies appeared to him as a means by which the truth of faith, as a truth from beyond man's reach, was confirmed. A Christian, so he concluded, must be continually in the process of becoming. As he is a forgiven sinner who, despite being forgiven, again and again falls in the sin of unfaith, so he is thrown into agonies of faith until the end of his days in order to test his faith by being compelled to fight for it. So Luther could say of himself: "I did not learn my theology all at once; I have had to brood and ponder over it more and more deeply; my *tentationes* have brought me to it for one learns only by experience."[33]

He once said that the greatest of these *tentationes* was to know of none at all;[34] for such an attitude appeared to him the height of self-deception. He believed it to be an incontestable fact that every man has a bad conscience in spite of all the masks of self-confidence he wears, for at the bottom of his heart he knows himself to be in the wrong before God. Even though he rebels against the gospel of the forgiveness of God, because faith in this gospel involves the surrender of his self and the undoing of his self-determination, he will nevertheless experience faith as a liberation not only from himself but particularly from his bad conscience.

Luther best described the human situation which leads to the agony of faith in the following words in which the fright and terror by which one can be seized at the sound of a rustling leaf serve as the symbol of all proud insecurities from which one can be liberated alone by faith.

"So it can happen that conscience feels all misfortune that befalls us as the wrath of God and that even a mere rustling leaf seems to be God's wrath. . . . . There is nothing more worthless and more despised than a dry leaf that lies on the ground; worms crawl over it; it cannot ward off even the smallest speck of dust. . . . . But there comes a time when its rustling will scare man and horse, spike and armour, kings and princes, the power of a whole army and even such spiteful and angry tyrants as cannot be scared either by the fear of hell or by God's wrath and judgment but only become still prouder and more hardened by such threats. Aren't we fine fellows? we do not fear God's anger but stand stiffly unmoved by it. But we can be scared and frightened by the anger of an impotent dry leaf, and the rustling of such a leaf can make the world too narrow for us and become a wrathful God to us."[35]

IV

From this analysis of Luther's faith we can conclude that his interpretation of the Christian religion corresponded exactly to his conception of the meaning of his mission in the world. In his faith he related himself only to God in Christ and he did not base it upon the content of his experiences. With respect to his work he relied upon the almighty Lord of history and not upon his own qualities of leadership, of which he did not think much anyway. In his faith as well as in his work as a reformer he really believed himself "more acted upon than acting."

This way of thinking has nothing whatsoever to do with quiet-ism, of which Luther has often been accused. Rather it is "prophetic"—through and through. This can be proved by the fact that Luther felt himself called to a most personal, active participation in the work which, as he believed, God performed in the world through him. It was God himself, the ever-active creative power, who, by means of the Reformation, made room in the world for his word, but Luther was drawn into this divine work with his whole person. He felt that God had overpowered him; he did not think that he had thereby been drawn into a heteronomous servitude. He was moved rather to commit him-self to him who had overpowered him and to co-operate with him. Such was Luther's own conception of his faith. His prin-ciples of action were: Do not rely on men but trust in God. Do not fear men but fear God. That is why Luther acted on the historical scene without special consideration of political and historical consequences. Whosoever wants "to help the cause of the gospel," he wrote in a letter to Wolfgang Capito,[36] must preach it without fear and regard of men, in order that "the free, pure, and plain truth" may assert itself by itself alone.

In explaining the beginnings and the course of the Reforma-tion to the people of Wittenberg after his return from his exile in Wartburg castle, he said: "All I have done is to further, preach, and teach God's word; otherwise I have done nothing. So it happened that while I slept or while I had a glass of beer with my friend Philip (Melanchthon) and with Amsdorf, the papacy was so weakened as it never was before by the action of any prince or emperor. I have done nothing; the word has done and accomplished everything. . . . . I let the word do its work."[37]

These words sound quietistic and politically naïve, but they were spoken by one who, in the name of God, changed the course of history. What Luther meant to express was that his decisions and actions were motivated only by his concern to serve the word of God, and not by political calculations and predictions. By, and on account of, his faith, he became a re-former. His work, the Reformation, will live as long as this faith finds a response in the hearts of men.

CHAPTER 3

Luthers Conception of the Church

THE Reformation produced new types of churches. Their
character was determined by many factors among which the
religious one was only one among several others. But the impetus that brought them into being was Luther's conception
of the church.

The times had long been ripe for a change. Medieval ideas
and institutions were on the point of exhaustion. Forces of a
new cultural activity, brought to the fore by the leaders of the
Renaissance and of Humanism, threatened to replace them.
They manifested themselves in the awakening of human autonomous initiative, in nationalism, in capitalism and in the Great
Discoveries. In the course of its development the Reformation
entered into a connection with these new cultural trends and
it thus became a factor in the "modern" phase of western
civilization. Indeed, it was a most significant factor because
it made it possible for the new cultural life really to prosper.
For it shattered the fundamental authority on which all medieval life had rested. It undermined the whole ecclesiastical
framework which had held medieval civilization together.

And yet, the Reformation was not born of the spirit which
motivated the new civilization. It was not a part of the Renaissance. Nor was it a vehicle of nationalism, much less an ally
of that enterprising individualistic spirit of acquisitiveness
which manifested itself in early capitalism. The Reformation
was born in a monastery, remote from the world. Its center
was a small insignificant university, situated on the fringe of
civilization and lacking all the prestige and splendor and tradition of the old medieval institutions of learning. Its source
was Martin Luther's rediscovery of the Gospel. He had made
this rediscovery long before he became prominent as a critic

of the church. Though, from the beginning, it endowed him with a high sense of mission, it led him in no way to suspect that he would be led by it to break with the institutions of the medieval church.

By the fresh understanding of the Christian gospel in terms of the Pauline doctrine of the justification by faith, Luther fulfilled at first only the personal "search for the merciful God" that had caused him to become a monk. But because the implications of his new interpretation of the gospel were revolutionary, he inaugurated a new period of church history. He by-passed the humanistic criticisms of the medieval theological and ecclesiastical traditions. From scholastic theology he broke through to the Bible. He became persuaded that it was the sole norm and authority by which Christian life and faith should be measured. He read it as the "Word of God," i.e. the Gospel of Jesus Christ in whom God is revealed as the merciful giver of the good which man is unable to acquire by his own efforts be they ever so noble, moral or religious.

In 1512, Luther began his public work as a professor of Biblical theology. Imbued with the ever increasing joyful certainty that he had rediscovered the Gospel, i.e. that he had found the true source of Christianity, and therefore regarding himself as a true son of the church, he lectured first on the Psalms and then on the Epistles to the Romans, the Hebrews and the Galatians. In the course of this exegetical work, he developed and formulated the basic ideas which he later was to defend in his conflict with the Papacy and Roman Catholicism. The teachings that were to become those of the Reformation and that were to serve as the source of a new Christian order in the world thus matured before their revolutionary character was made apparent to their author and to the world in connection with the publication of the Ninety-five Theses on Indulgences in 1517. It is due to this fact that later when Luther as the leader of the Reformation had to serve as the guide, interpreter and defender of evangelical Christianity, his views, proposals, and criticisms always showed a remarkable fundamental consistency, in spite of the fact that the pressure of the demands that were made on him impelled him to improvise most of his writings and to address them more or less spontaneously to the issues at hand.

I.

No idea was more important in Luther's whole work than
that of the church. It too had assumed definite shape in his
mind long before he was made to realize that, as he conceived
its meaning, it was in profound contrast with that prevailing
in Roman Catholicism. We find that the church-idea of the
Reformation, the source of all later Protestantism, was already
clearly developed in its essentials in Luther's first commentary
on the Psalms. The ecclesiological principles which he formulated at the very beginning of his career, still far remote from
the world-shaking conflicts of his later life, served him in all
his labors as a reformer as the guiding vision of a new and true
church in the world.

He saw then—and he held on to this insight always—that
the church is a "people," "God's people," the "community of
believers," the *"communio sanctorum."*[1] He disliked the term
"church," because it seemed to him not to convey any clear
meaning. He preferred to translate the Greek word *"ekklesia"*
and the Latin word *ecclesia* (which he continued to use, of
course) into the German terms *Gemeinde* (community), *Ge-
meine* (congregation), *Sammlung* or *Versammlung* (assembly),
Haufe (crowd; people), *Christenheit* (Christendom; the unity
of all Christian people).

By interpreting the church in this way, he recovered the
early Christian idea of it, that of the New Testament. Yet he
was not at all concerned to restore the New Testament church
or to plead that Christianity ought to be reformed in its church
life according to the pattern of the New Testament as many
Protestants were later to demand and as some did, even during
his own lifetime. He was merely persuaded that he had again
seen the true nature of the church. His thinking was moulded
by Roman Catholicism and the historical tradition of church
life. He learned much in particular from Augustine. It would
not be wrong to say that the fundamental Roman Catholic
concept of the church as the *corpus Christi mysticum* (the
mystical, i.e. spiritual body of Christ) remained the theme also
of his ecclesiology. He would not think of Christ apart from
the church and of the church apart from Christ. But while
the medieval Roman Catholics were wont to see the "body of
Christ" actualized in the priestly administration of the sacra-

ments (with the consequence that the church became identified primarily with the hierarchy or even the papacy), he interpreted the "body of Christ" to be the body, i.e. the unity *or* community of Christian believers. What, in the medieval church, had been secondary, the fellowship of the Christians with one another, now became primary. The church of Christ, as he saw it, was a universal fellowship of Christian believers who share with one another all their faith and love. He wrote: "The consequence of being one with Christ is that we are one also among ourselves. . . . . As the grains of corn are milled they are blended with one another. None of it keeps its own flour but it is mixed with that of others and is made part of it. . . . . (So also among Christians) none is for himself but everyone shows and spreads himself among his fellows in love."[2]

The most radical, i.e. most incisive feature of Luther's interpretation of the Christian religion was that he stressed its personal character. Faith was for him nothing else than a personal believing, the trusting conviction that what the gospel of Jesus Christ proclaims as God's way with men is true. It is to be appropriated by way of a personal commitment to it. Each believer must have the certainty that God is his own God and that his goodness and love are offered to him personally. Faith in the gospel, as Luther interpreted it, is a personal event that happens in the secrecy of the believer's own soul. As every one of us will have to die for himself, so he must also believe for himself. The Roman Catholic teaching of the implicit character of faith, i.e. that the individual believer may implicate (literally wrap up, entwine) his own believing in that of the whole church, so that it is unnecessary for him to be personally persuaded of the truth of faith, was thus radically rejected.

On account of this, Roman Catholics have been inclined to criticize Luther as a religious individualist and even as a religious subjectivist. And Protestants too have understood Luther's personalism as if it implied the reduction of the Christian religion to individual subjective experience. But the Roman Catholic criticism and this Protestant misinterpretation of Luther's conception of faith are based on a bad misunderstanding of his views. Luther never thought and taught otherwise of the Christian faith than on the basis of the confronta-

tion of the Christian with the word of Christ in whom the living
God speaks: Faith is always an encounter in which the Christian
is addressed by another, in the last resort by God himself.
Moreover, he was persuaded that, because God is the ever-active
giver of *all* the good in the world and as such the creator and
father of *all* living beings and things and because in Christ
he is disclosed as the merciful savior of *all* men, any man who
by faith has become one with Christ is by virtue of this faith
liberated from all isolation in himself and re-incorporated in
God's one creation and in God's one people. Luther therefore did not speak as an individualist when he emphasized the
personal character of the Christian life. What he taught was
that though one becomes a Christian only in the secrecy of his
own personal encounter with God in Christ, the Christian life
is never a life of self-secluded isolation but always one of fellowship and mutual self-giving love: to be a Christian and to
be in the church, the community of believers, is one and the
same. In this sense, he could adopt for himself Cyprian's slogan:
"Outside of the church there is no salvation."[3]

II

Luther's interpretation of the church as the *"communio
sanctorum"* was a deed of tremendous consequences. It became the dynamic resource of Protestant church-life, although
Protestants again and again lost the sense of its true significance. Luther himself found it difficult to elucidate its full
meaning, for he had to establish it in opposition to Roman
Catholicism and in connection with the formation of new
evangelical churches. The conflict with the Roman Church
involved the removal or revaluation of traditions, conventions,
practices and teachings which had grown up in the course of
centuries. And the building of a new church-order was attended by innumerable complications of a personal and impersonal sort and beset by all the uncertainties which commonly accompany the launching of new enterprises in history.

The key to the understanding of Luther's doctrine of the
church as he developed it in criticism of the Roman Church
and in justification of new church orders is his teaching
that the church as the communion of believers is constituted
in and by the word. *"Tota vita et substantia ecclesiae est in*

verbo Dei."⁴ This "word of God" is Christ as he lives in the witness of the Bible and as he comes to life again and again in preaching and proclamation based on the Bible. Because this word is the "sole vehicle of the grace of God,"⁵ and because by it the "Kingdom of God" is established in the hearts of men,⁶ it is the one and only true mark of the church.⁷ For "the word of God cannot be without God's people and, conversely, God's people cannot be without the word. For how could it otherwise be preached and heard!"⁸

The church is therefore truly constituted only when it lives of the word as its active constitutive principle. This was the norm by which Luther measured the ecclesiastical practices and ecclesiological doctrines. He did not conceive of the word as a legalistic and prescriptive norm as many Protestants were to do later. For just as he did not regard Christ as "another Moses"⁹ but as the "mirror of God's paternal goodness"¹⁰ and as "the revealed God"¹¹ who gives forgiveness and new life, so he read the Bible not as a book of rules and laws but as the written gospel of Christ. The Scripture, therefore, was normative for him in so far as all that could not be justified by its witness to Christ should not be regarded as Christian *de iure divino*. To be sure, in accordance with the universal conviction of all Christians of his time he believed the Bible to be divinely inspired (although he had no particular theory about the method of its inspiration and no dogma of its literal inviolability) and he therefore considered it as a divine source of truth. But the use which he made of it was determined by his conviction that, because it was the only reliable testimony concerning Christ, it was the authoritative standard of Christian faith and life. Yet in spite of the fact that he thus made the true knowledge of Christ dependent upon the Scripture, he read it in the religious awareness that Christ was the lord of its message. There is no authority of Christ except that which can be sustained by the Bible but the Bible is authoritative only in so far as it points and directs to Christ— such was Luther's conception of the normativeness of the Bible. He attributed no objective oracular qualities to it; rather he insisted that it should be properly "understood" in terms of its own meaning. That its true meaning, namely the gospel

of Christ, could plainly be understood, was never doubtful
to him.

Relying on this certainty, he became persuaded that the
Roman Catholic Church was not truly Christian. The whole
sacral apparatus of the Roman Church, the papacy, hierarchalism, the non-Scriptural sacraments, Canon law, monasticism,
etc. appeared to him (specifically since the year 1519) as human
historical "additions"[12] to the gospel. Because the Roman
Catholic Church held them to be of the essence of Christianity
they represented in his judgment an arbitrary deformation of
the Christian Church. When he came to recognize that the
claims of the pope to be the vicar of Christ could not be justified *ure divino* but at best only *humano iure,* he concluded that
the assumption of this "right" was inspired by blasphemous
presumptuousness. From then on and throughout his life he
fought the papacy as the Antichrist, indeed, as the "devil incarnate."[13] He charged that the exercise of the papal office
restricted the sovereignty of Christ. The Roman teaching that
obedience of papal authority was necessary to salvation led him
to suspect that the papacy hindered the free course of the gospel
in the world and blocked its unrestricted appeal to men.

What Luther here attacked was the view that the Christian
church is an institution of definitive forms, a constituted body
whose nature is unrealizable except by a permanent maintenance of integral outward forms. It was far from him to deny
that the Christian church required concrete orders of organization, polity, procedure, teaching, worship and morals, but
he broke with the principle to which all Roman Catholicism
conformed that the Christian church cannot live except in
unchanging forms as eternal as the gospel itself.

Luther did not yet perceive the far-reaching implications
of his thesis. Although he saw that in Roman Catholicism
relative historical decisions and developments were absolutized, he lacked the historical knowledge and insight (as all his
contemporaries did, because "historical understanding" was
not yet a cultural possibility, much less a discipline of knowledge) to interpret the Christian life historically. At a later
time, the historians amply proved his "historical" judgment of
the historical character of the Papacy and its church. Then the
fundamental question which Luther had raised but not fol-

lowed through became really acute, namely the problem of
"revelation and history," "religious truth and history," etc.
The people of the Protestant churches, the spiritual descendants of Luther, have not solved this problem, even in our day,
primarily because they still absolutize relative historical views
and facts of their own (the Christianity of the New Testament,
Luther's achievements, etc.) substituting them for the historical
absolutizations of Roman Catholicism. Thus they replace the
big historical pope of Rome by little historical popes of Wittenberg, Geneva, Canterbury, Boston and, most frequently, of
early Christian Jerusalem as seen in the perspective of many
different locales in Christendom.

Yet Luther coped with the problem as far as he could see its
implications. He dealt with it in terms of certain distinctions
which he made with respect to his fundamental conception of
the church as the "communion of believers."

III.

On the basis of the presupposition that the "word" is the
constitutive principle of this "communion of believers," he
asserted (1) that one must distinguish between its "internal"
and "external" character; (2) that there is a church in the
general sense (the "universal" community of believers) as distinguished from the church in the specific sense (the local
church congregation and its organization); (3) that this local
congregation must be organized around the preaching of the
word, yet in such a way that the principle of the "priesthood
of believers," which is in accordance with the character of the
universal church determines its constitution; (4) that next to
and together with the family and the political order the local
church congregation is one of the "hierarchies" in and through
which the church as the universal community of believers
is realized.

A detailed discussion of these aspects of Luther's ecclesiology
is in order:

(1) It was at the beginning of his career, and particularly
during the time of his conflicts with the Roman Church in
connection with the controversy on indulgences, that Luther
formed the concept of the twofold character of the church.
In the "Sermon on the Power of Excommunication" of 1518,

he wrote: "The communion of believers is twofold: on the one hand, it is internal and spiritual, on the other hand, it is external and corporeal. As a spiritual communion it is a unity of faith, hope and love toward God; as a corporeal (communion) it is participation in the sacraments, i.e. the signs of faith, hope and love and (this participation) is also extended (so that it becomes), a communion in things, usages, personal relations, habitation and the physical relationships."[14] The purpose he had in mind when he made this distinction was to affirm that while it is possible to exclude a believer from the external fellowship of the church and deny him the use of its "signs of faith" (the sacraments), it is impossible to deprive him of membership in the spiritual communion of believers. For this communion transcends all externalities and all limitations of time and place. It is a *religious* community inspired by faith and it is therefore independent of external circumstances and arrangements. One enters it only by a divine call; and since God is not bound to the external forms in which men may realize this fellowship, no denial of the use of these forms can separate a true believer from it. Here lies the root of Luther's idea of the invisible nature of the church. It is wrong to suppose that he ever seriously conceived of an invisible church as such. The very statement of his which we are here discussing is a refutation of such an opinion, for it defines the nature of the church as twofold, both inward and outward, or, as we may also say, both invisible and visible. Later on, Luther elucidated the duplex character of the church by analogically referring to the relationship of the soul and the body in order to suggest that just as the soul determines the character of the body, so the spiritual nature of the church is prior to and determinative of its external order.[15] He went on to emphasize specifically that while the internal community must be *distinguished* from the "external" one, the two must not be *separated* from one another.[16] Indeed, when one of his critics interpreted his explanation of the spiritual nature of the church as if it referred to an unreal, invisible, ideal church, he rejected this criticism, saying: "You make fun of me for having called the church a spiritual assembly, as if I wanted to build a church after the pattern of the Platonic state which is nowhere, and you are so well pleased with this whim of yours as if you had really made a point."[17] He stated this fundamental idea best in the following sentence: "Although the church lives in the flesh, it does not live according to the flesh, as Paul says in Galatians 1 and 2, and in Corinthians 10. So it has its being in a place and in the things and activities of the world, but it is not properly understood in terms of all this. . . . . For as in this life the church is not without eating and drinking and yet the Kingdom of God according to Paul does not consist of eating and drinking, so the church is not without place and body and yet the place and body do not make the church and do not constitute it."[18] The church, i.e. the community of believers, cannot exist without external forms and arrangements yet these are not of its essence.

With this insight Luther liberated himself from religious obedience to the ecclesiastical forms and laws of Roman Catholicism. When he also reached the further conclusion that the institution and laws of the papacy had developed under definite and delimited historical circumstances, he made it possible not only for himself but for all Christians to seek free forms to express their faith.

As we shall see, he himself was actually not able to realize this possibility but to this principle he always adhered: problems of external ecclesiastical arrangements are issues of faith only in so far as one must make sure that ecclesiastical forms and practices do not block the free course of the word of God in the world. He used this rule successfully in criticising the institutions of Roman Catholicism, but he did not abide by it when he had to apply it to the new church situation which his effective criticism of Romanism had produced.

Already in his first commentary on the Psalms he had written: "The church is perpetually born and perpetually changed in the succession of believers; the church is here one thing and there another, yet it is always the same."[19] In the succession of believers the church is real. In their believing it is actualized. In this sense it is invisible and spiritual (for faith is inward and therefore invisible). Yet this invisible faith of the believers is the ground of those visible expressions of love by which the church becomes the fellowship of the believers with one another, actualized concretely amidst definite human circumstances. Faith is therefore the test of the true church. By faith the worth of its institutions must be measured.

It was in connection with the constructive application of this point that, in the course of his career as a church-reformer, Luther came to violate his own principle of the freedom of the church. As we have stated, his whole ecclesiological teaching was based on the presupposition that the "word" is the constitutive principle of the church. He could therefore conceive of faith as the test of the true church only in so far as he coupled it with the "word." He was persuaded that the "word," namely God's self-disclosure in Christ, is an objective reality which affirms itself clearly, indubitably and inescapably to anyone who comes under its sway. It never takes hold of one except by the power of the Holy Spirit, i.e. by its own persuasiveness it removes all hindrances, such as doubt, unbelief, pride, self-sufficiency, self-righteousness which he to whom it comes may put in its way. In other words, through the "word" God establishes his reign in the heart of man and in doing so he triumphs over all obstacles by which the human mind may block his activity. Moreover, the "word" by which God (the Holy Spirit) acts upon man is always definite and concrete: It is Jesus Christ as he is witnessed to in the Bible. The picture of Christ God impresses upon man's inwardness when he takes hold of him is clear and distinct. Also the testimony of the Bible in so far as it conveys the gospel, i.e. the good news that in Christ God is revealed as a loving father who freely gives all that he demands, is unmistakable and not subject to any ultimate misapprehension. If properly read and interpreted, the Bible will impart the meaning of its message in such a way that it will confirm itself to the reader "as by itself most certain and easily apprehendable, indeed, as its own interpreter."[20]

Luther held these convictions in a religious way. They reflected his religious certainty in the reality of God. In other words: when he was persuaded that through the Bible he was brought under the sway of Christ and through Christ under the sovereignty of God, he did not regard that which thus controlled him as something mechanical as if it asserted itself upon him in an impersonal way. Nor did he consider it as something "factual," and as such as something either natural or supernatural or as something either historical or super-historical so that its objective given-ness would have to be proved by adequate proofs or demonstrations. Yet he was sure that he was confronted with the holy fountain of all life and good which though immanent in life and all its good transcends it as its creative source, as the standard by which its work is judged, and as the end of its perfection. He refused to be drawn into metaphysical speculations on this divine reality. He insisted that God should be encountered in the concrete context in which he had made himself accessible, i.e. in Jesus Christ, in the Bible, in Biblical preaching and in the Biblical sacraments.

Now he was aware of the danger that because God is accessible only through historical concreteness the forms of this concreteness may be considered as divine in themselves. He stated frequently that historical knowledge of Christ is not the same as faith in him and that it cannot even be the basis of faith. He also was conscious of the historical nature of the Bible and he therefore advocated that its text should be properly understood, that it should neither be absolutized in its literal-ness nor arbitrarily interpreted (as it was done, for instance, in allegorical exegesis by which a meaning other than its own was superimposed upon the text). He knew, furthermore, that the authority and true effectiveness of preaching, are not dependent upon the preachers' incidental skill of insight or eloquence. He believed that all these misunderstandings, against which he cautioned, had been committed in one way or another by Roman Catholicism. Indeed, so we may say, his fundamental criticism of Roman Catholicism was that it had imprisoned the gospel in man-made historical forms thus delimiting its freedom.

Nevertheless, it happened also to him that despite his thoughtful concern for this freedom, he too obstructed it. To be sure, he never lost the conviction that in the end the word of God would establish itself in the hearts of men by its own initiative and power. This confidence enabled him to attribute no ultimate significance to any human understanding, on behalf of the word of God. He was also willing to admit that the word of God could find true believers even under conditions that defiled it. Therefore he never denied that there were true

Christians in the Roman Church even though he believed
that Antichrist ruled it through the papacy. In the same way,
he did not hesitate to admit that there were true Christians
among the Protestant sectarians whose churches he felt it
necessary to oppose violently because he thought that they
misinterpreted the Christian gospel. But these broad-minded
insights never became the principles of his actions. That men
would honestly differ in their apprehension of the same reality
and that it might be possible to reconcile these differences
either by a reconsideration of their reference to the apprehended reality or by a toleration of them under maintenance of
mutual contact—these possibilities which were implied in his
fundamental conception of the power of the word and of the
nature of faith did not suggest themselves to him as real. He
replied to the exclusivistic dogmatism of the Roman Catholic
Church with a dogmatism of his own. He never had any confidence in the theological conferences which the Emperor
Charles V arranged in order to affect a reconciliation between
Catholics and Protestants. He suspected that these enterprises
were futile, quite apart from the fact that he saw that they
were undertaken primarily for political reasons. Also the in-
transigeance which he displayed toward Zwingli and the Protestant sectarians (whom he called Schwärmer [fanatics]) was
caused by his unwillingness to concede that their interpretation
of Christianity might be in accordance with the gospel or that
it was at least debatable, especially in view of the fact that they
as Protestants affirmed as resolutely as he did the desire to be
governed by the word.

Luther therefore insisted that the "word" could be the constitutive principle of the church only by means of "pure and
true doctrine." Thus he laid the foundation of the creedalism
that was to govern Protestantism generally and Lutheranism in
particular. It did not occur to him that "true doctrine" as he
understood it was debatable.

This attitude of his was not inspired by his personal stubbornness (though he had a good share of it) nor by an exaggerated sense of authority (he had a high consciousness of his
mission but he had no desire to aggrandise his name or his
power.)[21] It was due to the power that tradition held over him
and to the political practical necessity to maintain uniformity in

religion. In both respects, his position was in no way unique
but common to his age.

The power of tradition was so great that notwithstanding
the revolution which he himself had effected with respect to
Roman Catholicism, Luther felt it necessary to relate his
understanding of the Christian gospel to it. Whenever a dogmatic view of his was seriously challenged, he therefore fell
back upon a literalistic Biblicism, in spite of the fact that he
himself had overcome it. Moreover, he was so dependent upon
the traditional dogmas which, in many respects, he had religiously transcended that he did not permit a correction of their
tenets even in the light of his own special teachings; he did
not see to what an extent these teachings of his (particularly
that on justification by faith) necessarily implied modifications
of the old dogmas, even that of the Trinity and that of the
two natures of Christ. When he was involved in controversy
with fellow-Protestants who though they differed from him in
special points, fundamentally shared his understanding of the
Christian religion because they had learned it from him directly
or indirectly, he was unable or unwilling to base his thinking
on the principle of interpretation which he had developed for
the religious use of the Bible and which he applied also to
other Christian ideas and traditions, namely the twofold principle that the Bible must be read with the concern for Christ
and that no authentic knowledge of Christ can be had apart
from the Bible. Nor did he remember that over against Catholicism he had refused to bind his conscience to human traditions and customs.[22] Observance of these principles saved
him from literalism; it also enabled him to understand the
Bible and the Christian tradition in a dynamically religious
way. But, in the face of opposition in his own camp, he chose
to stand on static, fixed principles and he failed to give his
opponents the benefit of that religious understanding of which
he was so eminently capable. He could not cope with dissent.

The chief reason for this strange deficiency of his, if such
it was, must probably be sought in the fact that he refused to
consider himself a dissenter and that he fervently disliked it to
be regarded as such. In his judgment, Roman Catholicism
was the product of an evil dissent from the Christian gospel,
and he suspected that all who dissented from the interpretation

of the gospel that he had made possible as a reformer of the
church were guilty of a repetition of the Roman Catholic
schism.

The other factor that determined Luther's dogmatism was
the assumption that uniformity in religion was a political-social
and moral requirement. Again we must note that, in view of
the fact that his own refusal to recant had driven the most
effective wedge into the wall of medieval-Catholic uniformity,
his concern for uniformity in religion appears very strange.
He thought it impossible that Christians could engage in common action, particularly in the political arena, unless they held
the same creed. In this respect he was as uncompromisingly
untractable as the Roman Catholics were—and still are. His
thinking in these matters was undoubtedly determined by the
conviction that as Christ is one so also his gospel and its truth
are one. The idea did not suggest itself to him that this one-ness
of truth might be established in the creeds of the churches in
the way in which, as he himself ceaselessly taught, the believer
must apprehend the one lordship of Christ: in a repentant
willingness ever to rethink all attainments. He was prevented
from conceiving such an approach as a practical possibility, for
he was persuaded that social-political and moral concord could
prevail in a community only on the basis of uniformity in
religion. So Luther insisted on creedal uniformity among the
Protestants. (In this connection, one must remember that
wherever a transition from the Roman Catholic to the Protestant church order was effected, whole political communities
and not merely individuals made the change.) For the problem,
how concord could be maintained in the Holy Roman Empire
in view of the Protestant Catholic conflict he knew no human
solution. That it would have to be solved by force of arms,
the statesmen forced him to acknowledge. He agreed to this
solution with a reluctance that betrayed the religious listless-
ness of his consent. Yet he did not doubt that uniformity in
creed was the only way by which the unity of the church could
be maintained.

We conclude then that Luther's distinction between the
internal and external nature of the church, i.e. the universal
community of believers, helped him to explain and justify his
objections to Roman Catholic church-doctrine and practice but

he did not carry it over into the ecclesiological thought which he developed for Protestantism.

(2) His predicament was partly due to the fact that his thinking about the church was oriented to another fundamental distinction, namely that between the church "in the general sense" and the church "in the specific sense."[23] The former is the community of believers seen as the invisible-visible church universal; the latter is the local congregation of believers, organized in itself and as an organization related to other ecclesiastical bodies. There can be no doubt that Luther made the distinction, although he did not specifically formulate it. At any rate, one must adopt it in order to explain his ecclesiological ideas.

The problem here suggested is as old as Christianity. The New Testament idea of the church is not intelligible unless it is understood as having reference both to the "universal" people of God and to the local fellowship of Christians. In the course of the historical development of Christianity, this double aspect of the nature of the church continually asserted itself both in doctrinal thought and ecclesiastical practice. Roman Catholicism, however, effected a transformation of the church idea by combining the two sides of the church which at the beginning were ideally distinguished. By means of the episcopalization and finally the papalization of the ecclesiastical organization it developed a universalism in which congregationalism was absorbed. It is interesting to note that the same process can also be plausibly described as the absorption of individual local congregations in western Christendom by the Roman congregation or as the assimilation of these congregations to the universalist imperialism of the Roman congregation.

Luther re-discovered the double character of the church when he understood it again as the "people of God." The New Testament was, of course, his source and guide. But he was not interested to repristinate the New Testament church. In this respect, he differed from the Zwinglians as well as from the Anabaptists. Both these groups (and one must be mindful of the fact that the Anabaptists sprang from Zwinglianism) were influenced by the historical outlook of Humanism and therefore tried to go back to the true beginnings of Christian-

ity. Luther, who also had a sense of the historical character
of Christianity, as we have seen, did not care to derive any
norms from history. He therefore did not read the New Testament with historical eyes. For him it was the medium of God's
revelation and, sometimes at least, even the revelation itself.
By thinking biblically he naturally recovered many of the historical ideas of the Bible, but he did not understand them
historically.

This manner of thought is well illustrated by his ideas of
the church. When he was led by the New Testament to conceive of the church both as a universal fellowship and as a local
congregation, he was not conscious of having an historical
insight, but he interpreted this conception theologically and
constructively in terms of the doctrine of the justification by
faith which was the key to his understanding of the Biblical
revelation. At the same time, he oriented himself critically to
Roman Catholicism, regarding his Biblical ideas as theological
corrections of Roman Catholic errors. His view of the church
as a spiritual-corporeal (divine-human) communion of believers was thus a Biblical-theological re-interpretation of the
Roman Catholic idea of the church as "the mystical body of
Christ." The correction of the impersonalising that was implied in the Roman Catholic ecclesiology was of special importance to him. Luther really saw the universal church as one
God-created and God-inspired *people*. It was for this reason
that he emphasized also the congregational character of the
church. This too was a Biblical notion which he developed
critically and concretely against the background of Roman
Catholicism. Also his congregationalist emphasis was a Biblical-theological correction of Roman Catholicism and not a
repristination of the Biblical church.[24]

The problem of the authority of the Bible for church polity
was to trouble Protestantism throughout its history. We do not
need to concern ourselves further with it in this connection.
What is important for us here is to see that Luther made the
distinction between the church in the general (universal) sense
and the church in the specific (congregational) sense. This
distinction guided him in his work as a builder of evangelical
churches.

(3) The procedure by which reformed churches were

established was determined by the remarkable fact that Luther and the Protestants never thought of themselves as heretics, i.e. that they never acknowledged that they were really excommunicated from the church. Luther in particular was of the conviction that the papacy had unrightfully usurped power in the church and that, inspired by the devil, the enemy of God, it had misled and was continuing to mislead the Christians. He never doubted that there were Christians also in the Roman Church and it never occurred to him to treat Roman Catholics as heretics.[25] He was persuaded that in his fight against the Papacy he was pleading the cause of that Christian people (*Christenheit*) which since the days of the apostles had been in the world as the body of Christ, living of his "word." He looked upon the Papacy as a devilish intruder who, in the course of the six hundred years of his existence, had succeeded in building a *"Rottenkirche"*[26] (a schismatic sect) within Christendom, that illegitimately appropriated for itself the authority of the tradition of the ancient church. In so far as Luther attributed normative importance to the "tradition," he was sure that he could claim it for his cause, for he felt the Reformation to be in continuity with the church of the apostles and of the "Fathers" and with the church of those in medieval Catholicism who, like Bernard of Clairvaux, Bonaventura and Gerson, had preserved a sense of true Christianity in terms of the apostolic and patristic tradition and especially in accordance with the Bible,[27] the only true source and norm of the church.

Determined by such an attitude, he proceeded with the work of reformation. This meant that as a reformer he took a position *within* Christendom, *within* the historical body of the Christian church in which by virtue of Christ's and the Holy Spirit's activity through the word the true church, the *communio sanctorum,* was existing, even though not everybody who belonged to the external-historical ecclesiastical body was a true Christian and even though many products of the historical church were unchristian. He thus believed to occupy a position within the church, concretely speaking, within the Roman Catholic church, and he felt called upon to purify it by setting it free from the errors of Rome which had come to adulterate its true nature. In the depth of his mind, Luther always thought that there was only one church. He felt called upon (by God and not by his own choosing) to purify it so that, liberated from the unevangelical and therefore unauthorized institutions, practices and teachings of the papacy, it might again freely live of the fountain of its life, Christ the Word, its Head. That is why he resented it that his opponents called his teaching "Lutheran" and he got no satisfaction from the fact that his followers called themselves by his name. "Who is this Luther?" he wrote. "My teaching is not my own and I have not been crucified for anyone's sake. . . . Why should it happen to me, miserable stinking bag of worms that I am, that the children of Christ should be called by my name that cannot save anyone? I am not and do not want to be anybody's master. Together with the church I have one universal teaching of Christ who alone is the master of us all."[28]

All these considerations became of direct practical importance when the actual work of the reformation was undertaken in the local communities. The changes that were made in accordance with the teachings of Luther and the reformers were effected from within the existing ecclesiastical conditions. The Lutheran Reformation in particular has rightly been described as a "conservative reformation," because under Luther's leadership it was undertaken with the purpose of conserving all prevailing traditions, customs, rites and doctrines that were not in conflict with the word. To be sure, a tremendous reduction of ecclesiastical traditions took place: the papacy and the entire hierarchical administration and apparatus were abolished, the monasteries were dissolved, scholastic theology was condemned, the sacraments and the whole complex of ritualistic traditions and practices were reduced to Baptism and the Lord's Supper, etc. But many conditions and institutions remained intact and became the basis of the new order: The church was regarded as a people's church (every infant was baptized soon after his birth; thus everyone was born a Christian or born in the church); church-property remained at the disposal of the church-congregations or church bodies (much of it, however, was secularized when it was assigned to educational and charitable use); church services continued to be held in the traditional houses of worship and the altars, pictures, organs and other symbolisms were preserved; the new Lutheran liturgy was fashioned after the pattern of the mass, though great care was taken that "Roman errors" were eliminated from it; the Lord's Supper, though no longer regarded as sacrifice, was still a celebration of the presence of Christ; the fundamental dogmas formulated by the ancient church were retained as the main substance of Christian doctrine though they were interpreted with reference to the Bible and not to church tradition, etc.

The church-order of Lutheran Protestantism thus bore the marks of Catholic historical tradition, precisely by virtue and not in spite of the fact that it was instituted as a corrective reformation of Roman Catholicism. Luther and his followers believed that the true church that had been hidden in the corruptions of Romanism should be brought to light and established in the very midst of the ecclesiastical and religious life that the Roman Church had nurtured. Luther himself never ceased to remind those by whose initiative the reformation of the church was accomplished that they were doing the work which the pope and the bishops should have been expected to perform if they had had a right conception of their responsibility to the word of God. That he expected the conventional officers of the empirical church and not the people themselves to assume leadership in the establishment of the true church was a concession on his part to historical actuality. For the same reason, he appealed to the Christian princes as the actual leaders of the laity to assume responsibility for the reformation when the high clergy refused to act.

But according to his innermost conviction, the task of establishing a true church order in the world belonged to the "Christian people" themselves, not the men and women who happened to be members of historical Christendom and its organizations but the Christian believers among them who had been apprehended by the word of God. He was certain that as truly as by God's grace the gospel of Christ had always and under all circumstances drawn believers to itself transforming them into victorious doers of faith and love, there had always been in existence a real Christian community, a true church. He therefore concluded that these true Christians should be free to institute the external church in accordance with the spirit that motivated them as Christian believers. This was the substance

of Luther's teaching of the universal priesthood of all believers. Acting as priests, i.e. as true mediators of the word, toward
one another, they would, he was persuaded, realize the true
church in the world not only by manifesting its spiritual nature
in a community of love but also by creating an external order
for it which would make it possible for them and all men freely
to be nourished by the source of their priesthood, namely
the word.

Luther proposed to reform the church in the light of this
conception of Christianity. A twofold task had then to be
fulfilled: The Christian order must be of such a character
that (1) it was possible for the word to be freely preached and
heard and (2) the members of the Christian congregations could
assume the responsibilities of the priesthood of believers. Luther
was aware of the fact that the freedom of the word could not
fully be accomplished by human arrangements and that the
local congregations were not actually made up of mature Christians really able to exercise the rights of universal priesthood.
But he trusted that, in his own time, God would fulfill his
purposes among men if, in so far as it was possible to do,
churches were established around the preaching of the evangelical word and organized on the basis of the principle of the
universal priesthood of believers. He hoped that within such
an order there would grow by the grace of God and in God's
own season the true church: the community of the people of
God. He was confident that if Christian worship was reformed
so that the proclamation of the word was its center, the word
would establish its truth among men by its own divine power,
and that if church congregations were given the right to determine their own affairs true believers created by the word would
have the possibility to live and act as Christians without hindrance.

In guiding the work of the Reformation, Luther therefore
did not conceive the reforming methods and accomplishments
as final: The conserved Catholic traditions and customs as well
as the newly-instituted evangelical orders were regarded by him
as the conditions in which God would establish his reign among
men.

But also in this connection, the actual achievements in the
reforming of the churches fell behind these principles and

intentions. The free preaching of the word was bound to the definition of pure and true doctrine; the dynamic character of the word was almost entirely restricted by rigidly defined and fixed doctrines, and the revelation of the living God which was expected to attend the preaching of the word was misinterpreted as a system of knowledge once for all supernaturally disclosed. Luther himself was not chiefly responsible for this development, although he did much to set the stage for it. But already during his lifetime, the theologians of his church, most of them his own pupils, began to engage in theological controversies in a dogmatist spirit. Thus they anticipated and prepared the rise of Lutheran Orthodoxy which for more than a century was to enervate preaching by circumscribing the divine word in the rationalism of theological dogmatism.

The realization of the priesthood of believers through the exercise of church responsibility on the part of the local congregations also remained unfulfilled. Luther himself was again and again uncertain how far he should go in this respect. At times he insisted that the congregations should have the full right to call their own pastors and to judge the true preaching of the word; at other times, he toyed even with the idea of encouraging the formation of *ecclesiolae in ecclesia,* made up of people who were active believers (he very quickly abandoned such proposals because he feared that they implied sectarianism which he detested); and, at still other times, he feared that nothing could be done as long as there were not enough Christians in the world. But nevertheless, he was so sure that a real community of believers belonged to Christ and the gospel and that in this church there should be no distinction between Christians of different ranks and rights (clergy and laymen) that he insisted that the reformed churches should be so organized that the congregations should have the right to call their own ministers or at least that they should have no minister assigned to them against their will and that the pastoral office should be so defined that it could not be regarded as establishing a Christian status in the church different from that of any Christian believer. With these demands he did actually prevail but not to the extent he had originally hoped for: The Lutheran churches were finally organized by the authority of the princes. According to Luther's teaching, these princes were supposed

to reform the churches by virtue of their position of prominence and power among the members of the church and as
emergency bishops. But in fact, they assumed control over the
entire organization of the churches by virtue of their political
power, respecting religious freedom only in so far as they did
not presume to control right preaching and teaching (which
they left to the theologians). So territorial state-churches came
into being whose local congregations enjoyed only nominal
rights of self-determination. The principle of the universal
priesthood of believers had been a good tool of criticism directed against Roman Catholic clericalism. As a constructive
ideal for congregational church life it was actualized so little
that for a long time it served the Lutheran churches only as a
reminder of what might have come to pass among them. Its
most important result for ecclesiastical practice was that the
ministerial office was interpreted as a function which set its
bearer apart in the Christian congregation only in so far as
he was charged (on congregational assent) with a task (preaching and the administration of the sacraments) that by virtue of
its nature (it requires special training) and for the sake of
order not every Christian could fulfill although as a member
of the church everyone was by spiritual right entitled to hold it.
The ministerial offices in Lutheranism thus assumed a character radically different from that of Roman Catholic clericalism. It was of special importance that, from the beginning of
the Reformation, ministers were encouraged to marry. By
their family life they became therefore closely related to the
people among whom they served and the families in the parson-
age became centers of the social life in the Christian communities.

(4) The relation of the church to the social order was of
special concern to Luther, and his definition of this relation
points to aspects of his ecclesiology different from those which
we have discussed so far. We have seen that his fundamental
doctrine of the church was built around the idea of the *"communio sanctorum,"* the "Christian people," who are in the
world because Christ always draws believers to himself and
because the word which proclaims God's revelation in him
always finds believing hearers. We have also observed that
Luther asserted that this community of believers has a twofold

character in so far as it is both internal and external, spiritual and corporeal. These two "sides" of the church correspond to those of the "word," the life-source of the church. For just as the spiritual, divine nature of the "word" cannot realize itself anywhere except by physical human speech and auditory reception, so also the church as an inward community of faith cannot become actual except by an outward organization. The visible form and character of this external side of the church must be determined by the invisible spiritual reality of the inward community of faith which they are to express. There is only one way in which God makes himself known: the outwardness of his revelation is the cloak under which he hides his true nature. Accordingly, the rule of the Christian life, so Luther taught ceaselessly, is that "good works do not make a man good, but a good man does good works."[29] So also the church as the holy people of God is hidden in the external ways and orders in which it is manifest.[30]

From this distinction in the nature of the church, Luther derived the ecclesiological rule that though it is never possible to establish the true church among men merely by making external ecclesiastical arrangements, no ecclesiastical practices must be permitted which are contrary to the nature of the word as it is clearly known or which make it impossible for Christ to reach men and to incorporate them in his body. As a reformer he therefore advocated the abolition of those Roman Catholic institutions and practices which, according to his conviction, were contrary to what everyone who read the Bible with an objective and open sense for what it said could recognize Christ and his gospel to be. He insisted furthermore that the "external" church should be so reformed that it was possible for the "internal" church to be realized within it: The "word" must be its center and the community of believers must be the form of its life. These considerations guided him in the work by which local church organizations were reformed.

But to all this he added still another thought: The true church of the community of believers must manifest itself not only in external ecclesiastical institutions but also in the whole of social life. Luther therefore had to define the place of the church in the social order.

Again it is important to see to what an extent the concrete

presuppositions of his thinking were determined by his own
Roman Catholic background and how he interpreted his new
conception of the Christian gospel with reference to this background. We have seen that his idea of the church as the *"communio sanctorum"* was a Biblical-theological corrective of the
medieval Roman Catholic conception of the church as the
corpus Christi mysticum. He therefore defined the divine social
reality which is in the world by virtue of God's revelation in
Jesus Christ not as a mystical super-personal institution of
priesthood and sacraments but as a personal interrelationship
of the believers in Christ with one another that is ever produced
and nourished by the word.[31] While this definition entailed a
radical deviation from the Roman Catholic tradition (as the
course of the Reformation showed), it nevertheless preserved
the ecclesiological notion (which, in ancient times, Augustine
had most forcefully expressed) that the church is an objective
divine "given." On the basis of this notion, the medieval
Roman Church had tried to accomplish the *Verkirchlichung*
(ecclesiasticalization) of the whole social order. Proceeding on
the same general assumption, namely the objective "given-ness"
of the church but interpreting its nature as "the community of
believers," Luther too was persuaded that the church must
interpenetrate the whole social order. And just as the medieval
church had understood the society which it dominated as the
"corpus Christianum," so he too conceived of the social whole
as the *"corpus Christianum,"*[32] for he took it for granted that
every person in European society was a Christian because as a
child he had been baptized and thus incorporated in the
body of Christ. But, because of his conception of the church
as the community of believers, he was compelled to define the
interpenetration of the social life of this Christian society by
the church in a way radically different from that of Roman
Catholicism.

　The most important innovation he introduced was that he
replaced Roman Catholic asceticism by the ethic of the "calling." Every Christian is able, he taught, to actualize the ethic
of love in the secular work and responsibility to which he has
been "called." In this teaching, Luther's doctrine of the universal priesthood of all believers found its most concrete expression. For while in the doctrine of the priesthood of believers

he referred to the duty of every believer to seek his neighbor's good and to serve him unselfishly in all his needs of body and soul, he suggested in his teaching on "Christian calling" the practical implementation of this demand: the social status and responsibility in which the Christian stands give him the concrete opportunity to help his neighbor.

But at this point there arose for Luther the difficult problem that the callings are often actually of a nature contrary to the ethic of Christian love. He thus seemed to teach that the communion of believers as realized in the secular callings cannot be a real fellowship of love. In a way, this was actually Luther's true conviction. For he was in fact persuaded that the believers' fellowship of love (identical, we should remember, with the "internal" side of the church qua *"communio sanctorum"*) can be realized in this life only within circumstances (which are part of the "external" side of the church) that appear to render the true accomplishment of love impossible.

Here the "dualistic" character of Luther's theology comes drastically within view. In the context of our discussion, we cannot explain it in detail. It must suffice here for us to state that he saw the whole Christian life as a conflict between faith and unfaith, determined ultimately by the cosmic conflict between God and the devil. This battle has in principle and in fact been decided in Christ's death and resurrection by the victory of God over the rebel who commands hell, sin and death and who though defeated nevertheless continues to disturb the divine sway over the world. So the tension in which God's reign stands marks also the Christian life. The Christian *is* justified *propter Christum* and is endowed with the blessings of the divine victory over sin, death, and the devil. But throughout his life on this earth he must withstand the assaults of these enemies from within and without. Though forgiven and declared righteous, he still is actually a sinner; though incorporated in the one community of faith, hope and love, the people of Christ, he still finds himself in the world of idolatry, despair and selfishness. He *is* a Christian only in the sense that, within a life-long battle against the enemies of God which, to be sure, he is able to oppose victoriously by virtue of his union with Christ, he *is becoming* a Christian.

Now it was in the light of this interpretation of life under

God that Luther interpreted the character of the social-historical order of the *corpus Christianum,* in which through callings and the practice of neighborly love and helpfulness the community of the Christian people is to be externally realized. He saw the whole of social life so ordered and determined by God that Christians would be *enabled* to realize membership in the communion of believers in the fallen, sinful world of nature and history: The family *(oeconomia)* is the natural order *(ordinatio),* the state or magistrate *(politia)* the protecting order, and the church *(ecclesia)* the spiritual order, and by submission to them the communion of believers can be actualized in this world. Conformity with the laws and requirements of these *hierarchies* (so Luther also named them) does not produce the church qua *communio sanctorum* but *enables* it to come into being.

This becomes most apparent with respect to the political order, for it is evidently impossible to regard the coercive power and the use of force that constitute its authority as directly Christian. But nevertheless the function of the state to protect the good and to restrain and punish evildoers enables the Christian community to exist at all in human society, for if there were no restraining and ordering power, human society would consume itself in a war of all against all. Luther was always very emphatic in stressing the distinction between the "two kingdoms" of the state and the church, but he also related them closely with one another. He liked to describe the state as the kingdom of God's left hand, intending to suggest by this figure of speech that the church as the kingdom of God's right hand could not be established among men without the state.

But all this is of secondary concern to us in this discussion of ecclesiology. Our interest is drawn to Luther's conception of the church as one of the three "hierarchies" or "orders." What he had here in mind was the church "in the specific sense": the local church congregation. But not its congregational character was the object of his attention, but its nature as an historical order constituted for the purpose of the right preaching of the word and the right administration of the sacraments. By placing the church next to the family and the state as one of the three essential social orders, he therefore meant to suggest that unless there is provision made for the proclamation of the "word," the creative ground of the church qua *communio sanctorum*, the Christian life cannot be developed at all in human society. Also the "church" as seen as an institution in which divine service through preaching takes place *enables* the church as the community of believers to come into being.

It was highly characteristic of Luther that in describing what he conceived to be the specific character of the "church" as one of the "hierarchies" or "orders," he emphasized the determining role which the ministers as the administrators of the word and the sacraments had to play in it. As he saw it, the authority of the preachers in the church corresponded to that of the prince or magistrate in the political order and to that of the parents, especially the father, in the family. He was persuaded that unless these authorities properly exercised their responsibility in their respective spheres, not interfering with one another but also mindful of their common task in the God-ordered world, the Christian character of society could not be preserved and its destiny to become the scene of the communion of believers could not be realized.

This part of Luther's doctrine of the church later became prominent, if not central, in Lutheranism. It regarded the church primarily as a "preaching church." The Lutherans believed to be in continuity with the Augsburg Confession, the creed which, since 1530, was the norm by which they measured the rightness of Christian teaching. In it Melanchthon, its author, had defined the church in the formula: "Where the word is rightly preached and the sacraments are rightly administered, there is the church" (Art. VII). This interpretation certainly agreed with Luther's ecclesiological teaching. Though it reflected particularly his view of the church as the "order" of preaching it could also be read in the light of his whole doctrine of the church. For in the context of his entire ecclesiology the preaching of the word was the necessary condition that had to be fulfilled, the one means that had to be used in order to bring the church into being: the community of believers. Constituted by the divine word made vocal and audible in right preaching, this community is made up of those who on hearing and believing the word know themselves as a spiritual people. Through them God redeems the world by causing them to establish the fellowship of love in human society through the practice of the universal priesthood of mutual spiritual and physical helpfulness, made visible primarily in the church congregation but permeating the lives of men everywhere.

The formula "Where the word of God is rightly preached (we should add: "and heard") and the sacraments are rightly administered (we should add: "and received")" can therefore be read in the light of Luther's whole complicated ecclesiology thought it seems to state only certain of its parts.

In concluding the analysis of Luther's teaching we raise the question why it was that his ecclesiology, though based on the apparently simple principles of "the preaching of the word" and the *"communio sanctorum"* was so complex. It is important to raise this question because Luther's doctrine of the church contains most of the notions which guided the whole Protestant movement in its manysided and variegated concern with the true nature of the church.

The fundamental fact we have to keep in mind is that in order to justify first the demand for a reformation and later the reformation itself, Luther had to develop a doctrine of the church of his own. It reflected necessarily the rather complex understanding of the nature of the "reformation" that was formed in his mind in the course of the gradually deepening conflict between him and the Roman Church and in connection with the unpremeditated founding of a new church order.

Luther's conception of the "reformation" was determined by the fact that in objecting to Roman Catholic Christianity in the name of a biblical understanding of the Christian religion he preserved the sense of historical continuity with Roman Catholicism. All his teachings, but particularly his doctrine of the church, were therefore biblical-theological corrections of the traditions that had been developed in the course of Christian history. Believing that his teaching was in accordance with what the Christian gospel had been not only *in* the beginning but *since* the beginning and certain therefore that he spoke in the name of Christ from within the one church which had been in the world since the days of the New Testament, he nevertheless was compelled (by the fact that the Roman Church excommunicated him and his followers) to found new churches and to provide them with an order according to the principles of the reformation. The new order he was able to produce and permitted to develop—in the form of the Lutheran Evangelical churches—reflected this double character of the reformation, namely, on the one hand, the reduction of the old faith and order of historical Christianity to its true nature in accordance with the "word" and, on the other hand, the introduction of a new faith and order embodied in a non-Roman form of Christianity made necessary by the exclusion of his cause and movement from the Roman Church.

Luther regarded the "Papists" as innovators who, so he charged, had done violence to the Christian gospel by the arbitrary and blasphemous invention of unchristian religious laws, institutions and practices. The thought never occurred to him that his own mission and work of a "reformer" was that of an innovator.[33] But the Roman Church condemned him as such and, by virtue of that fact, it compelled him actually to become the innovating founder of a new church. He involuntarily accepted this role, but he never ceased to be convinced that the evangelical churches of the Reformation and especially those that came to be known as Lutheran churches were ordered in accordance with the word and that as such they were in continuity with the true church that had always been in the world though under the Papacy it had been and was hidden under unevangelical corruptions.

Luther communicated to Protestantism as a whole this peculiar consciousness to represent the one holy catholic church in continuity with the true Christian tradition of the word which the errors of the Roman Church had spoiled but not broken. Thus Protestants came to regard the churches they founded not as novel Christian groups or as sects but as embodiments of the one church, as old as the gospel. As a matter of fact, however, the Protestant churches, formed under the diect or indirect influence of Luther's Reformation, were new historical creations just as Luther's own church was. This was made obvious to all of them by the constant reminder extended to them by Roman Catholicism that it represented the mother-church with whose historical tradition they had broken and from whose historical continuity (allegedly preserved since Biblical times) they had seceded in order to begin new churches. To be sure, Roman Catholicism did not regard itself as a historical church (as it does to this day, it denied that it was the product of historical human decisions) but as a miraculous extension of the Incarnation into history.

It was not until modern men became consciously and critically aware of the historical nature of all human life that the relation between the "old" and the "new" amidst the changes of tradition was understood. Then it became clear that also the life of the church is historically determined, i.e. that what prevails among believers of a certain time as the definition of the nature of the church and as the expression of this nature in ecclesiastical forms and practices is the result of decisions which they have made in their specific situation under the guidance of their faith.

CHAPTER 4

Calvin's Institutes

O N ACCOUNT of its influence upon many generations of Protestants, Calvin's *Institutes of the Christian Religion*[1] may be regarded as the classical statement of the Protestant Christian faith. It reflects more clearly than any other book produced by the Reformation the thought which inaugurated the whole Protestant movement.

This is all the more remarkable in view of the fact that Calvin was a member of the second generation of the Protestant Reformers. When, in 1536, he appeared on the scene of history as the author of the *Institutes of the Christian Religion,* the Protestant Reformation was firmly established not only in Germany and in Switzerland but also in other European countries. In contrast to Luther and others of his contemporaries, Calvin did not have to plow new religious grounds. He could rely upon what those who had preceded him had already stated and affirmed. In the light of all this, it is all the more remarkable that, in the course of time, the *Institutes* came to be regarded as *the* theological exposition of Protestantism.

One may say that this book reflects Calvin's total career. It does not represent his entire life work as a writer, for he was the author of numerous volumes of sermons and Biblical commentaries and of essays dealing with theological and ecclesiastical controversy, and particularly of innumerable letters—numbering several thousands—in which he instructed his contemporaries of all European lands in the meaning of the Christian faith as he saw it.

Nevertheless, the *Institutes* reflect Calvin's total work. This is true also in the sense that the book accompanied him throughout his life. In 1536 it established his fame; when, in 1559, he produced the last edition, the little book of the beginnings had grown into a volume of large size containing all the theological wisdom that Calvin had gathered in the course of his career.

In order that we may understand this book best, let us consider it in terms of the stages of its growth. The first edition was published in Basle in the early part of 1536. It was conceived as a catechism, i.e., as an introduction to the Christian faith. Yet it was meant to serve also another purpose, namely a political one, for it was dedicated by a letter of introduction and dedication to the King of France, Francis I. The latter, for political reasons, was a staunch defender of Roman Catholicism, resolved to exclude the influence of the Lutheran Reformation from his land. But such prohibition was unsuccessful in view of the fact that during the Reformation age the printing presses had become very quick means of communication all over Europe. Since the beginning of the Protestant movement, Lutheran influences had thus made themselves felt on French public life.

One of the first tasks that Calvin, as a spokesman for the Protestant faith, assigned to himself was to justify his religious conviction and to prove to the King and all who were willing to listen that the Protestant faith was not subversive. This is how the *Institutes* came into being.

It is significant that all the editions of the *Institutes* were provided by Calvin himself with the letter of dedication addressed to the French King in 1536:

"I beseech you, Sire,—and surely it is not an unreasonable request,—to take upon yourself the entire cognizance of this cause, which has hitherto been confusedly and carelessly agitated, without any order of law, and with outrageous passion rather than judicial gravity. Think not that I am now meditating my own individual defense, in order to effect a safe return to my native country; for though I feel the affection which every man ought to feel for it, yet, under the existing circumstances, I regret not my removal from it. But I plead the cause of all the godly, and consequently of Christ himself.

"It shall be yours, Sire, not to turn away your ears or thoughts from so just a defense, especially in a cause of such importance as the maintenance of God's glory unimpaired in the world, the preservation of the honor of divine truth, and the continuance of the Kingdom of Christ uninjured among us.

This is a cause worthy of your attention, worthy of your cognizance, worthy of your throne. This consideration constitutes true royalty, to acknowledge yourself in the government of your kingdom to be the minister of God. For where the glory of God is not made the end of Government, it is not a legitimate sovereignty but a usurpation."[2]

These statements reflect the true spirit of Calvin. They are especially remarkable in view of the fact that the author of the challenging book that contained them was only twenty-six years old.

The book itself was divided into six chapters. The first three dealt with the "Law," in the form of an explanation of the Decalogue; with "Faith," by way of an interpretation of the Apostles' Creed; and with "Prayer," on the basis of an exposition of the Lord's Prayer. Then followed three other chapters, one dealing with the sacraments, namely Baptism and the Lord's Supper, another containing a discussion of the five other Roman Catholic sacraments, the validity of which Calvin denied; and finally there was a chapter on "Christian Liberty," the power of the church and of the political magistrate.

This organization of the earliest edition of the *Institutes* indicates that Calvin was under the influence of the writings of Luther. Indeed, he followed the order of Luther's *Catechism*. The Decalogue, the Apostles' Creed, and the Lord's Prayer had been used for centuries as the chief subjects of religious instruction, and depending upon this old tradition, the Reformers, and especially Luther, had used these statements as the means by which to explain the faith which they held.

But it was characteristic of Calvin that going beyond the limits generally set by the writers of catechisms, he dealt extensively also with the church in his interpretation of the Christian faith. What he said about the character of the church and also of the nature of the state he retained unchanged in all the later editions of his book. From the very beginning his mind was so definitely set that he had no need to modify any of the opinions he articulated in his youth.

He showed himself in all respects a true disciple of the early Reformers, especially Luther. The doctrine of justification by faith, according to which no man may trust in his own power to achieve the good but rather must rely upon the mercy of God in order to be enabled to fulfil the moral law, was adopted by Calvin as his major theme. But he added to this interpretation of the Christian faith something very characteristic of his own religious nature: the religious life, he taught, is one of complete obedience to God. What God's will is is laid down in the law, the law of the Old as well as of the New Testament. That the fulfilment of this law in terms of absolute obedience is the highest good was guaranteed to Calvin by the faith in the merciful God, who in his revelation in Christ shows to anyone who believes that he is not only just but also forgiving.

Throughout his career, Calvin insisted upon this understanding of the nature of the religious faith: unreserved obedience to the law of the divine Lord, who, in Christ, has proved himself trustworthy.

The second edition was issued in 1539, and printed at Strasbourg, where Calvin was then a resident. The first issue of the *Institutes* had established his fame. When he happened to travel through Geneva in the year 1536, he was recognized as the author of a widely read and representative Protestant book, and his friend and compatriot, Farel, drew him into the service of the Geneva church. This first activity of Calvin in Geneva ended in a fiasco. He did not succeed in persuading the leading citizens of the city of the validity of his conception of Christianity and the principal organization of the church implied therein, and so, in 1538, he resigned his offices and went to settle in Basle, from where he was called to Strasbourg.

He became the minister of a congregation of French Protestant refugees and, at the same time, a lecturer in the Reformed church of Strasbourg. Of all the German cities, Strasbourg at that time was the most decidedly Protestant. Under the leadership of the two reformers, Butzer and Capito, its whole common life had been transformed according to the principles of the Reformation. The Protestant faith was not only taught in church and school but it was expressed in organization and discipline.

Calvin, who in Geneva had endeavored to build a city of God in the civil community because he was persuaded that the whole individual and common life of men should be one of obedience to the divine commandments, was profoundly im-

pressed by the accomplishments of the Strasbourgers. He attached himself particularly to Martin Butzer, whom he revered
as a father until their friendship was terminated by Butzer's
death in 1551.

In the new edition of the *Institutes,* this Strasbourg experience was clearly reflected. The six chapters were extended to
seventeen. The parts that were now added were inspired by the
studies that Calvin had made in reaction to his own Geneva
experience and in response to the stimuli that he received in
Strasbourg.

He had undertaken a new study of Paul's Letters, especially
the Epistle to the Romans. Even more definitely than before he
had come to the conviction that it was Paul's interpretation of
the Christian Gospel which had to be regarded as the central interpretation of Christ to be found in the whole New Testament.

Inspired by this Paulinism, he had turned to a study of the
Church fathers, and particularly to Augustine. Thus he had
become an accomplished Augustinian, finding in Augustine,
however, primarily what agreed with his own Paulinist outlook.
From Augustine he directed his attention also to the Greek fathers, especially Chrysostom. Using this knowledge very skill-
fully, he undertook now to add to the earlier chapters of his *Institutes* certain discussions of what he believed to be the major
themes of the Christian faith.

He still talked primarily of the law and of faith and of
prayer and of the sacraments and the church, but the work assumed an entirely new character. These are the chapter headings:

The Knowledge of God; The Knowledge of Man and of
Free Will; The Law; Faith; Penitence; Justification by Faith
and the Merit of Works; On the Similarity and Difference Between the Old and the New Testaments; On Divine Predestination; On Providence; On Prayer; On the Sacraments; On
Baptism; On the Lord's Supper; On Christian Liberty; On
the Power of the Church; On the Five False Sacraments; and
finally, On the Life of the Christian Man.

Inspired by Paul and by Augustine, Calvin had added to
his earlier exposition interpretations of those themes of faith
which in the mind of the Reformers were the most decisive and
characteristic ones.

He began his exposition with chapters on the knowledge of God and the knowledge of man. This was in accord with the deepest explanations of the religious life as they can be found in the literature of all ages, for religion is always a relation between God and man, a response of man to the action of God made known through a Revealer. The interpretations of this commitment of man to God have always been, generally speaking, of two kinds. One either tried to explain how the soul could rise to God—then the religious life was seen as an interpretation of human existence in so far as it is governed by its own deepest levels. Or one attempted to show that the knowledge of God is the pre-supposition of the best self-knowledge at which man can arrive—then religion was seen as the service of God. The first way of speaking of religion is characteristic especially of the mystics; the second way may be called that of the prophets. The mystics begin with human experience and then cause their mind to be elevated in the search for the vision of God, but the prophetic way of speaking of religion is one in which human existence, and particularly human self-knowledge, is understood in the light of the divine self-disclosure. When religion is thus interpreted, God-knowledge becomes the basis of self-knowledge.

It was highly indicative of Calvin's bend of mind that he chose this second way of interpreting religion. The knowledge of God, he insisted, must be firmly established before one can comprehend the meaning of the divine will for human life. That is why he began this second edition of the *Institutes* with a chapter on the knowledge of God, and for the same reason he ended it with a chapter on the life of the Christian man. In order to give an impression of the flavor of this second edition, one can do nothing better than to cite two sections from the chapter on the Christian life. This chapter, entitled "The Life of a Christian," has been overlooked by many of the interpreters of Calvin's ethics. If it were read more often, many of the common misinterpretations of Calvin's ethics would not occur. Calvin wrote[3]:

"Although the divine law contains a most excellent and well arranged plan for the regulation of life, yet it has pleased the Heavenly Father to conform men by a more accurate doctrine to the rule which he had prescribed in the law, and the principle of that doctrine is this: That it is the duty of believers to present their bodies a living sacrifice, wholly acceptable unto God, and that in this consists the legitimate worship of Him. Hence is deduced an argument for exhorting them: "be not conformed to this world; but be ye transformed by the renewing of your mind, that ye may prove what is that will of God."

"This is a very important consideration that we are consecrated and dedicated to God that we may not hereafter think, speak, meditate, or do anything but with a view to his glory, for that which is sacred cannot without great injustice toward Him be applied to unholy uses . If we are not our own but the Lord's, it is manifest both what error we must avoid and to what end all the actions of our lives are to be dedicated. We are not our own. Therefore, neither our reason nor our will should predominate in our deliberations and actions. We are not our own. Therefore, let us not propose it as our end to seek what may be expedient for us according to the flesh. We are not our own. Therefore, let us as far as possible forget ourselves and all things that are ours.

"On the contrary, we are God's. To Him, therefore, let us live and die. We are God's. Toward Him, therefore, as our only legitimate end let every part of our lives be directed. Oh, how great a proficiency has that man made who having been taught that he is not his own, has taken the sovereignty and government of himself from his own reason to surrender it to God."

One may say that this passage can serve as a motto for the entire interpretation of the Christian faith that Calvin offers in his *Institutes*.

In the light of these words expressing the theme, "We are not our own, but we are God's" one can also appreciate why Calvin felt compelled to attribute so much significance to the two doctrines of predestination and of providence, doctrines which have been regarded by many as the central themes of Calvinist Christianity.

Calvin was naturally led to emphasize predestination and providence because he could not but be consistent with himself. He felt it necessary to say that because in all respects man depends upon God, so that he is always God's and never his own, he must let the divine will govern his reason. He was further

driven to say that the divine sovereignty is so absolute that
every single aspect of human existence, and also the ultimate
end of human life, must be viewed in the light of this divine
initiative. In the doctrine of providence Calvin taught, therefore, that a believer must learn to be assured that nothing
at all happens in the world without the express will of God.
Not being afraid to say too much rather than too little, Calvin
chose to be so specific in the explication of this doctrine that
he declared that not a single hair falls from the head of a man
without the express will of God and that no drop of rain falls
from the skies without the direct volition of the divine Father.
But when he spoke in this way he did not mean to be understood as a determinist, much less as a fatalist. He wished merely
to interpret the Christian faith as an absolute confidence in the
omnipotent Creator who is the Father. When, therefore, he
dealt with the question, to what extent the doctrine of providence is applicable to the daily events of life, he said that one
who believes in the all-ordering divine providence does not
need to be anxious or filled with dread. He may always be
sure that nothing can befall him that is not provided for his
benefit by the omnipotent will of God who is good.

It is this same spirit that led him to speak so affirmatively
concerning predestination.

He warns again and again throughout the *Institutes* and
in all its editions of the danger (to which all men are so easily
prone) of speculating concerning the divine nature. Just as
Luther he was persuaded that religion has nothing whatsoever
to do with speculation. It is nothing but an answer to what
God has done in his revelation.

In this light, one must see predestination: just as man lives
by the gratuitously given grace of God, over which he has no
control whatsoever and which he must receive in faith, so he
must understand his ultimate destiny as being in all respects dependent upon the will of God. Predestination, therefore, was
for Calvin merely an appendix to the doctrine of justification
by grace. He was a predestinarian because he believed absolutely in the initiative of the God of mercy. If a man cannot
rely upon himself for his salvation but must throw himself
upon God's merciful goodness, then he must also be willing

to acknowledge that in all respects he is God's and not his own —particularly with regard to his eternal destiny.

Calvin was so consistent in making his explications that he also drew the negative conclusion which makes it appear as if he had been speculative, after all. In other words, as a predestinarian he spoke as one who believed in rejection as well as in election; yet, when he thus stressed double predestination, he did not mean to yield to the temptation of one who thought speculatively about the divine will, as if he were able to say what was hidden in it. Rather, as a teacher of double predestination he desired to be understood as one who explained what he believed to be actual occurrences. Throughout his career, he had tried to teach men obedience to God. He became most concretely impressed by the fact that some men were utterly incapable, as it seemed, of such obedience. No services of the spokesmen of the divine word could persuade them to yield in their disobedience. So, in the light of the fact that some show a strange propensity for religion while others seem to be excluded from the possibility of opening themselves to it, Calvin believed that it was possible for a theological interpreter of the religious faith to say that some were affected by the saving will of God and others were not.

All these convictions which are characteristic of Calvin's entire work were for the first time most clearly expressed in the second edition of the *Institutes* of 1539.

In 1543, there appeared a third edition. It was again enlarged, although all that the former issues had contained was preserved. In the meantime, Calvin had returned to Geneva. He had arrived there in September, 1541. He had made it the condition of his acceptance of the call of the citizens of Geneva to be their chief minister of the word of God, that they should order the church life of their city according to the "Ecclesiastical Ordinances." Therein Calvin had laid down the principles of that church organization which, throughout the centuries, has proved effective in all Calvinist church groups.

He was interested to establish a church that should be free as far as possible from interference of the state or the political magistrate. He wanted to see the church organized according to what he believed to be the will of God. He knew the will of God, as has already been suggested, through the law. The law

was given to him in the Bible, in the Old as well as in the New
Testament. The New Testament, according to his conviction,
merely clarified all that was enunciated in the Old Testament.
particularly in the passages dealing with the moral law. Therefore, Calvin believed that a church organized according to the
will of God had to conform to principles of polity that were derived from Scripture: and he interpreted the ecclesiological
chapters of the New Testament, Romans 12 and I Cor. 12, in
such a way that he saw therein prescribed four church offices,
namely, those of the pastors, the elders, the teachers, and the
deacons. No church, he was persuaded, conformed to the law
of God unless it was established in these four offices, the purpose of all of which was to be the proclamation and the expression in deeds of the word of God.

According to these principles, he built the church of Geneva, and in this concern he consumed his strength. When, in
1543, it was necessary to bring out a new edition of the *Institutes,* he added to the earlier chapters on the church certain sections in which he made plain his own convictions as to the
character of church polity. Furthermore, he took occasion to
reject more forcefully than he had done before, the Catholic
church order which he believed was contrary to the word of
God.

In the form of this third edition the book was issued repeatedly, but more or less unchanged, in 1545, 1550, and 1554.

When the year 1558 came around, Calvin was forty-nine
years of age. He believed that the end of his life was near. He
suffered with many illnesses. Throughout his career he had
been ailing with severe indigestion. In 1558, he suffered not
merely of this stomach ailment and of gout, but also of the
quartan fever. He was unable to attend to his regular duties
and was confined to his house; but, as was characteristic of him,
he used this leisure, as he called his sickness, to revise his
major book, the *Institutes.* Working on his sick bed, he re-
arranged the material of all the former editions. He made corrections as he felt the need. He added to what he had written
before, particularly that wisdom which had come to him as a
Biblical exegete.

The *Institutes* of the first edition of 1536 had been conceived by him as a catechism. In 1539, he had stated that he

wished that the book should be used by the students of theology as an elementary text which might help them to understand the major themes of Christian thought. In 1559, when he was able to print the completely revised edition which was to remain the final one of his work, he said that he desired the book to be understood as a statement of Biblical theology. As such he wished it to be used as a basis for the work of interpretation, particularly in exegesis of the Biblical books. The additions he made in this last edition were therefore primarily taken from the Bible.

He believed that as a Protestant thinker he should prove to the world that the only source of his faith was the Bible and nothing else. On this basis he argued against those who fundamentally disagreed with him: turning to the right, he endeavored to refute the Roman Catholics who unjustly, he believed, added to the authority of the Bible that of the tradition; and turning to the left, he criticized just as vehemently the "radicals" of the Reformation, the Anabaptists, who believed it possible to order their lives primarily on the basis of a direct inspiration from God and only secondarily on the basis of the Bible.

The book was now organized in what he called "four books." The first book (in eighteen chapters) dealt with the knowledge of God ,the Creator: the second book (in seventeen chapters) treated "the knowledge of God the Redeemer in Christ, which was revealed first to the Fathers under the law and since to us in the Gospel"; the third book (of twenty-five chapters) was entitled "On the Manner of receiving the grace of Christ, the benefits which we receive from it and the effects which follow from it" and the final book (of twenty chapters) was devoted to a discussion of "the external means or aids by which God calls us into communion with Christ and retains us in it."

All in all, the work now contained eighty-one chapters. In 1536, it consisted of merely six. Now, the fullness of the Calvinistic faith was disclosed. No major theme that was of significance in the Reformation was omitted. One cannot say that the argument of the work is one of continuity. Calvin presents himself as a writer who was able to deal with many diverse subjects. Yet, in spite of the fact that these subjects do not appear to hang together, they are written about by a man

who had a clearly delineated intellectual and spiritual character. The interpreters of Calvin's *Institutes* have tried to describe and analyze this character. Some have said that Calvin
was primarily oriented to the sovereignty of God; others have
attempted to show that the doctrine of predestination was the
hinge on which all his arguments turned. Still others believe
that providence should be emphasized centrally; and still another group has endeavored to show that Calvin was but a true
disciple of the Reformation and that therefore "justification by
faith" was his one great theme, articulated in various ways.

I believe that the truest way to describe Calvin's manner
of writing and of arguing is to see him as a Biblical theologian.
To be sure, he read the Bible in the light of the doctrine of
justification by faith and in terms of the absolute lordship of
God, but he left room in all he wrote for the great variety of
religion that is embodied in the Biblical books, believing that
the Bible was a spiritual unity. Accordingly, one will understand him best as a Biblical theologian.

He did not care to speculate on divine themes or to write
as a philosopher. He wished nothing more than to be obedient
to what he was persuaded was the voice of God directly made
audible in the words of the Bible. Indeed, if one desires to
gauge the manner in which the Bible as a whole formed the
thought world of a great Christian thinker, one can, I believe,
do nothing better than to study Calvin's *Institutes*.

CHAPTER 5

Luther and Butzer

T HE STRASSBURG reformer Martin Butzer (1491-1551) is remembered only by scholars who in their research deal with the history of early Protestantism. He does not live in the memory of Protestants as one of their great leaders. But in his day he was a very influential person. Not only Strassburg, but all Germany, needed his energy, his practical advice, and his political skill. Many a diet and many an ecclesiastical conference heard him phrase formulas and doctrines which were intended to relieve tense situations and to work for progress in religion. But the result of his work has been forgotten, it seems, with the memory of his energetic, spirited face. The few copies of his books that have been carried over to our generation adorn the rare-book rooms of great libraries. The catalogues of common book collections remember him only by a chapter on divorce that he incorporated in his swan song, *De regno Christi,* written for the English king, Edward VI, which young John Milton happened to discover when his divorce kept his mind occupied with appeals to the parliament.[1] His secretary planned to publish his collected works after his death in ten big folio volumes, but he succeeded in getting only the *Scripta anglicana* (Basel, 1577) into print. The mass of the other material rests in Strassburg. Perhaps one day it will be revealed to interested historians, enabling them to judge thoroughly the man, his thoughts, and his influence. The writings of his that are now accessible have been studied mainly in reference to Calvin, and there seems to be proof enough that Butzer was Calvin's foremost teacher. They reveal, not an original mind, but one rich in many very suggestive ideas which, in their full scope, remained unrealized and not successfully applied by Butzer himself. Therefore they were forgotten

67

and left to emerge in the minds of later generations under new conditions. Anglicanism and Puritanism alike could rightly claim him as their godfather.[2] The ideas to which we here refer are concerned with practical religion, with the church and state in their essential nature and in their relationship to each other.[3] These ideas we shall here compare with those of Luther in order to exhibit them in their full character and to estimate them at their own value. Perhaps the result will be a clarification of our own thought about the principles of practical religion as it is seen in its relation to the secular order. Such ideas are generally comprehended under the concept of the Kingdom of God. It may be well, therefore, to commence our comparative study with Luther's and Butzer's understanding of this notion.

Luther identifies the Kingdom of God with the invisible church, the *communio sanctorum,* i.e., the communion of those who have accepted the word in faith,[4] who have become real children of God through their God-given faith. Driven and inspired by the Holy Spirit, they love God and their neighbor because they cannot do otherwise. Through their faith they are able to fulfil the commandments of the Sermon on the Mount.[5] The Kingdom of God is "that which binds hearts and consciences together in a living communion." "It is a communion of love of purely spiritual character which comprehends all times and all lands."[6] The constitutive element of the Kingdom of God is faith. This conception is thoroughly religious. The citizens of the Kingdom are thought to be those to whom God grants, out of his mercifulness, justification by sanctifying them with the Holy Spirit and by assuring them in the preaching of the word of full certainty of salvation. "The Kingdom of God is a kingdom of grace in which through the name of Jesus all sins are to be forgiven."[7]

In his thought on the Kingdom of God Butzer emphasized its *moral* character. He understood the gospel primarily as a moral phenomenon. It was to become a moral power. When by the fulfilment of the Scripture the communion of love is established among men, the Kingdom of God is realized; Christ rules.[8] He does not stress, like Luther, the religious content of the Gospel as being of very first importance. That accounts for the different conception of the relation between

Gospel and law. Luther sharply distinguished them from each other. But Butzer appreciates the Gospel also as a law.[9] The Old and New Testaments belong closely together.[10] The Scripture as an entity is obligatory.

Roughly speaking, then, the two reformers have a different concept of morality. For Luther, it is mainly a good inner attitude put into action, nourished by the grace of God. Butzer has the attitude originate out of the conscious and strict observation of the Will of God given in the Gospel, which is to be realized as such in all orders of life and is to comprehend the whole social and cultural life of man.[11]

This general difference must be proved in detail.

It is to be noted that Butzer's concept of the Kingdom of God is not unified. Two circles of thought are interwoven with each other. The Kingdom of God has come when the commandments and the truth of the Bible have permeated *all* human conditions; but, on the other hand, it is present only in the church of the elect, the invisible communion of the predestinated saints.[12]

If we observe how by using the narrower concept the two circles are combined with each other, we touch the fundamental difference between Luther and Butzer.

Both of them consider the Kingdom of God as the communion of the true believers, whom Christ governs and whom he leads to love. This means for Butzer that the Kingdom of God consists of the elect. But how can their communion appear as real? The election can never produce a vital contact between men, but concerns only individuals. It seems as if this "communion" lacks that connecting link which Luther finds in the word, given and effective in history. How does Butzer find it? He considers the election realized by incorporation of the Christian in the Corpus Christi, the church of Christ. The idea of predestination is combined with a peculiar idea of the church: Christ, who grants election by his spirit, has by his word constituted a church, an organization with offices and constitution, so that his elected followers might form a communion.[13] In this church, which is ordered by Christ himself and which is directed by himself through his instruments, the *ministri*, the flock of saints represents a communion of sanctification and of love. From now on membership in the Kingdom of God, now identical with the visible organized church, reveals itself in love, in ethical obedience to the commandments of God and Christ.[14]   In such thinking Butzer's strong emphasis on church discipline originates.   The principle of election, however, is changed and enlarged.   Everyone can consider himself elected who is a member of the Christ-ordered church and who contributes to the common welfare by leading a life which conforms to biblical prescription, thereby promoting God's glory and mankind's salvation.   Furthermore, because Christ's order is superior to all human orders, his word and his discipline are of highest significance for the formation of human life.   In all human conditions the word must be obeyed as a law.   Even the state is bound to it and obliged to propagate the kingdom of Christ on earth.[15]

At the center of Luther's church concept stands, not predestination, but the word of salvation.   Members of the true church and of the Kingdom of God are those believers who have received their justification in the word and express such a gift in an evangelical morality.   They also are elected, but that is not decisive for the formation of the church concept. The church, in its invisible character as a *communio sanctorum,* cannot exist without the word.[16]

The office of the pastor or preacher is therefore a necessity; the development of a visible church is required.   Its only purpose is the preaching of the word and the administration of its sacraments which are based on it.   The form, order, and constitution of this earthly organization, the visible part *(Kultgemeinde)* of the invisible church *(Gemeinschaft der Gläubigen),* is absolutely voluntary and incidental.[17]   Christ has given no special orders for it; the Bible does not prescribe its external character.   No discipline can be exercised in this church; only the word in its saving character must be made effective.   The Holy Spirit uses it as a means to gather the communion of the Christians who live in free expression of their faith.   A church discipline does not make this morality obligatory for a wider circle.   The Gospel, truly received and accepted only by a minority, cannot be made a moral law for a disinterested majority.   The communion of love, called the *regnum Dei,* is limited to the small number of the *fideles* or *sancti.*

If one thinks that Luther unjustly enlarged this concept of the church in his idea of the general priesthood of believers, one may well remember the statement of Holl: "Since the Kingdom of God is an invisible entity and it is reserved for God to call into it whom he will, no man has a right to deprive any other person of membership therein, or of the possibility of such membership, and thus to deny him participation in the communion of love."[18] The idea of the general priesthood of all believers indicates the incidental character of all church organization and the relative religious significance of ecclesiastical offices. Furthermore, by claiming that a secular profession could not hinder the perfection of a man's Christian character, Luther came to appreciate the religious importance of all secular callings.

Butzer took these notions over from Luther, but he emphasized almost more strongly the religious character of the professions and vocations. Religion's calling to salvation and the calling to a profession go hand in hand.[19] He sees the realization of the communion of love, required in the "word," guaranteed in professional and vocational work for the benefit of the commonwealth.

Luther stresses much more energetically than Butzer the idea that a calling, a vocation, is Christian only in so far as the persons engaged in it are Christians. In their Christian consciousness the orders of the world are Christianized. All orders of the world as such are non-Christian. Luther regards also state and magistrate as such an order. It is akin to the family and artisanship or craftsmanship. It is merely the divinely controlled, natural world-order that is fulfilled in these "offices." A non-Christian is capable of administering them just as well as a Christian, if the task is accomplished with "reason." "The procedure becomes Christianized only in the consciousness of the Christian person who knows that in filling his office he serves his neighbor."[20] As if directly refuting such an opinion, Butzer writes in the discourse on the magistrates: "The task of a magistrate is another task than to make shoes, clothes, and such things which fulfil bodily needs."[21] Here we touch upon a very important point of difference between Luther and Butzer, particularly with reference to their concept of the state.

Luther separated completely the sphere of the Kingdom of God from the sphere of secular orders.[22] State and Kingdom of God stand in strict contrast to each other: in the latter is freedom; in the former, coercion; the latter is dominated by love, the former by force; in the latter there is freedom for the inner man, untouched by external power, while the former disciplines the outer man.[23] What has the inner communion of love, fulfilling the Sermon on the Mount, in common with the external order, founded upon compulsion, right, power, and authority of the sword! But, nevertheless, the state is a God-ordained, natural order.[24] It even stands in the service of the Kingdom of God.[25] Without the state, i.e., the power of the civil magistrate, the flock of the true Christians could never exist, because they would be suppressed by evil men. The state furnishes to the Kingdom of God (not only to the church!) the possibility of growth, since it uses its coercive power to limit the expansion of evil and because it creates by its laws a morality which protects the extension of the Gospel. In its fight against crime, the state is related to the Kingdom.[26] As a "police régime" it becomes a "left hand" for the Kingdom of God.

How different Butzer! He also knows of the limitation of political power in regard to conscience, which it cannot rule.[27] But under no circumstances does he put it in antagonism to the Kingdom of God. The political magistrate has a spiritual task. By having received with the power of the sword the power over the *lives* of its subjects or citizens, it is responsible for the best *living*. It has to see to it that life be lived *bene beateque*. According to its utmost ability, it must promote the highest type of morality, not only peace and concord on the principles of "law of nature." Because the highest morality is founded on religion, it is the duty of the magistrate to establish the true religion in his country, i.e., the moral powers of the Kingdom of God shall have absolute influence in the lives of its subjects. Butzer does not hesitate to declare that the secular government must propagate the Kingdom of God by its own means. However, the presupposition is that the true magistrate is Christian. All others he calls tyrants. The State is in the service of the Kingdom of God, directly not indirectly. It does not only prepare for the highest morality; it is obliged to spread the true and best one among its subjects. "It is the duty of the government to see that its subjects live right and well. That is not possible where they are not, above all else, drawn to the true service of God. On this depend all virtues, as well as all felicity and well-being. For they who seek the Kingdom of God and his righteousness will themselves obtain all good things, said Christ the Lord. The pious rulers must therefore not use religion as a means for the maintenance of external peace as impious tyrants do, but the establishment of religion itself must be their aim. Therefore they will leave nothing undone which glorifies the name of God among their subjects by their activity of governing and which propagates His Kingdom and builds it up in the best way."[28] So it follows that the state promotes and serves the church and that it stands beside her, is even inferior and subject to her, as it hears from the ministers of the church the word of Christ. The result is a Christian state which endeavors to develop all its life under the law of the biblical word. A distinction between the political and ecclesiastical power is recognized, but their separation is not stated.

For Luther, it was a principle that church and state comprehend two strongly separated spheres.[29] The idea of a Christian state is for him impracticable, if not inconceivable.[30] The Gospel, to be experienced only by a small number of men and in its moral applications first of all valid for the individual, can never become, as for Butzer, a rule of the political laws. Throughout his lifetime Luther complained about the fact that there were not enough Christians. Although he also related the life in the world to the highest moral communion (the *communio sanctorum*) by saying that love ought to regulate and permeate all secular orders, he hesitated to make it obligatory or binding. He only wanted to see the moralizing influence of the Kingdom of God at work in yielding practical results. Butzer had probably the same aim in mind. But it can easily be felt that he wanted to make religion and its moral expression a law, thereby tending to secularize religion itself. Luther wanted to prevent just that.

Luther gives to religion its own sphere, clear and precise, and leaves to the secular orders a legal status of their own *Eigengesetzlichkeit*, which shows his profound insight into the reality of things, for as long as economics are economics they are ruled by economic laws, and as long as politics are politics they are governed by political laws. Luther sees that the connection between the secular orders and religion can come about only through persons who in their Christian consciousness may raise secular affairs to a higher moral level, while the church in preaching the word enables them to review things *sub specie aeternitatis,* under the aspects of the invisible Kingdom of God.

Butzer's ideal of state is a "commonwealth"[30a] wherein the common welfare is best guaranteed by the Christian nature of the state and its actions. Thus he blends two spheres that are essentially foreign to each other. The true Christian communion seeks more than welfare. Butzer's own ideas regarding the realization on earth of the Kingdom of God promoted by the state display traits which concern happiness and utility. He claims that a Christian state will be the most *powerful* and the wealthiest one,[31] not feeling that the very existence of *such* a state would destroy the most distinctive features of the Christian religion.

One may read, as though a direct answer of Luther to Butzer, the rather pessimistic, gloomy words: "But see to it that you fill the world with true Christians before you rule it in a Christian and evangelical way. You will never be able to do so, for the world in the mass is un-Christian and will remain un-Christian, although all are baptized and are called Christian. But the Christians (as it is said) live far apart from each other. Therefore it cannot be in this world that a Christian government becomes common everywhere, not even over a country or over a good number of men."[31a]

That is why Luther feels no justification for demanding that a prince *must* be Christian.[32] He recognizes—surely in contrast to Butzer—that an unbeliever can sometimes rule and govern in a better way than a Christian.[33] Though, naturally, he would greet a Christian prince with joy, he is of the opinion that the office of government *per se* is not influenced by the Christian character of its responsible leader. It is his function to maintain power in his country, to keep right and peace, to punish the criminals, and to protect the orderly citizens. Legislation is therefore governed by the common "positive law," and not—as Butzer advised—by Christ's precepts or by the decalogue. For the Gospel does not contain a rule about the method of government; it prescribes only that one shall honor the civil magistrate. How superior is Luther, with his profound description of the Mosaic law as the Jews' "Saxon Code," which may be used as a pattern of a law code and as a good example,[34] to Butzer, who was always inclined to consider the Mosaic law, not as a code of natural or common law, but as a law of God, deserving preference to all human laws! How much superior is Luther to Butzer when he writes: "Thus God has subjected secular government to reason, because it is not supposed to rule the soul's salvation or eternal things, but only goods of body and of time which God has subjected to men (Genesis, chapter 2). That's why the Gospel does not teach how to govern and how to rule. It merely commands that one shall honor the magistrate and not rebel against him."[35]

However, that is not to say that Luther does not want the preacher to exhort the prince to morality and fear of God. Such attitudes are required on the basis of the natural world-order. Hence the combat against atheism, the punishment of blasphemies, the fight of the state against heretics, as far as they are unbelievers of God's existence and skeptical of the fundamental truths of Christianity.[36] In this respect, owing to the point of view of their time, Butzer and Luther follow the same lines. A compulsory oppression of members of another Christian group, e.g., Catholics, a coercion of conscience, was unacceptable to them both, but they were of the conviction that a state with two confessional groups could not be governed.

This law against heretics suggests that the state has to pursue positive politics in regard to religion. It is a task according to the "law of nature." On the same basis Luther considers it the state's duty to insure the welfare of its citizens. Establishment of universities and schools, the issuance of marriage laws, propaganda for relief of the poor, suppression of begging and vagabondry, of usury and exorbitant luxury,[37] belong to its program. These propositions for civic improvement, published in the "Manifest to the German nobility," are identical with those of Butzer in his "De Regno Christi" for the reorganization of social and cultural life in England. But the presuppositions out of which they grow differ radically from each other. The place of religion in their plans for a *Kultur- und Wohlfahrtsstaat* is not the same.

Finally, we have to deal with the ideas concerning the relationship between church and state. It has been made evident that Butzer never felt the contrast between the two orders as sharply as did Luther.

When in the course of time, in order to complete the work of reformation, Luther saw himself compelled to use the help of the prince in church matters, he did not thereby surrender his principles. The duty to *reform* is conferred upon the prince as the *praecipuum membrum ecclesiae,* on the basis of the general priesthood of all believers and as *Notbischof.* It is true, all this led finally to the establishment of a church government appertaining to the sovereign, but Luther did not desire this result. According to Butzer, the sovereign is obliged, in fulfillment of the divinely ordered purpose of his office, to promote a reformation and supervise the church. He formulated the first Protestant theory for the church supremacy of the English kings.

If, in conclusion, we state that the difference between Luther's and Butzer's church concept is the result of a difference in world-view, we are led to a general historical comparison. Though Butzer became a Protestant reformer through the direct influence of Luther, he remained, throughout his life, a loyal disciple of that school to which he was introduced as a student at Schlettstadt and Heidelberg. He never ceased to be a Humanist.[38] Hence the moralistic color of his Christian ideal. The difference between his and Luther's concept of the Kingdom of God is, therefore, largely due to the antagonism between Humanism and Lutheranism, between Erasmus and Luther, between an anthropocentric, rationalistic, and moralistic use of the Bible and a theocentric biblicism.

CHAPTER 6

Calvin and Butzer

C ALVIN belonged to the second generation of Protestant reformers. It does not necessarily follow from this fact that he was an epigone; that he was not, is proved by the existence of the type of Protestantism which is generally called Calvinism. But it cannot be doubted that he owed decisive stimuli to anti-Catholic predecessors and that, in the development of his theological and ecclesiastical system, he was not entirely original. It is the general opinion of historians that Calvin depended—at least in the first years of his career as an evangelical theologian—largely upon Luther; particularly the latter's idea of justification is, it is claimed, better understood by no one than by Calvin. Neither will one go very far astray, if one assumes that Melanchthon and especially Zwingli exerted some influence upon the reformer of Geneva. During the last decades, one has begun to pay attention also to another man with whom Calvin is known to have entertained a cordial and close friendship: Martin Butzer of Strassburg.

It is the merit of Seeberg and of Lang to have first related Butzer to Calvin. They were preceded by Usteri,[1] who dealt with the ideas and customs of baptism, common to Strassburg and Geneva; by Erichson,[2] who proved that the Genevan order of worship which, later on, became of world-wide importance by the expansion of the calvinistic sects, is of Strassburgian origin; and by Scheibe,[3] who called attention to the identity of Butzer's and Calvin's doctrine of predestination. Seeberg[4] claims that "Butzerianism was the preparatory stage for Calvinism," and Lang declares that without Butzer the roots of Calvin's religious system cannot be clearly understood.[5] He also stresses the fact that the most significant ideas in Calvin's theology, namely those on predestination and on

church organization, show a direct influence of Butzer.[6] That
the latter has nearly been entirely forgotten as an original
thinker in comparison to Calvin is explained by the statement
that Calvin deepened the thoughts of the Strassburg reformer
not only by including them in a clear and consistent theological system, but also by making them effective in a successful
practical application. The findings of Lang were emphasized
by Anrich, who wrote the first, short biography of Butzer. He
asserts boldly that "the triumphant course of Calvinism
throughout the world signifies to a continuous influence of the
ideas of Butzer," who must be called "the father of Calvinism
before Calvin."[7] All these suggestions were finally found fruitful by O. Ritschl in his discussion of Butzer and Calvin in the
History of Protestant Dogma. He not only gives a full representation of Butzer's theology, but in his chapters on Calvin
he refers also very frequently to the influence from Strassburg to Geneva, and to the identity of Calvin's and Butzer's
thoughts.[8] He even goes so far as to declare that the latter
was superior to the former in "theological originality."[9]

The proof of such assumptions, however, is somewhat difficult. It must be achieved by a more or less indirect conclusion;
to a large extent one must be satisfied with the demon-
stration of similarities. This becomes most evident in connection with the doctrine of predestination, which stands in the
foreground of the interest. The community of thought seems
to exist since Calvin's first Protestant publication, the *Insti-
tues* of 1536. Mr. Van den Bosch,[10] who made a careful investigation of Butzer's concepts of predestination before the
appearance of Calvin in the Protestant public, reaches the
conclusion that "in the first edition of the *Institutes* Calvin
attributes to the doctrine of predestination the same religious
significance as Butzer." It is interesting to note that he feels
unable to claim a direct dependence of Calvin upon Butzer.[11]

In order to avoid the difficulties involved, it has been
attempted to eliminate Butzer entirely. Scheibe,[12] and especially Holl,[13] have pointed out that in order to understand Calvin, it would suffice to refer to Augustine and Luther, from
whom also Butzer received the first stimulus to pay attention to
God's "Alleinwirksamkeit." But in contrast to such an opinion, which, at the first glance, seems to be quite conclusive, one

must seriously consider the interpretation of Lang, who calls
attention to an original trait in Butzer's and Calvin's idea of
predestination. The idea of election was to them of the same
value as the idea of conversion was to the Pietists and the
Methodists.[14] It explains to them why a great number of men
accept the Gospel and why others do not.

The practical sociological observation of the religious status
of a human group, of the fact that there seem to be non-
religious individuals, led Butzer to develop his doctrine of
predestination. Only later he was compelled to accept its full
theological consequences. It is noteworthy, however, that he
never admitted that the predestination idea excluded the possibility of belief in free will.[15] Although a considerable change
took place in his theological development, he never surren-
dered those features of his theory of predestination which he
exhibited in his earliest writings. His predestination dogma
was based on his idea of the spirit, an idea which gives to all
his thoughts a characteristic, regulative note and which distinguished him particularly from Luther, while it related him
closely to Zwingli. It is not at all impossible that Butzer is
here indebted to the reformer of Zurich. The elect are those
who have the spirit, and those who have the spirit are enabled
to believe in the word and to express it by good works in a vir-
tuous life according to the Scripture. The foundation of the
church is not the word, but the spirit, which renders the word
effective.[16] Both supplement each other since both emanate
according to the order and the will of God from Christ, to
whom he has given all power. The Kingdom of Christ is his
rulership over those whom he has elected, i.e., those to whom
he has given the spirit so that they can gather around the word,
preach, and do it. In this respect the Kingdom of God is identical with the church. The same interest prevails in Calvin's
thought; not only his doctrine of predestination, but also that
of the word and the spirit are first to be found in Butzer.

But in spite of this community of thought in connection
with these leading phases of their theology, a dependence of
Calvin upon Butzer could hardly be maintained, if there were
not indications of an actual relationship between them. The
literary influence of Butzer on Calvin cannot be doubted. The
latter expresses his gratitude to the Strassburger in most com-

plimentary words in the Prefaces to his commentaries on the
Epistle to the Romans,[17] on the Psalms,[18] and on the Gos-
pels.[19] Lang supposes also that Calvin used Butzer's works
already in preparation for the first edition of the *Institutes*.

To what degree Calvin can have received a knowledge of
the Strassburg reformer during his years of study in France,
cannot be made out with certainty. The traditional opinion
refers frequently to the famous discourse of Nicolaus Cop
(All Saints Day 1533, Paris), which Calvin wrote for his
friend, the rector-to-be. Lang[20] has shown that the author
used a sermon from Luther's church postil in Butzer's Latin
translation. But, of course, that does not prove anything about
the kind or even the possibility of Calvin's acquaintance with
Butzer's books. Pannier[21] thinks that young Calvin heard his
cousin Olivétan, who seems to have studied in Strassburg,
speak of Butzer (in 1528)[22] and that, at Bourges, his professor Volmar fully introduced him to the work of the latter. The
first certain indication of Calvin's knowledge of Butzer, which is
in our reach, is given in a letter of Calvin to Butzer, which
Herminjard[23] dates on September 4, 1534, and which is written from Noyon to the "Bishop of Strassburg," imploring him
for help in favor of a poor minister. In conclusion Calvin
writes: "Hoc pro tempore. Vale erudissime vir"[24] as if he had
had previous connections with Butzer. It is much more probable that he was on friendly terms with Butzer's fellow-pastor
Capito, as the first letter from Butzer to Calvin (Strassburg,
November 1, 1536)[25] seems to suggest it. It is written in a
tone of respect which very significantly contrasts itself with the
familiar language of Capito.[26] Its purpose is to arrange for a
meeting with Calvin (now at Geneva) at a place of his con-
venience where all mutual and common problems shall be discussed until an agreement of opinion is established. The last
sentences read as follows:

"Farewell, most learned and holy man, and do not despise
my request, giving me thereby new cause of sorrow. For it cannot be said how much I regretted that I was not privileged to
make your acquaintance and to speak to you when you were
here. At other times, Capito shared everything with me. I do
not know which dark spirit made him so forgetful that he did

not think of introducing you to me. Now he himself is very sorry about it."

These words refer to Calvin's visit in Strassburg at the end of 1534,[27] or, what is more probable to that of October, 1536.[28]

It is most probable that the two reformers did not become personally acquainted with each other until the synod of Bern, which took place in 1537. Calvin refers to this meeting in his letter to Butzer of January 12, 1538,[29] written under the impression of the dismissal of Megander from the church of Bern, while the lutheranizing pastors Peter Kuntz and Sebastian Meyer, whom Calvin despised, were retained. He felt that Butzer's efforts toward a union between the Swiss and the Wittenbergers on the basis of the Wittenberg Concord of 1536 were responsible for this upheaval at Bern. He addresses Butzer in a way that continued to be characteristic of his attitude toward the busy and famous man from Strassburg even after their relationship had developel into a cordial friendship. He reviews the opinions of Luther and of the Swiss from an impartial point of view, asserting that he is vitally interested in a church union. However, he still favors the Swiss in contrast to the Lutherans. He appeals to Butzer that he attempt to bring the obstinate, narrowminded Wittenbergers to their senses. He himself takes—with some superiority—the position of an impartial although interested observer. As such he, a man of twenty-nine years, has the courage to extend a severe admonition to the renowned theologian and church-man, seventeen years his senior. Butzer is criticized for his diplomatic carefulness in theological discussion, which originated out of a desire to provoke no one. Calvin writes to him:

"If you want a Christ, who is acceptable to all, you must not fabricate a new gospel for that purpose. . . . After you have said that the veneration of Saints is produced in human superstition rather than founded in God's word, you add at once, that one must, nevertheless, consider the writings of the church-fathers, and that a veneration, recommended by them, ought not to be entirely condemned. Thus you re-introduce constantly that authority to which every error can be represented as truth. But does it mean to keep God truly holy, if one grants so much to man, that His truth does no longer rule over us?"[30]

The letter shows the royal freedom and superiority of Calvin.

He was willing to co-operate wherever, without danger of sacrificing fundamental views, he could see a promise of success. This emphasis upon clarity in theological purpose and this impartiality are characteristic of him in his relationship to Butzer to the end.

Butzer does not seem to have been offended by the severity of the criticism—he was accustomed to such a treatment! For when Calvin was forced to leave his position at Geneva during the year 1538, he and Capito stretched every nerve to persuade Calvin to come to Strassburg. Butzer's forceful appeal was finally successful.[31]

While in Strassburg, Calvin was exposed to the full influence of Butzer. In his letters to his friends,[32] one discovers an attitude much friendlier than before toward the man who bore not only the burden of the ecclesiastical reform of Strassburg and of Hesse, but also that of the upbuilding of a Protestant consciousness throughout the European world. Although he still emphasizes differences of opinion between them and his unwillingness to follow Butzer in every respect, he defends him with a cordiality and with the forcefulness that indicates clearly that their acquaintance has become close and intimate. This was the more important as Calvin spent a highly formative period of his life in this attachment to Butzer. It is, therefore, quite right that Pannier, in his admirable study on Calvin in Strassburg, stresses the possibility that Calvin became, during the years from 1538 to 1541, in many regards Butzerian.[33] He had many precious experiences; he deepened his theological views; and he made valuable observations of practical church-organization. His views on predestination and on the Lord's Supper became more precise. In regard to these doctrines, he was, when he left Strassburg, a pupil or follower of Butzer. Furthermore, there can hardly be a doubt that, in Strassburg, Calvin was introduced to the idea of a universal Protestantism, for the cause of which he worked so enthusiastically and ceaselessly during the last years of his life. It was Butzer who called him to Frankfurt and asked to be accompanied by him to the memorable religious peace-conferences, synods, and disputations of Hagenau and Regensburg in 1541. Through the mediatorship of Butzer, Calvin came into contact with German Protestantism and especially with

Melanchthon. From that time on, he was almost another Butzer in his interests for a union of the Protestant churches.[34] In
many respects, he brought to Butzer's plans at least a partial
realization. However, he never became Butzerian in the sense
of losing himself entirely to his cause. He always refused to
attempt a church union at any price. He became rather more
himself. Pannier has well said:[35] "Calvin was, when he left
Strassburg, more himself; he was more Calvinistic—and that
due to the nearness of Butzer." Whatever he took away with
him, he had made fully his own. Indeed, one cannot say that
he transplanted thoughts or institutions into his world without correcting or improving them. Whether it is baptism, the
Lord's supper, predestination and the whole type of theology
for which it stands; whether it is the idea that the school is
most significant for an effective church-discipline, and the
picture of the Strassburg Academy; whether it is the order of
worship or church-organization itself, and the idea of a united,
world-wide Protestant church—he made them all Calvinistic
when he accepted them for himself and took them to Geneva.
But nevertheless in all this lives Butzer. What he thought out
and planned and recommended and inspired in all these
respects becomes real through the understanding mind and
the efficient hands of Calvin.

The type of church which we call, in our day, Calvinistic
or Reformed, is really a gift of Martin Butzer to the world,
through the work of his strong and brilliant executive Calvin.[35a] The very peculiar relationship between the two men
becomes quite clear in connection with this institution of ecclesiastical organization. Gustav Anrich published a study[36] on
this very subject and has shown very convincingly indeed how
strangely the two worked hand in hand. Being of a fundamentally equal religious disposition—both of them were under
the influence of Humanism—thinking and acting, therefore,
more or less in the same direction, tied to such cities as Strassburg and Geneva, so similar in character and need, they finally
found themselves. What the elder wanted to see fulfilled in
plans that had busied his life, the younger eagerly made his
own, erecting a building which he could rightly call his own
property, but which never could have been thus built without
the enhancing, stimulative, productive thought of the other.[36a]

As we describe the building and its growth we represent the arguments of Professor Anrich: When Calvin returned to Geneva in 1541 he proposed at once to the city-magistrate a new church organization, and within a few weeks, he had won his case in the "Ordonnances ecclésiastiques." Their most characteristic feature is the instalment of the four offices of pastors, teachers, elders, and deacons. The pastors are combined in the Congrégation, later on called the Vénérable Compagnie. The soul of the whole organization is not this pastoral group, but the Consistoire, consisting of the ministers and the elders. Its task is the execution of church discipline, which it may independently put into practice even unto excommunication. Only for these two outstanding offices the method of appointment and election is clearly stated: A pastor is selected by the Vénérable Compagnie, presented to the magistrate, and, if accepted, elected by the congregation, this election being ratified by the magistrate. The twelve presbyters are appointed upon the proposition of the pastors; all are members of the city-council. If one asks for the origin of this order, one is inclined to follow Calvin, who points to the New Testament. In the 1543 edition of the *Institutes* he has given the scriptural proof by using the enumerations of the offices and gifts of the spirit in I Cor. 12 and Eph. 4. But after a careful study and examination of these references, it becomes evident that not the early Christian situation has been applied to the conditions of Geneva, but rather that the needs of the Genevan situation have been projected into the New Testament. Since a scriptural origin of the church order seems not possible, it might be found, one thinks, in Calvin's own proposal for church discipline of 1537. But therein one does not encounter the term "elder," nor the doctrine of the four offices as *ius divinum*, nor collegial ecclesiastical magistrates. Neither do the *Institutes* of 1536 or 1539 present the case differently, nor is the hint at other cities where church discipline had been introduced before, e.g., Basel, of value, since the characteristics of the Genevan order are lacking. One has to turn to Strassburg.

Begun in 1531 under the leadership of Jacob Sturm as the representative of the magistrate, church discipline had been fully constituted in the church order of 1534, with the collab-

oration especially of Butzer. Three Kirchenpfleger or elders
assist the pastor of each parish in his work of discipline. All
pastors and three of the helpers, who take turns in attending
the meetings, form the church assembly, convening twice a
month. Pastors are called in the following way: After having
passed an examination, the candidate preaches before the congregation, and the elders of the parish with twelve members
of the congregation undertake the election, which has to be
ratified by the magistrate.[37]

This order was developed in protection of the church
against the anabaptist sects. It resulted from a practical necessity. It is most interesting to note that Butzer devised the
theological theory for these institutions. In the Strassburg
Catechisms of 1534, 1537, and 1543, in his book "De vera
cura animarum" of 1538 and especially in his church-order for
Hesse (accepted at Ziegenhain in 1538, published in 1539),
he deduces from I Cor. 12 and Eph. 4 the theory of the divinely ordered offices of pastors, presbyters, deacons and also that
of the teachers, although they became never so prominent as
in Geneva. That these Strassburg offices were not installed
upon the authority of the Bible, but that this biblical authority was applied to a more or less accomplished organization is
seen in the fact that deacons as city-officials had been at work
since the twenties, when the city had undertaken the restoration of reorganized poor relief. Ecclesiastical poor relief was
really never established in Strassburg, in spite of Butzer's
theory.

These orders, it is true, were not fully realized. Butzer
could never attain to the full co-operation of the magistrate—
only in Hesse he was quite successful. But there can be no
doubt that Calvin was introduced by him to the Strassburg
system of discipline. From Butzer he learned the theory of
the *ius divinum* of ecclesiastical offices, especially that of the
presbyters. So far Anrich .

It is, then, quite evident that the so-called Calvinistic type
of church organization originated very largely in Strassburg
and in Butzer, whose ideas Calvin could put into practice. The
growth of this organization illustrates better than anything
else the fact that Calvin was Butzerian in order to be himself.
Professor Von Schubert has rightly said:[38] "What the contact

with the spirit of Rome was to the founder of the order of the
Jesuits, the contact with the spirit of Strassburg and of Butzer
was to Calvin." If one adds to the community of all those theological and ecclesiastical attitudes which we have mentioned
also their identical estimation of social ethics, which Klingenburg has fully investigated,[39] and particularly also Calvin's dependence on Butzer in his defense of elective government,[39a]
the affinity of the two reformers appears as truly astonishing.
But whether that minimizes the originality of Calvin or Butzer,
is a question that cannot be answered. One will have to be
satisfied with the fact that there existed between them a very
close relationship of viewpoint. "Bucer et Calvin," says Pannier,[40] "étaient bien faits pour se comprendre."

We know that since these Strassburg days, this friendship
was cordial. But its expression in correspondence is largely
unknown to us, because only a few of their letters are preserved. It is characteristic of both of them that, when Calvin
was about to return to Geneva, Butzer wrote to Bern that Calvin was needed in Strassburg for the French congregation and
the Academy as well as for the great tasks of Protestantism,"[41]
and that Calvin wanted Butzer to accompany him to his city.[42]
A few examples of the intimacy that marked their relationship
are still existing. On October 15, 1541, Calvin wrote to Butzer
in a letter of thanks for his reception in Strassburg:[43] "If I
should not live up to your expectations, you know well that
I am in your power. Admonish, chastize, do all that a father
is permitted to do to his son." And Butzer, who held Calvin's
brilliance equalled only by that of Melanchthon,[44] and who
longed for Calvin just as much as for Capito, who had been
taken by the plague of 1541,[45] was no less intimate in his letters to Calvin. Thus he ends a hearty letter of consolation and
encouragement:[46] "*Sed tu meum cor, meus animus* (thou,
my heart, my soul), *semper tuo, imo Christi bono, omnium
omnia mala vinces, quo ad licuerit . . . Tuus totus* (thine
wholly) *Bucerus.*"

A few letters of Butzer, written during the following
years, which are still in existence give chiefly information
about political and ecclesiastical affairs.[47] Only with the year
1547, the letters became more frequent and also more immediate and open in tone and emotion. The dark days of the

Emperor's warfare against the Protestants and of the Interim were approaching. Butzer saw his life-work endangered: God's avenging hand was stretched out over his unfaithful people.[48] God himself was demanding the supreme sacrifice for the sake of faith. Butzer was willing to give it.[49] In these years, he proved that he was a man of firm, courageous decision. But his heart was trembling, and in his sad letters he deplores the situation of the German church, beseeching his friends for their prayers, so that the vain, faint hope for a victory of the Gospel might perhaps be fulfilled.[50] He prepared himself for exile. He learned that he would have to leave the city which he loved with all his heart, in order to dwell in a foreign land. But in the fall of 1548, he expressed the hope that in such a case the Lord might give him an opportunity to see the churches of Geneva.[51] When his fate became more certain and when he had probably already decided to go to England, he had still the wish to bid farewell to the friend personally.[52] Evidently Calvin was again close to his heart, for he signs his letters again: Tuus totus Bucerus.[53] His hope was not to be fulfilled; he fled to England, never to return, on April 6, 1549.

None of Calvin's letters of this period are preserved. But we can still read a few which he wrote to England. They are examples of his fine, noble sensitiveness and tact, for it cannot have been easy to deal with Butzer, who was broken in health and in spirit and who saw his course ended. But Calvin's affection was still strong and fresh.

Butzer was homesick in London and in Cambridge. He longed for his family and for his friends, and he suffered because they did not write to him. He suspected that they had left him, turning to the Zurichers under the leadership of Bullinger, who saw in him a menace to the cause of the Gospel, blaming him for having obscured the doctrine of the Lord's Supper. The Swiss animosity against Butzer had turned into hatred. Already in 1546, referring to the death of Luther (February 18, 1546), Bullinger had written to A. Blarer,[54] who was not only his but also Butzer's friend:

"But I would begin to hope for the better, if Butzer also would be called by the Lord; for there lives no other man in our days, who gives more hopes to the Papists and who disputes

about the Lord's supper in an obscurer way than this Butzer.
. . . So much is certain: Now that Luther is dead, Butzer will
dive deeper into his union efforts, because until now he was
miserably afraid of Luther, in his cause."
About Butzer in England he wrote:

"Butzer is in England and remains fully himself. What Germany had accepted from him, England will also accept. May
the Lord protect her from evil and may He give him a better
mind or a better end *(meliorem mentem vel meliorem metam)*.
In such an ungrateful and bad time, however, there must be
instruments of anger and corruption. The Lord Jesus may
have mercy with his people."[55]

Calvin knew all about this. He not only consoled Butzer,
but he defended him also. He requested Bullinger,[56] informing
him of Butzer's complaints, that he should tell Hooper, who
was taking Bullinger's side, to treat Butzer as he, one of the
foremost servants of Christ, deserved. He assured Bullinger
constantly of his friendship with Butzer: "I should do wrong
to the church of God, if I should hate or despise him, not to say
anything about his merit for me personally."[57] Or: "Of course,
I am sometimes of another opinion than you, but my heart is
not at all estranged from you; just as I keep friendship with
Butzer, although, in all freedom, I think sometimes otherwise
than he."[58] To Butzer himself he wrote cordial letters, not
quite as intimate as one might expect. He wrote to Edward VI
and to the Lord of Somerset,[59] assisting Butzer in his efforts
for a reformation in England. He expressed his regret that he
could not have asked Butzer's advice in connection with a letter to Melanchthon.[60] He advised him—the best council to a
homesick man—to write books in order to make his wonderful
gifts useful to the church.[61] And what was probably of more
value to Butzer than anything else: He succeeded in having
the *Consensus Tigurinus* accepted. Not without having asked
for Butzer's opinion and not without praising his assent,[62] he
pursued a work that was dearest to Butzer's heart. When he
announced the friend's death (February 28, 1551) to Bullinger he said that he felt lonesome like an orphan.[63] No doubt
he loved him much. If we remember that Butzer had been
one of his chief teachers, we know why.

After having observed this friendship and the indebtedness of Calvin to Butzer, one wonders why the latter never received the proper credit for his contributions and how it could happen that Calvin so entirely overshadowed him. An answer to this question can be found by a comparison of the goal that the two men had set to themselves and to their work.

During the controversy of 1544 between the Lutherans and the Swiss, Bullinger once used the expression *bucerisare*[64] *(verbutzern* or *butzern),* having in mind Butzer's method of reconciling the divergent views on the Lord's Supper. By coining that word, he testified to the fact that Butzer represented an original type of Protestant theologian. It was because of this very fact that the Strassburger had so many enemies and that even his friends disagreed with him. He himself was well aware of the animosity his activity and viewpoint caused, but although he grew sometimes weary, he never ceased to pursue his ends. He was driven on by a decision which he had clearly defined to himself and which was the heart of all his work. Its note is prominent in all his writings, in commentaries, pamphlets, and letters. For our purpose it may suffice to concentrate our attention on the correspondence with the Blarers, of whom at least Ambrosius (of Konstanz) always understandingly tried to take his side.

Butzer was blamed for conceding too much to the Lutherans or to the Catholics. But he declared:[65] "I condemn the Erasmian caution and the Saxon ambition; I seek the simplicity of Christ." What he meant by this he explained at another occasion:

"My aim is, although I pursue it not always with the necessary warmth and broadmindedness, that the Christians recognize and embrace each other in love; for all defects in customs and judgment result from the fact that because of weak concord the spirit of Christ misses its effect. . . . How well do I understand now, since my attitude toward Luther, Philipp (Melanchthon) and others is purer, their pious writings at which I had before so much to criticize."[66]

He intentionally wanted to overcome the differences in theology, because a theological faith as such did not seem to comprehend all the essence of Christianity. "In true theology," he wrote,[67] "everyone knows so much rightly as he expresses in life." The same principle is described in the gospel Commentary in these beautiful words:[68] "True theology is not theoretical or speculative. Its aim is rather action, i.e., a godlike life." Through a faith that was effectively expressing itself in love, he wished to see the realization of the *communio sanctorum*.[69] "Communion"— that was his great ideal. Everything had to serve to this end.

"For nobody truly knows Christ who does not feel the necessity of a communion, of mutual care and discipline among his members. . . . Christ suffered and taught for no other purpose but that we should be one and embrace each other with the same love with which he embraced us, and that we should seek our mutual salvation with the same eagerness with which he sought ours."[70]

Hence his emphasis upon church discipline. No communion of love could exist, he thought, without discipline.

Such an ideal was new and original in the compass of Protestant theology. It is interesting to note that Butzer attributed the ideal of communion now to the local congregation and then to the church at large. In this latter respect, he was still under the powerful impression of medieval ecclesiasticism and universalism. Christ, the head of the one church, the corpus Christi—to this medieval church concept he gave a Protestant flavor. He pointed out:

"Christ, the head, is working in one body which is connected with him and consists of well connected and co-operating members. O pernicious blindness, that even the best Evangelicals do not recognize what it means to believe in a catholic church and in a communion of saints, and to be members of Christ."[71]

These are terms and words in which the medieval Catholics used to define their universalism.[72] When Butzer spoke or wrote them, he filled them with a new passion, described by "faith and love,"[73] which he had learned from Luther and Zwingli. For him, this passion culminated in the doctrine of predestination and thereby he broke with medievalism. But one senses still the atmosphere of the Dominican order, in which Butzer received his education, and one hears, if ever so softly, the great Thomas, when one reads:[74] "The Kingdom of God is the church of Christ"; but the Protestant explains: "It lies in nothing that is external *per se*, but in faith and justice, and in such a use of external things as faith dictates." Butzer was a Catholic with a Protestant heart.

As such he desired to be a Paul to his contemporaries; and he also had the wide-open heart of the great apostle.

"If we cannot agree *(congredi)*, we are neither against nor of Christ. He promised that he would be in the midst of those who gather together in his name; if we cannot come together in his name, we cannot pray to him either.[75] All who read Paul, must know how Paul and all true Christians promoted the protection and the development of the communion of saints and their agreement *(consensus)* in all things. By the ministry of the word faith is born and nourished; that is why the apostle traversed land and sea and sent out his (pupils) with such eagerness; now another spirit is at the helm, which flees all union *(congressum)*."[76]
The same passion that sent Paul restlessly around the world was driving him on to make Christ the ruler "to whom the Father has given not only some regions of Germany but the whole globe."[77] One is almost tempted to say, that like the apostle, he desired to be a Jew to the Jews and a Greek to the Greeks, in order that Christ might become true king of all his believers.

But another Paul was claimed by Luther and by Calvin, a Paul that knew no compromise. If Butzer stressed the words "love" and "communion" most of all, Calvin emphasized, one may say, "faith" and "faithful." The famous saying of Hundeshagen: *"Die Dogmatik ist bei den Reformierten nur ein locus in der Kirche, bei den Lutheranern umgekehrt die Kirche nur ein locus in der Dogmatik,"[78]* is more appropriate in regard to Butzer than to Calvin.

Butzer—if it is permitted to speak in very general terms— thought of religion first of all as ministering to man's salvation, while Calvin related it primarily to the eternal God. Butzer was a humanistic, social biblicist, Calvin a theocentric biblicist. Calvin could always hold fast to one steady firm pole, which he called *majestas Dei*, but Butzer was shifting and changing for the sake of the *communio sanctorum*. That is why the doctrine of predestination finds a clear logical place in Calvin's theological system, while Butzer started out to use it as a means to analyze and to command a practical sociological situation, later on compelling himself to think it out to its full theological consequences. That is why Calvin could afford either to differ from others in his opinions and yet keep friendship or to differ and break radically, while Butzer could neither stop to seek in friendship also some agreement of opinion nor radically break with anyone. Calvin could be cruel; Butzer could not and he was no less energetic than Calvin!—for the *cura animarum* came first.

All this leads us to understand why Butzer was barely remembered by the side of Calvin. And yet—he was the father of Calvinism.

CHAPTER 7

Protestant Reactions to the Council of Trent

THROUGHOUT the period of the Reformation the demand for an ecclesiastical council resounded throughout Germany and, indeed, throughout Europe. In such an assembly there seemed to reside the only hope for a reform of the church based on a reconciliation between Roman Catholics and Protestants.

The Council which was finally convened at Trent did not fulfill these expectations. Its canons and decrees re-established the Roman Catholic church on the basis of its medieval doctrine and polity. They also rendered final the breach which the Reformation had made in Christendom. Far from effecting a reunion between Protestants and Roman Catholics, the Council of Trent caused the adherents of the Reformation definitely to become separated from the Roman church.

I

It was a tragedy that the very council that was convened in order to settle the issues raised by the Protestant Reformers should become the dividing mark between their churches and the Roman church from which they had sprung. They themselves had taken the initiative in calling for a council but it was impossible for them to submit to the Council of Trent.

The main reason for this fundamental disagreement was that the Protestant conception of an ecumenical council differed profoundly from that held by their opponents, especially the pope and the emperor. In order to understand the reactions of the Protestants to the Council of Trent, these different conceptions must be properly distinguished from one another.[1]

On November 28, 1518, a little more than a year after the publication of the Ninety-five Theses on Indulgences, Luther appealed to a free universal council. He asserted, almost in the very language of the declaration of Constance, that "a sacred council lawfully assembled in the Holy Spirit, and representing the whole catholic church, is superior to the pope in matters of faith."[2] There can be no doubt that he relied on an understanding of the authority of a council which was similar to that of the conciliarists of the fourteenth and fifteenth centuries. Two years later, on November 17, 1520, he repeated the appeal in anticipation of receiving the bull *Exsurge Domine* which threatened him with the ban. In the meantime, he had come to the conclusion that the office of the papacy represented Anti-Christ in Christendom primarily because the pope claimed the exclusive right to interpret Scripture authoritatively and to be superior to a council. At the disputation at Leipzig, Johannes Eck, who was to be his life-long opponent, had forced him to examine the history of the papacy and the councils. As a result of this study, he came to regard the medieval councils as fallible. Nevertheless, he continued to appeal from the pope to a free Christian council. He was persuaded that a representative gathering of Christians free from papal control had the ability to define what was Christian on the basis of the word of God, the only ultimate norm of Christian truth he was willing to recognize.

A "free general Christian council" became the concern of the evangelical spokesmen at the numerous diets, called during the reign of Charles V in order to deal with the religious question. Again and again, the Lutherans declared themselves ready to submit to a council truly representative, i.e., general; uncontrolled by the pope, i.e., free; and subject to the authority of the word of God alone, i.e., Christian. In this understanding of the nature of a council, they were, of course, inspired primarily by the teachings of Luther. They relied upon his conception of the Christian faith that had resulted from the rediscovery of the free gospel and the new emphasis upon justification by faith alone and all that was implied therein for the conception of the church as the fellowship and universal priesthood of believers.

The Roman Catholic idea of a council was diametrically

opposed to this Protestant conception.[3] All Roman Catholic advocates of a conciliar settlement of the issue of the Protestant Reformation took it for granted that it should be assembled only upon the initiative of the pope and on the basis of the recognition of papal authority and that all conciliar decisions should be in conformity with the traditions of the Roman church. This view implied a totally different conception of Christian truth than that which guided the Protestants. Moreover, the Roman Catholic advocates of a council insisted that the Protestants should acknowledge their errors before they could get a hearing before the council and that they should agree beforehand to accept the principle that decisions of the council were final and definitive.

The Protestants from their point of view were unable to yield to these demands. They repeated again and again that the papal interpretation of the authority of the council implied the untenable possibility that those who were to come under the judgment of a free Christian council would themselves be the judges. In the light of these differences, it is apparent that the two groups did not mean the same thing when they spoke of the council.

The situation was further complicated by the fact that the Emperor Charles V and many others of the German leaders held still another view of the council.[4] They by-passed the question of truth which was basic in the papal and Protestant conceptions. They attributed primarily a functional authority to the council. They believed that the religious differences between the Protestants and the Roman Church were capable of settlement by negotiation. They were sure that these differences had arisen at all because the Christian church was in need of a reformation with respect to certain practices and that a reunion of the conflicting parties could therefore be effected by religious-theological conferences to be followed by concessions and compromises in the realm of ecclesiastical organization and religious practice. Charles V acted on the assumption that the followers of Luther could be compelled to return to the Roman Church as soon as certain formulæ had been found on the basis of which they would re-align themselves with the old church. His brother Ferdinand was persuaded that if the papacy could be induced to grant the chalice and priestly marriage to the Protestants, the main cause of the conflict would be removed. Others (Protestants and Catholics alike, but persons who were under humanistic influences) were confident that a German national council would be able to effect an understanding between the conflicting parties. This view implied that the medieval conception of the *corpus Christianum* as a priestly-political society should be maintained but that certain changes in the structure of national or territorial churches, particularly in Germany, should be permitted.

In contrast to the advocates of this plan, both Luther and the leaders of the Curia were aware of the fact that the issue of the Reformation was primarily dogmatic and not practical. They therefore assigned to the Council the task to decide upon the norm of Christian truth and they wished it should deal with the fundamental Christian doctrines rather than with practical reforms.

Throughout his career, Luther maintained the attitude which, at the Diet of Worms on April 18, 1520, had caused him to declare that unless his view were refuted by reference to the word of God he would not recant. He therefore made all negotiations about religion dependent upon statements of faith.

In the same way, Pope Paul III saw to it that the Council of Trent concerned itself primarily with questions of faith and only secondarily with the problems of the practical reformation of the church.

II

In view of the fundamental contrast between the opinions held by Luther and the Protestant reformers on the one hand and by the papacy on the other hand, it is not conceivable that a reconciliation between them could ever have been effected. It is also vain to speculate on ways by which, at the very beginning of the Reformation, the split of Christendom might have been avoided. Luther certainly had no schismatic intentions when he demanded a discussion of the problems raised by the sale of indulgences. He was right, when as he later on looked back upon the gradual development of his estrangement from the papal church, he was persuaded that he had been acted upon rather than acting himself, and that

God had led him on as if he were a horse, putting blinkers on him so that he would not see who came running up upon him.[5] When the Council of Trent finally began its deliberations at the very end of the year 1545, a few months before Luther's death, it was much too late to undo the results of his preaching of the Word of God and of his attacks against the papal church. By then the lines of division were too firmly drawn. The different conceptions of the nature of the Christian religion and of the function and authority of a general council within Christendom could then no longer be reconciled.

To be sure, both the Papacy and the Holy Roman Emperor could possibly have avoided the division of Christendom which they had to confront when the Council of Trent convened. If Leo X and his immediate successors had followed up the excommunication of Luther, pronounced in the bull *Decet Romanum Pontificem* (January 3, 1520), say by placing an interdict upon Frederick the Wise and his realm (as the papal advisers Aleander and Campeggio repeatedly suggested) and if Charles V had seen to it that the Edict of Worms which put the imperial ban upon Luther (May 25, 1520) was executed, the Reformation would probably never have developed in the way it did. As matters actually stood, neither pope nor emperor was able to enforce his decree. They both lacked the moral and political strength to oppose the Reformation at a time when the division of western Christendom might have been prevented. Throughout his career Charles V was preoccupied with the task to secure the realization of his dream of a universal Christian monarchy of the Habsburg dynasty.[6]

His high sense of mission as Holy Roman Emperor and Protector of the Church required of him that he should maintain the unity of Christendom. When he finally undertook the war on the Schmalcaldic League of the German Protestants on the ground that they refused to attend the Council of Trent which he had caused the pope to convene, the occasion had passed when he could realize his ends. Despite his victory over the Protestants, he was unable to disestablish their churches. The Interim-settlement which he imposed upon them at the Diet of Augsburg in 1548 proved to be ineffective.

The Council of Trent to which he had expected the defeated Protestants to submit had been disbanded by papal

order in the midst of the Schmalcaldic war. When the council
reconvened in 1551, he ordered representatives of the Protestant estates to appear before it, but before it could seriously
take up negotiations with the Protestants, it was again ad-
journed on account of the treasonable attack of Maurice of
Saxony upon the Emperor at Innsbruck in the winter of 1552.

The Peace of Augsburg in 1555, by which the conflicts of
the German Reformation were concluded, granted the Protestants terms on which their territorial churches were legally
recognized. The Protestants therefore had no need to concern
themselves with the last sessions of the Council of Trent held
during its third period in 1562 and 1563.

That this situation had come about was due not only to
Charles' failure to subdue the Protestants but also to papal
political activity. The popes had been involuntary allies of the
Reformers, permitting them to extend their influence in the
absence of effective opposition. Leo X, Clement VII, and
Paul III found themselves often entangled in European politics
in order to protect their Italian interests against the Emperor
and consequently they neglected their spiritual duty to deal
with the Protestant criticisms of the church.[7] The perennial
conflict between the houses of Habsburg and Valois occupied
their primary interest.

Throughout his reign, Charles V was faced with the danger
that the popes would align themselves with his arch-enemy,
Francis I of France. The Council which the Emperor and the
German diets again and again demanded in the hope that it
might end the religious conflict was treated by the popes not
primarily as a religious-ecclesiastical issue but as a political one.
Clement VII was forced by the Emperor to consent to the calling of a council, but he never took his own promise seriously,
not only because he feared the possibility of conciliarist opposition to papal monarchy but chiefly because he was apprehen-
sive of the political danger which imperial domination of the
council might entail for him. Paul III was elected to the See
of Peter in the expectation that he would finally convene the
long-delayed council. One of the first acts of his reign was to
set in motion the process of preparing the council. He chose
to rely upon the support of the advocates of church-reform
who, in the meantime, had arisen within Italian Catholicism.

In the end, it was this group which saw the Council of Trent through to its conclusion, thereby setting Roman Catholicism on the road to that unified strength which it has maintained until our times. But Paul III was always wary of the influence which the Emperor might exercise upon the council. For political reasons, he postponed its opening again and again, even after he had officially convoked it. To the last, he was suspicious of Charles V, just as the latter never trusted him entirely.[8] He looked with fear upon the policy of temporary concessions and theological conferences which the Emperor pursued toward the Protestants; and he refused to permit the Council of Trent to concern itself exclusively with problems *de reformatione* as Charles V wished but, in defiance of the Emperor, he caused the Council to devote itself to questions *de fide* as its primary agenda allowing it to prepare reforms of ecclesiastical practice at the same time.

On account of these imperial and papal policies, which, moreover, were aggravated by the Turkish threat to Christian Europe and by the French king's ever-changing stratagems toward the Empire and the Papacy, the Protestants gradually gained the impression that it was the purpose of the popes to do all that was possible in order to avoid a council. They suspected that the leaders of the Roman church were unwilling either to come to terms with the issues of the Protestant Reformation or to undertake the reform which spokesmen of Roman Catholicism had declared necessary ever since Adrian VI had caused the legate Chieregati to acknowledge the faults of the church at the Diet of Nuremberg in 1523. At the diets held during the first part of the reign of Charles V, they declared themselves willing to participate in a council. They assumed that if it would actually be convened it would be constituted on a basis acceptable to them. When, on March 3, 1537, the Schmalcaldic League officially rejected the invitation of Paul III to a council that was to meet at Mantua on May 3, 1537, it did so on the ground that the terms of the papal invitation did not guarantee that the council would be free, general and Christian. They pointed out that the discussions and resolutions of the diets had led them to expect that the papacy would not have the decisive votes at a council. The fact that eight more years were actually to pass before the Council of

Trent actually commenced its sessions definitely confirmed
them in the conviction that their opponents did not seriously
desire a council.

III

In the light of these factors, the Protestant reaction to the
Council of Trent must be seen in the following way: 1) The
Protestants interpreted the nature and authority of a council
in their own terms. They asserted that they would never agree
that a council convened by papal authority and held according
to the customs of the Roman church was a true and free council. 2) The fact that the council which finally met at Trent
was called only after many delays and that when it was finally
convoked, it was postponed several times, confirmed them in
the conviction that the papacy refused not only to come to
terms with the interpretation of the Christian gospel which
they had developed but also to undertake a reform of the
church.

A twofold attitude toward the papacy was the expression
of these opinions: 1) Following Luther, all Protestants came to
regard the papacy as the Anti-Christ who prevented the word
of God to run a free course in the world. 2) To these religious-
theological criticisms of the papacy they added the opinion
that the popes did all they could in order to avoid a council by
craftiness and deceit.

In numerous Protestant writings published prior to the first
sessions of Trent these reactions came to expression. Luther
set the pace and the tone. In 1533, when the papal legate Hugo
Rangone of Reggio[9] invited the Saxon elector John Frederick
to a council, Luther advised his prince that if the Protestants
were to consent to attend a council which could not be regarded as free and the deliberations of which were to be
guided not by the word of God but by arbitrary human rules,
they would repudiate their evangelical confession.[10] Two years
later, the papal nuncio Pietro Paolo Vergerio was sent to Germany by Paul III in order to sound out the German princes
about their attitude toward a council.[11] He had a personal
meeting with Luther at Wittenberg and received the following
statement: "We do not need a council for ourselves and on
behalf of our cause, for we have the evangelical doctrine and

order, but Christendom as a whole is in need of a council and that part of it (namely the papal church) which is still caught up in error must learn how to distinguish between truth and error."

In the last days of 1536, Luther wrote the so-called "Schmalcaldic Articles" in preparation of the meeting of the Schmalcaldic League in February 1537, at which the Protestants definitely declined to attend the council called to meet at Mantua.[12] He composed these articles at the request of the Elector who regarded it as necessary that, on the basis of Holy Scripture, Luther should state those teachings of his on which he would absolutely stand either before a council or in God's last judgment and from which he would not deviate under any circumstances. At that time, John Frederick toyed with the idea that Luther and his Protestant fellow-theologians should take the initiative in calling a "general, free, Christian council." Luther complied with the request and wrote the statement of faith later known as the "Schmalcaldic Articles." At the meeting of Schmalcald they were not used according to the original plan. Because of a severe illness, Luther himself could not participate in the discussions. The theologians present reaffirmed the Augsburg Confession and its Apology and they adopted a statement written by Melanchthon entitled *Tractatus de potestate et primatu Papae* in which the papal claim to rule in the church *iure divino* was rejected. Luther published the "Articles" in 1538 under the title *Artikel so do hetten sollen auffs Concilion zu Mantua, oder wo es wurde sein, uberantwortet werden von unseres teils wegen. Und was wir annemen oder geben kundten oder nicht.* In the meantime, the council had been postponed. Luther suspected that papal fear of a free church assembly was the reason.

In the year 1538, the problem of the council occupied him continuously. He had definitely come to the conclusion that the pope did not really desire a council, in view of the fact that, since 1536, he had postponed it three times. When, early in 1538, Luther got hold of a copy of the *"Consilium delectorum cardinalium et aliorum praelatorum de emendenda ecclesia S. D. N. Paulo III petente conscriptum et exhibitum* (anno 1537),"[13] the famous memorandum of the Cardinals' Commission under the chairmanship of Casparo Contarini on the reform of the church (the memorandum which outlined the principles which later guided the Council of Trent in its reforming work), he doubted its sincerity. He decided to publish it in translation and provided it with a preface and sarcastic marginal notes. He insinuated that though the Curia was aware of the need of a reformation of the church it intended to do nothing about it.[14] By that time he had become completely disillusioned about the possibility that a reforming council would ever be assembled under the auspices of the papacy. He therefore set to work on a long treatise which he published in 1539 under the title "Of Councils and Churches."[15] In it he tried to show once more that the Roman church could not claim to be a true church because it had permitted the popes to arrogate to themselves the right to convene councils and to interpret the Christian gospel on the basis of their own arbitrary authority. He also endeavored to demonstrate that no council presided over by the pope could be a true and authoritative one. He undertook an extended analysis of the four first ecumenical councils of the ancient church, and he concluded that they had been convened by the Roman emperors in order that through them the sole authority of the Biblical word might be re-established in the church. Moreover, he argued that the decrees of the ancient councils were normative in Christendom only in so far as they agreed with the word of God, because no council had ever had or could have the right to promulgate statements of faith or to impose new laws upon Christian believers beyond the authority of the word. Luther therefore arrived at the conclusion that, in the light of the Scripture and the four ancient councils, the popes had no authority whatsoever to convene councils or to preside over them.

This judgment came to be shared by all Protestants, even by those among them (Butzer, for example) who, in contrast to Luther, continued to hope that by means of theological conferences as Charles V sponsored them, a reconciliation between them and the Roman church might be brought about. From then on, the Protestants lost all real interest in a council convoked by papal authority. This explains in part why their concern for the deliberations and decisions of Trent was so slight.

Luther's irreconcilable hostility against the papacy came once more to the fore a few years later. At the Diet of Speyer in 1544, Charles V found himself compelled for a political reason (a new outbreak of the old conflict with Francis I) to make considerable concessions to the German Protestants. He guaranteed them their acclesiastical establishments. Ignoring papal authority and disregarding the fact that the invitations to the Council of Twent, which was to convene on March 15, 1545, had been issued, he also promised to convoke before the year ended either a diet or a national synod at which the religious conflicts in Germany were to be definitely settled. Paul III caused a Breve to be prepared in which he bitterly expostulated with the Emperor for having presumed to promise a council without consulting him and for having illegally appropriated for himself jurisdiction in matters of religion.[16] By some indiscretion this document came to be generally known. Thus also Luther heard of it. He was so aroused by the Breve's reaffirmation of papal sovereignty in matters of religion, that he wrote in reply his intemperate book "Against the Papacy of Rome, founded by the Devil."[17] In it he summed up once more all the reasons against papal authority in the church which he had formulated in the course of his career, at the same time heaping abuse upon the Curia for the immoral conditions which it permitted to prevail in Rome.

Luther died less than a year after the publication of this book. He had been the most vociferous and passionate opponent of the council among the Protestants. The few pamphlets which other Lutherans wrote on the conciliar question contained the same arguments which he ceaselessly repeated.

IV

The Breve which had occasioned Luther's last anti-papal outburst brought another fighter to the fore who was to become the only Protestant leader of the period of the Reformation to concern himself directly with the Council of Trent — none other than John Calvin. He was to become Luther's successor as the most representative leader of the Reformation movement during the period of the Council of Trent. He too felt it necessary to protest against the papal pretensions expressed in the Breve. He published it in toto and added a series of critical remarks.[18] He sharply attacked Paul III on account of his personal life, emphasizing the pope's political concerns for his family, namely his son Pier Luigi and his grandsons.[19] Directing his arguments specifically to the sentences of the papal document, it was his purpose to demonstrate that the claims made by the pope in the Breve were the expression of tyrannical ambitions. Neither the Scriptures nor the customs of the ancient church, he insisted, sanctioned papal authority over councils. Moreover, the condemnation of the Protestants as heretics without an objective and fair examination of their cause seemed to him unjustifiable.

Calvin's attacks upon the papacy differ in no way from those of other Protestants. The following specific examples of his criticism of papal assertions may illustrate his manner of argument:

On the statement of the pope that Charles V "proposed laics to have power in spiritual things, and not only laics, but laics indiscriminately, even the asserters of damnable heresies," Calvin remarked:[20] "As if the Emperor had wished the decision to be given according to the caprice of each individual, and not to be taken from the Holy Word of God, after duly weighing both sides of the question! As if, too, he had committed to laics the office of deciding for themselves, and not rather of inquiring into what was taught by the word of God. If this fact is new to Farnese, he must have very little acquaintance with antiquity."

"If this view of Farnese is adopted, there will be no occasion for a Council. The matter will be quickly disposed, if those who come forward to give an account of their departure are, while the cause is unpleaded, to be declared assertors of damnable heresies. Nor, in sooth, does the most Holy Father act imprudently. For what is more desirable than to slay your enemies with a single word? But there is this inconvenience that those who are so atrociously condemned nobly and strenuously defend themselves against the calumny, while, at the same time, they charge home upon the Pope himself the guilt not only of impiety and wickedness of every kind, but prove him to be Anti-Christ, the head of all the wicked."

Paul III had pointed out in his letter that he had repeatedly called a council and that at the moment when Charles V had chosen to make concessions to the Protestants the Council of Trent was pending. Exhibiting the common Protestant suspicions concerning the papal intentions and demonstrating the complete irreconcilability between the Protestants and Roman Catholics, Calvin replied to these passages in the papal letter as follows:[21] "It is true Farnese has sometimes made a show of calling a Council, but anyone who believes that he ever thought seriously of holding a Council, has not a particle of soundness in his brain. He knows that the world, as if famishing, has long been gaping eagerly for a Council, and he knows that all accuse him of extreme cruelty, in so long dragging out the time by endless evasions."

"As if he had called the Council with any hope of assembling it, and had not rather intentionally selected the time which would be unsuitable for peaceful consultation. When he was well aware that the two principal monarchs of the Christian world were kept asunder by war, and that in several places the trumpet for battle was almost sounding, then he pretended that he wished a council. Who will believe that he was such a fool as to hope for it? Hence one may easily conjecture that he never acts without dissimulation, etc. . . . ."

On December 13, 1545, the Tridentine Council actually began. It remained in session until March 11, 1547, when it was transferred to Bologna. During this first period, seven sessions were held at which important canons and decrees *de fide* and *de reformatione*, which had been prepared by committees of theologians, were officially adopted. The dogmatic decisions related to Scripture and Tradition, Original Sin, Justification, and the doctrine of the Sacraments, particularly Baptism and Confirmation.

Calvin subjected these canons and decrees to a close critical analysis in a work which he published in 1547 under the title "The Canons of the Council of Trent, with the Antidote."[22]

This work is a piece of closely reasoned theological polemics. Calvin seems to have forgotten all his former arguments concerning papal and Protestant conciliar politics. He concentrates entirely on the purpose to refute the Tridentine teachings from the point of view of Protestant dogmatics.

He commences with an introduction in which the problem of submission to human authority (he thinks of the papacy, of course) in matters of religion is briefly considered. He defends the Protestant principle that the Scripture is the only infallible standard. However, he admits that the veneration in which the authority of an ecumenical council is held in Christendom is by no means unfounded, especially in view of the fact that the ancient church benefited greatly from the decisions of councils. Indeed, he expresses the opinion that if, in his own time, a General Council (a title which he denies to Trent) could be instituted, there would be ground to hope that it might command general respect and obedience and thus restore peace to Christendom. Unhappily he sees no means by which such a council might be convened, for the pope who would have the power to summon it, is himself the great offender. Hence any council dominated by him would be far more disposed to perpetuate abuses than to remove them.

Calvin tries to prove such an assertion by examining the actual composition of the Council of Trent. He points to the fact[23] that the Council was only sparsely attended and chiefly by Italian prelates. He also subjects the mode of procedure used at Trent to criticism. He insists that the theologians and canonists who formulated the decisions were not a representative and competent body and that they accepted too readily any changes demanded by the papal legates and the pope himself. Moreover, he feels that the "fathers" of the council gave these decisions the dignity of canons by merely giving a mechanical nod of assent.

After thus dissecting the procedures of the Council with the intent to demonstrate that it had no right to allocate to itself the sanction of the authority of the Holy Spirit, Calvin proceeds to consider the Opening Address of the legates.[24] Making the most of their confession of the need of a thorough reformation of the church, he shows that the corruptions and abuses of the papacy more than justified the Protestant withdrawal of allegiance from Roman Catholic authority.

Preliminary matters thus having been disposed of, the canons themselves come under review. Each is first given verbatim and then refuted in detail. Calvin dwells particularly upon the doctrines of Scripture, Original Sin, Justification, and the Sacrifice of Christ. He expresses the common Protestant deviations from Roman Catholic doctrine. His particular ire

is aroused by the Tridentine doctrine of Scripture. He is horrified at the anathema pronounced upon those who deny the
inspiration of the Apocrypha. He is most caustic in his criticism of the conciliar decision to make the Vulgate the authentic
translation of the Scripture. He writes:[25]

"As the Hebrew and Greek original often serves to expose
their ignorance in quoting Scripture, to check their presumption . . . they ingeniously meet this difficulty . . . by determining that the Vulgate translation only is to be held authentic.
Farewell then to those who have spent much time and labor
in the study of languages that they might search for the genuine
sense of Scripture at the fountainhead! . . . Is not this to subdue Greece and all the East?"

After a minute examination of the whole decree of the
fourth session, Calvin concludes:

"They cry out that the whole authority of the church must
fall if it is denied the right of interpreting Scripture—that a
door could thus be thrown open to lascivious minds, allowing
them to break through every restraint. Nay, in order to cast
obloquy upon us, they are wont to charge us with arrogating
the interpretation of Scripture to ourselves, in order that there
may be no check upon our licentiousness. Modesty will not
allow me to speak of ourselves as fact would justify; and yet I
will most truly declare that we have thrown more light upon
the Scripture than all the doctors who have appeared under
the Papacy since its commencement. This praise even they
themselves cannot deny us. Still there is none of us who does
not willingly submit his lucubrations to the judgment of the
church. Therefore we neither contemn nor impair the authority of the church; nor do we give loose reins to men who dare
what they please. I wish they would show us such a church as
Scripture itself portrays; we should easily agree as to the respect
due to it. But when, falsely assuming the name of Church,
they seize upon the spoils of which they have robbed it, what
else can we do than protest."

In this vein Calvin examines the whole of the Tridentine
canons and decrees of the first seven sessions. He argues from
a point of view diametrically opposed to that of the fathers of
Trent.

It is evident that when he wrote his treatise, the religious

and theological estrangement between Protestants and Roman
Catholics had become so fixed that mutual understanding was
no longer possible.

V

During the Reformation period, no other Protestant theologian took it upon himself to state his reactions to the Council of Trent. When, in 1551, after the Council had resumed
its sessions, Charles V insisted that the Protestants should appear before it, no detailed examination of the decrees of the
earlier sessions was undertaken by any of them. Melanchthon
acted and spoke like all of them when he refused to acknowledge the authority of the Council because it had been called
by the pope.[26] He also demanded that everything which had
been decided by the Council in the absence of the Protestants,
should be gone over again, if the Protestants were to be given
a fair chance of participating in the proceedings.[27] Moreover,
in order to prepare for a Protestant representation at the Council, he wrote in 1551, "The Repetition of the Augsburg Confession," also called "The Confession of the Doctrine of the
Saxon Churches."[28] His assumption was that the Lutherans, if
they appeared in Trent, would do nothing else but stand on
the re-affirmation of their classical confession. In this respect,
he exhibited an attitude which was common to all Protestants.

Henceforth, the relations between Protestants and Roman
Catholics never ceased to be polemical. The Roman Church
relied on the achievements of the Council of Trent, and the
Protestants depended upon their own creeds and confessions.
Thus each group felt compelled to refute the teachings of the
other one.

For the Lutherans the pattern of these polemics was set by
Martin Chemnitz, a pupil of Melanchthon, who, in the second
half of the sixteenth century, became one of the founders and
defenders of Protestant Orthodoxy. Between 1565 and 1573,
he published his famous work *"Examen concilii Tridentini"*
in four parts.[29] For a long time, this book remained the most
complete and detailed Protestant criticism of the Tridentine
doctrines. It was a product of Chemnitz's controversy with certain Jesuits.[30] In 1560, Jesuit theologians of the University of
Cologne had published a polemical writing against a Protestant
catechism. It bore the title *"Censura de praecipuis doctrinae*

caelestis capitibus." To this Chemnitz replied in a little tract of 1562, "*Theologia Jesuitarum praecipua capita*" in which he compared the Jesuit teachings with the Protestant *loci theologici* on the basis of the Scripture and the doctrines of Augustine. This treatise called forth replies from the Portuguese Jesuit Jacob Payon de Andrada, who had been one of the theologians of the Council of Trent. In 1564, he published two works entitled: "*Orthodoxarum explicationum de controversiis religionis capitibus libri X*" and "*De societatis Jesu origine libellus contra Kemnitii cuiusdam petulantem audaciam.*" In the first of these writings, Andrada claimed that the Council of Trent had authorized him to reply to Chemnitz's criticisms of Jesuit theology and in doing so he referred explicitly to the canons and decrees of Trent. Thus Chemnitz was induced to answer Vandrada by subjecting the entire Tridentine decisions to a close critical analysis. With great thoroughness and an impressive display of learning in historical theology and without any of the passionate hatred and intemperance that had characterized the polemics of the Reformation age, he endeavored to prove that the Roman Catholic doctrine was against Scripture and the teachings of the ancient Fathers. It was his major purpose to demonstrate that not Protestantism but Roman Catholicism could justly be accused of having fallen away from the teachings and practices of the ancient church.

The work made a deep impression not only upon Protestants but also upon Roman Catholics. Andrada wrote a reply under the title "*Tridentinae fidei quinque libris comprehensa*" (1578), but he did not succeed in upsetting the high esteem in which the Protestants, especially the Lutherans, held Chemnitz's book. Translated into German and French and frequently republished, even in the nineteenth century, it remained the most useful Protestant criticism of the Council of Trent.

A modern Protestant treatise on the Council still remains to be written.[31]

Part II

Protestantism

CHAPTER 8

The Nature of Protestantism

THE NAME "Protestantism" is not definite. It is derived from the "Protestation" of the German evangelical estates at the Diet of Speyer in 1529. In it they refused to accept the majority decision invalidating the unanimous vote of the Diet of Speyer in 1526 which at least provisionally had made possible the establishment of territorial evangelical churches in Germany. The term "Protestantism," therefore, signifies a reaction against the attempt to regulate religious affairs by political action, disregarding the voice of conscience. The declaration of the evangelical estates that "in things which concern the honor of God and the salvation of souls, everyone must stand for himself before God and be responsible to him," is filled with the same spirit which (at Worms in 1521) had induced Luther to defy the authorities of pope and emperor in the name of conscience. But it would be wrong to regard the signers of the "Protestation" as defenders of the religious freedom of conscience. They fought primarily for the political right of territorial regulation of church affairs in contrast to medieval papal and imperial universalism.[1]

It is not the protest against coercion in things of faith but rather the protest against the institution of Roman Catholicism which has characterized the Protestant groups throughout their history. Few of them have ever applied the name "Protestant" to themselves. Many, particularly the Lutherans, prefer to designate themselves as "evangelical." In this connection it is interesting to note that the English dissenters called themselves "Protestant Nonconformists" and that, in 1783, even the American offshoot of Anglicanism adopted the official name of "The Protestant Episcopal Church." The common feature of all Protestants is that they are not Roman Catholics.

This opposition to Roman Catholicism involves first of all the rejection of the claim of the Roman church to represent the direct continuation and embodiment of the divine work of salvation through Jesus Christ. While acknowledging their indebtedness to Roman Catholic history, Protestants deny that the perpetuation of this history in ecclesiastical institutions and practices, without conformity to which the Christian faith is deemed unrealizable, is reconcilable with the gospel of Jesus Christ. Protestantism as a whole represents a response to the gospel of Jesus Christ which in contrast to Roman Catholicism is not qualified by the claim that the historical media and channels through which this gospel reaches men are endowed with an authority derived from Jesus himself. To be sure, this principle has been and is being violated by many Protestant individuals and groups. Numerous Protestant beliefs, doctrines, and institutions appear to be so hallowed as if they were the only and exclusive vessels of the lordship of Jesus Christ. Indeed, it may be said that the Bible, which certainly is a product of human history, is so central in Protestant religion that the absolute lordship of Jesus is delimited by it. There always has been in Protestantism a Biblicism which violates the principle of Christocentrism no less than Roman Catholic traditionalism does. But nevertheless, Protestant Christianity has lived of the daring willingness, if necessary, "to urge the authority of Christ against the authority of the Bible," as Luther, the very founder of Protestantism, once expressed it.[2]

As the example of Biblicism so subtly shows, an unmediated confrontation of the Christian with the person of Jesus Christ is impossible, but this impossibility does not imply that the means of mediation must share in the authority of Christ himself. This is the secret of the Protestant protest against Roman Catholicism.

The fundamental difference between Protestant and Roman Catholic Christianity may be described as follows: Protestants believe that a man becomes a Christian not by partaking of the miraculous power of the seven *sacraments* but by the confession that the New Testament message of the revelation of God in Jesus is true. The sacraments which Protestants celebrate add nothing to the "word"; they merely bring it, as it were, directly and personally to the believer.

The *grace* which Protestants believe to receive from the "word" is not a supernatural, *quasi*-physical substance with healing power from Christ, as the Roman Catholic church claims to communicate it to man by the sacraments, but the divine assurance of the forgiveness of sins which freely given by God through Christ makes possible a new *personal* relationship between man and his maker.

The Protestant is convinced that *faith* alone, i.e., an absolute reliance upon God and a complete trust in him as he has made himself known through Jesus, is the proper attitude of man toward God. He rejects the Roman Catholic teaching that man possesses powers by which he can make himself acceptable to God.

For he regards *sin* not as a defect of human nature due to the loss of the supernatural gift of fellowship with God but as a rebellion of man against God, by which man tries to appropriate the divine power for himself as if he could be self-sufficient.

In the understanding of the *nature of man,* the Protestant is therefore more pessimistic than the Roman Catholic. He does not share in the latter's belief that there is a continuity between man as he is and God.

In theology and in ethics he rejects the principle of the classical and now authoritative Roman Catholic teaching of Thomas Aquinas that the realms of the natural and supernatural can be co-ordinated and that reason and faith can supplement each other. Instead, he teaches that there is a *tension between man and God* which is only dissolved by God's act of forgiveness.

In complete reliance upon God and not upon himself, the Protestant proclaims the freedom of the Christian man. Therefrom he derives the doctrine of the *universal priesthood of believers,* convinced that everyone who has come under the lordship of God through faith in the gospel of Jesus Christ and thereby become a free man, subject to God alone, can be a priest who through his words and deeds brings the liberating gospel to his fellowmen. Thus the Roman Catholic distinction between priests and laymen is destroyed.

The *church* is then understood as a fellowship of believers and not as a priestly institution of salvation. And the power of the *papacy* is broken. For as a believer the Protestant relies only upon God's act through Christ on his conscience, and not, like the Roman Catholic, upon God's act bound to the tradition of the church as it is defined and protected by the pope.

These fundamental differences between Roman Catholicism and Protestantism, here broadly stated in the terms of the teaching of the Reformation, have determined the inner history of Protestantism. They have, of course, not excluded the continuation of many teachings and practices of early and medieval Catholicism in Protestant religious life.

II

The total phenomenon of Protestantism is, of course, much more complicated than is indicated in these generalizations. Its main features must now be elucidated.

I wish, first of all, to point to the religious genius of Martin Luther. It should not be denied that the Reformation took its beginnings in his inner struggle for salvation, that its primary cause was religious. To be sure, Luther's discovery of the way to salvation by faith was conditioned by medieval piety and the expression of his faith in the new doctrinal, cultic, ethical, and institutional forms which laid the foundations of Protestantism was fashioned by the political, social, and cultural circumstances of his age. But the decisive experience was his very own, arising from the depth of his soul. In a most unique manner, he was apprehended by the numinous power of the divine. The reality of God overcame him in a way in which only few men can feel it. Throughout his life, he gave prophetic testimony of the power of the divine which had touched his soul with such a strength that it transcended testing explication by thought or conscience. Only Augustine is his equal in the capacity of expressing in words the depth and paradoxical complexity of religious emotions. Who but one who had felt the terrifying yet inescapable pangs of the "wholly other" could write the following words:[3]

"I too have known a man who told me that he had often experienced these tortures, though only for a short time, but so strongly and infernally, that no tongue can speak of it, no pen write of it—yes, that no one can believe it who has not himself experienced it. They were of such a kind that if they had increased and had lasted for only half an hour or even for only the tenth part of an hour, the man would have wholly perished and all his bones would have burned to ashes. At such moments God appears in his terrible anger and all creature as one stands before him. Then there is no escape and no consolation, no within and no without, but all accusation of all. Then man cries out as it is written: I am smitten by the glance of thine eyes. He does not even dare exclaim: O Lord, do not deal with me according to thine anger. In such moments, strange to say, the soul cannot believe that it might ever be redeemed; it only feels that the torture is not yet complete. But it is an eternal torture—impossible to hold it a temporal one. So there remains nothing for man but the naked longing for help and the terrible cry of fear and he does not know where to ask for help. Then the soul is stretched out (on the cross) with Christ, so that one could count its bones. And there is no particle in it which is not filled with a most awful bitterness, fear, anguish, and sadness—and all this is eternal."

A person who had thus encountered God could not but declare concerning his beliefs: *Opus est ut omnia quae creduntur abscondantur.*[4]

He had to confess God before men in such a way as to feel the full force of a conflict with the world:

"For whosoever wants to give God honor and glory, must condemn the world's honor and glory. He must say that man's words and works and all honor he has therefrom are nothing and that God's words and works alone are worthy of honor and glory. Alas, the world cannot tolerate this. And so you must suffer and be a heretic, a revolutionary, a blasphemer, because you do away with so many good works and with so much spiritual worshipful life. Then you are silenced and put to the stake. The world will not tolerate you, because it does not want to be disturbed. But it is just as impossible for you to be silent, and with a great voice you confess alone God's glory and honor in his words and works—and so you go to the stake and burn. . . . For they do not want to hear of God's name, glory and honor, because they and their interests would come to fall thereby. If God alone were wise, good, just, truthful, and strong, *they* would have to be fools, evil, unjust liars, false, and weak. . . . The world does not want to be foolish and wrong; therefore God does not want to tolerate it and sends his messengers to it and punishes it. And because of this, the saints must spill their blood. Thus it is a great thing to praise and magnify God before the world with a great voice."[5]

It is this prophetic surrender to the divine which has caused the Reformation and inspired Protestantism throughout its history. Only against this background its gospel of salvation by faith can be understood. Before such a piety all sacramental hierarchial mediatorship between man and God had to fall. Here lie the sources of the protest against every earthly and materialistic encasement of the holy, against all forms of a sacred canon law, against the combination of Pelagianism with Augustinianism, against all sacramental encounter with God. Here are the reasons for Luther's lifelong condemnation of the papacy as the Anti-Christ. This is the background for the English non-conformist cry: No popery! It is also the foundation of the Lutheran doctrine of the justification by faith and of the Calvinist doctrine of predestination. God's is the initiative—this is the primary presupposition of it all. Under its influence, Protestantism has become the prophetic, dynamic expression of Christianity. It has renewed the Jewish heritage within the Christian tradition. The prominence of the Old Testament, particularly in Calvinism, was not an arbitrary contribution of Calvin but an essential expression of the religion of the Reformation. Throughout its history, Protestantism has suspected idolatry in all attempts to confine the absolute in relative forms.

III

The religion of the *sola gratia* had to assume an historical form. It is a most interesting problem for the philosopher of history to discuss whether Protestantism can ever become incarnate in historical life.[6] But we are here confronted by the question of how Christian Protestantism related itself to historical life. It is significant to observe that it did not occur to Luther on his own accord to break with Roman Catholic traditions. Even after the opposition of the papal church had forced him to take the fatal step, he failed to formulate clear principles of a new organization. The expectation that "the word would do it" and the prayer that "God should give him Christians" were his mainstay.[7] Until the end of his life, he believed to belong to the one holy Catholic church. He did not wish to be considered as a separatist although he actually was one. In the same manner, the ideal of Catholicity has been preserved by Protestants of all ages.

One must distinguish between those elements of the Reformation which linked it to the medieval church and those which pointed to the civilization of the future. The discussion of the nature of Protestantism is frequently confused by a failure to recognize this distinction. For the religious spirit which I have just described expressed itself in both directions.

In order to begin with the remnants of medievalism within the Protestantism of the Reformation, it must be pointed out that the Reformers could not think of Christianity as embodied in an objective institution of salvation. They rejected Roman Catholic sacramentalism and substituted for it the authority of the Biblical word objectifying its meaning in confessions. They continued the medieval Augustinian interpretation of the Christian religion as a religion of grace, although they interpreted grace not as *medicina* but as *favor,* as Melanchthon put it. They continued the medieval Roman Catholic compromise between the ethic of the gospel and the ethic of the world, although they carried it as a tension into the world, instead of distinguishing between the perfection of the monks and the imperfection of the people of the world. The phrase, "intramundane asceticism of Protestantism," introduced by M. Weber and E. Troeltsch, is quite apt. The Reformers also continued the advocacy of the mutual responsibility of church and state for the true religion and its realization in life, although they destroyed the Roman Catholic principle of the supremacy of the church over the state by distinguishing and even separating the domains of the church from those of the state.

On the other hand, it is clear that the Reformation released powers which have gone into the making of the modern world. To be sure, its immediate cultural effects were negative rather than positive. It dealt the death-blow to the papal universal monarchy—which neither the rise of nationalism, nor the development of capitalism, nor the Renaissance, nor the humanistic return to the sources of antiquity, had been able to achieve. But the suspension of the hierarchy and of monasticism, the exclusion of canon law and the confiscation of church property for political and cultural purposes caused a new development in politics, economics, and home life. All this was grounded in the power of new religious ideas. Religion became inwardness, thought, spirit. As such it was the response of the free individual to the objective act of God through Jesus Christ, the gospel of forgiveness. The much praised religious individualism of the Reformation was everything but subjectivistic. However, it involved a tremendous simplification of the Christian faith. The question of the Reformers was how to obtain a merciful God and *quomodo bona opera fieri possint,* and they answered it by reference to the bold faith of the personal conscience which is bound to God alone and does not depend upon a complicated ecclesiastical apparatus of supernatural substances of salvation. From this there resulted a new conception of the church (the universal priesthood of believers; the emphasis upon the *communio sanctorum*) and a new conception of vocation. The world as it actually is was thus opened to the conquest of the Christian. For by activity in the orders of the world he had to prove his faith.

IV

It is not my purpose to show the development of these ideas in new institutional practices and in new cultural forms. But I wish to explain that the world orientation of early Protestantism was threefold.

(1) It depended upon the new religious stimulus which had broken forth from Martin Luther. The prophetic spirit which contrasted itself to the sacramental spirit of religion has invested Protestantism with a religious attitude of a unique character.

(2) Because this religious revolt was directed against Roman Catholicism not only in so far as the latter represented a religious principle but also in so far as it was a cultural institution, it had to express itself in forms that were shaped by the anti-Catholic cultural forces of the sixteenth century. Thus the Reformation became linked with the political forces of nationalism and territorialism, with the educational movement

of Humanism and—in the case of Calvinism—guardedly also with early capitalism. The Roman Catholic church too had to reckon with these realities and, largely stimulated by the Protestant revolt, it entered into an alliance with them. It adjusted them to its own tradition, while Protestantism had to accept them in their full independence. These connections shaped its future much more radically than that of the Roman church and affected its character often in contrast to the intentions and ideals of its founders. Luther would have been the first to protest against the later German Lutheran state-churches. And Calvin certainly did not anticipate that centuries after his death it would be possible to prove an inter-connection between the Calvinist ethic and the spirit of capitalism. Although he gave recognition to the new commercialism of his day, he sought with all his might to prevent its immoral, un-Christian implications.

(3) The religious movement of the sixteenth century called for a reformation of the church, not a revolt against it. For this reason it preserved many of the institutional forms which Christianity had developed in its historical course. The work of the reformation was to proceed in terms of the re-discovered Bible, one-sidedly interpreted according to the norm of Paulinism, but it was not intended to be a repristination of first century Christianity. The Protestant sects which came into being as a result of the Lutheran movement moved in this direction. They were rejected by the Reformers primarily because they were so radically individualistic that they threatened to violate the historical continuity with the Christian past which the reformers endeavored to preserve. Ultimately, these sects and their offsprings were to achieve a glorious victory of recognition with modern Protestantism. But the persecution of them during the sixteenth century by Protestants and Catholics alike proved that, in spite of their contrast, Protestants and Catholics were closely allied in the concern for the preservation of Christianity in the forms of objective institutions of salvation.

In consequence of the togetherness of these three elements within early Protestantism, three tendencies have struggled against one another in the entire Protestant history. They may be described as theonomous, autonomous, and heteronomous attitudes of mind.

(1) In so far as Protestantism lived of the religious genius of Luther, it was endowed with the spirit of complete obedience to God which causes man to lead a life of restless devotion to the eternal and infinite—a devotion which qualifies all acts as temporal and finite. Life is then understood in the terms of the first of Luther's ninety-five theses of 1517: "When our Lord Jesus Christ said: 'Repent ye . . .,' he meant to say that our whole life should be repentance." This theonomous orientation renders impossible every static conception and practice of religion.

(2) In so far as early Protestantism linked itself to the forces of its cultural environment which were inspired by the Renaissance, it gave room within itself to the spirit of autonomy. It cannot be denied, of course, that the theonomous attitude, because it results in that supreme freedom which Luther described in his pamphlet *On the Liberty of the Christian Man,* and which Calvin had in mind when he developed his teaching of election, is similar to the autonomous attitude which grounds man in that which is within him, especially reason. But Luther's antagonism to Aristotelianism and his hostility to the spiritualists and radical evangelicals in whom he suspected an autonomous religious subjectivism indicates that there must be a deep difference between prophetism and self-determination. Nevertheless, the Reformation opened itself to the spirit of autonomy. Luther's aversion toward Erasmus did not prevent the introduction of humanism into Protestant culture. Later historians could refer not only to the similarity between Luther's *"Hier stehe ich, ich kann nicht anders"* and Descartes' *"Cogito, ergo sum,"* but also to the kinship between Luther and Kant.[8] It may also be pointed out that when, during the eighteenth and nineteenth centuries, liberal theology defended the autonomous principle of the continuity and kinship between God and man, it believed to carry on the work which had been begun by the Reformation.[9]

(3) But it is precisely such an understanding of their endeavor which Luther and the Reformers had tried to prevent. That is why they clung to the heteronomous authorities of the Bible, dogma, and institutional church, thereby defying both

the theonomous and autonomous attitudes. Luther's theological and cultic conservatism, Calvin's rigorous Biblicism, and the traditionalism of the Anglican church must be interpreted from this point of view. The orthodoxy of the Protestant state churches was the expression of the heteronomous spirit. Much of that which, in the name of the eternal, unconditioned God had been attacked in Roman Catholicism thus found entrance into Protestantism.

The conflict between these three principles is the most interesting aspect of the history of religion. The greatest enemy of the autonomous man who, ignoring the limitations of creatureliness and finiteness, and oblivious to the abysmal power of sin, circles around his own self-sufficiency is the theonomous prophet who proclaims salvation in the name of the eternal, infinite unconditioned Lord of all life. But as prophetism must incarnate its eternal reference not only in moral judgments, but also in the temporal forms of speech, symbolisms, and sacramental signs, it tends to result in arbitrarily absolutized forms and laws which sooner or later perpetuate themselves for their own sake. They may be attacked as idols in a new prophetic onslaught in the name of the invisible God, and thus the full power of true religion may again be released, but general experience shows that they are brought to fall not by the theonomous man, but by the autonomous man when he emancipates himself from the slavery of the arbitrary traditionalist heteronomy of religious teachings and institutions. Thus the prophet, the priest, and the humanist struggle with one another.

This conflict has characterized the history of Protestantism in a unique way.

V

The Reformation occurred at a time when an autonomous secularist opposition against the heteronomous, sacral authoritarianism of the medieval church was already in progress. The Renaissance was a movement of the maturing European man who had been trained by the church and who, in the name of the ancient secularism which had been blended with the church's theology and ethics and transcended by it, declared his independence from his teacher. The Reformation had nothing in common with the Renaissance. It opposed its spirit. Indeed, for a time, Roman Catholicism succeeded in absorbing the

Renaissance in the same manner by which it had domesticated other rebellious movements in the past, while Protestantism developed life-forms of an inner-worldly asceticism and of a moral discipline which curbed all Renaissance expressions, particularly of art and philosophy, within its midst. Nevertheless, the Renaissance and the Reformation, which historical fate had designated as contemporaries, were to become allies. It was Renaissance England which fought the victorious battle that paved the way for the progress of Protestantism in Northern Europe and America. Capitalism developed its full strength in the countries where Protestantism was established. The Enlightenment, made possible by the almost uninterrupted continuation of the Renaissance culture in modern France, by the politically necessitated practice of tolerance in Holland, by the assertion of the Renaissance spirit in England where it had been permitted to flourish side by side with Protestantism—began its march through the countries of Northern Europe. It was eagerly accepted by men who, during the confessional wars, had lived by ecclesiastical absolutism sand upon whom the barren systems of orthodoxy could not bestow a zest for living.

Now the autonomous spirit could unfold its power. It proudly declared its emancipation from the supernatural authorities which until then had dominated Western civilization. Kant spoke for generations of modern men when he wrote:[10]

"Enlightenment is the advance of man beyond the state of voluntary immaturity. By immaturity is meant man's inability to use his understanding except under the guidance of another. This immaturity is voluntary, when it is due to want of resolution rather than want of intelligence. The motto of enlightenment is: *Sapere aude!* Courageously use your understanding!"

The new learning expressing itself in the modern disciplines of mathematics and natural science, philosophy and psychology, history and literature, political and economic science, took recognition of the liberation which already had taken place in the policies of the absolutist state and the conquests of commerce. With ever increasing aggressiveness, the intellectual revolution which we call "the Enlightenment" established the autonomy of man. Protestantism made its contribution to this victory—but not through its established churches, but by way of Humanism, the methods of which it had accepted, and especially by way of the sectarian radicalism, which the churches of the Reformation had suppressed. The humanists and the English nonconformists who, during a complicated historical development, had become the heirs of the sixteenth century sectaries, were more directly connected with the modern age than the orthodox Protestants. They became the defenders and propagators of tolerance, and they cultivated an individualism which, while it gave them religious liberty, secured freedom also for other activities of man.

The most important *practical* effect of the emancipated civilization upon Protestantism was the separation of church and state which was either directly or indirectly accomplished. The most significant *theoretical* result of the new culture for Protestantism was the breakdown of theological orthodoxy. Rationalism and Pietism had undermined the rigidity of its teachings from within—either by the appeal to reason or to personal experience. Thus the way was prepared for an undogmatic theology which by historical and psychological analysis endeavored to interpret the meaning of the Christian faith and by use of the new scientific methods tried to adapt it to the modern consciousness. Kant's theory of knowledge which was the turning point of modern philosophy exercised a deep influence also upon theological thought. His claim that human knowledge can contain only sensate experiences as they are moulded by the *a priori* forms and categories of the mind and his proof that all possibility of a *knowledge* of the supernatural must be excluded from the realm of reason, were to become fundamental principles of modern theology. Furthermore, Kant's teaching that the object of knowledge, the *Ding an sich,* must remain unapproachable and unknowable and that objects of faith in particular can never become objects of knowledge at all, forced theology to pay attention to the subject of faith. Schleiermacher, by placing religion in the realm of feeling and by defining theology as the description of religious feelings, inaugurated the period of psychologism in theology. It was he who first declared[11] that the idea of revelation be "better applied only to the region of the higher self-consciousness." Since then modern theologians have interpreted the Christian religion primarily in terms of human experience. By emphasizing an historical orientation they have related this experience to the his-

torical Jesus of Nazareth who was thus seen as the founder of
the Christian movement and only in this sense as the revealer
of God to man. Under these influences, a very complete and
thorough analysis of the religious life was made possible but
its objective validity became more and more questionable. The
God-idea was interpreted as a function of the human mind
rather than as a recognition of the reality of the existence of
God. Thus the spirit of autonomy entered the most fundamental part of the life of the church.

However, its effects made themselves only gradually felt.
During the reactionary period which followed the era of the
French Revolution the Protestant churches all over the world
experienced "a great awakening." Pietism, which, by dissolving orthodoxy from within, had paved the way for the Enlightenment thus enabling it to take hold of the thought of Protestantism, now became the weapon by which the churches defended themselves against this intruder whose foreign influence
they felt. Under the guise of personal religious experience,
understood in terms of Pietism and not in terms of modern
philosophy, orthodoxy established itself again, preserving traditionalism within the churches and guaranteeing to them the
continuity with the past. For this achievement, however, they
paid the price of losing more and more influence upon modern
life. The new theology became the concern of a minority group
within the churches. But it served directly and indirectly the
ever growing number of those members of the educated middle
classes who, estranged from the life and teaching of the churches,
dedicated themselves to an ecclesiastical religiousness in which
the moral emphasis of the Christian teaching were preserved as
the central core of an adequate philosophy of life. Only during
the present century, this New Protestantism began to determine
also the life of the churches themselves. Today it has produced
a crisis which becomes more and more agonizing as it is complicated by the apparent sickness in the whole body of autonomous Western civilization. Modernist theologians themselves
have reacted against the new Protestantism. Barth and the
large group of his more or less Barthian followers have de-
nounced the theological development of the last two centuries
as a betrayal of the Christian faith. This reaction appeared
first as a theonomous protest against the impossible interpreta-

tion of the Christian religion in terms of an autonomous spirit, but it has developed more and more in the direction of a Neo-Lutheran and Neo-Calvinist confessionalism in which the medieval heteronomous aspects of Reformation life and teaching are re-asserted. Thus modern Protestantism experiences again the conflict of early Protestantism between the Renaissance and the Reformation. But it seems that today this conflict cannot be resolved by a return to heteronomous ecclesiastical authorities, but only by a theonomous, prophetic criticism of the whole of modern civilization.

VI

The situation of modern Protestantism has been made possible by the development of the modern state to which the Renaissance and the Reformation made decisive contributions. In conclusion, I wish to deal with this development, because the nature of Protestantism is closely determined by it.[12]

The fundamental idea of the Middle Ages had been the co-ordination of church and state as the co-operating organs of the *corpus Christianum*. The three main groups of early Protestantism, Lutheranism, Calvinism, and Anglicanism, did not discontinue this system in spite of the fact that they distinguished more clearly than Roman Catholicism had done between the state and the church. For they transmitted the care for the cultural life into the hands of the political magistrate, definitely trusting that its action would conform to Christian standards. But this arrangement was ended by the secularization of the modern state, which Troeltsch has called the most important event in modern history.

I cannot deal with the causes of this secularization. They lie in the rise of national states within the medieval empire, in the development of city states, in the reception of Roman law and its idea of the uniformity and absoluteness of political power, in the humanistic revival of ancient political ideals and their interpretation in the theories of Machiavelli and Bodin, in the emergence of territorial powers within the larger territorial units, also in the glorification of the state in the Protestant theories. Under the impact of these early influences, the modern state grounded itself upon the principle of sovereignty, i. e., the principle that the state is the highest and ultimate authority on earth and the self-sufficient source of all political power. Its

purpose is defined as *salus publica* or *raison d'état,* consisting
of the maintenance of peace in relation to other states, the preservation of interior order, the protection of commerce, the care
for public health, and the increase of political strength. In a
way, this purpose does not differ from that given in classical
ecclesiastical doctrines but it is now entirely secularized. Political sovereignty and autarchy represent a drastic contrast to the
old Protestant teaching that the state is subject to the judgment
of the word of God and that it is its duty to preserve order and
welfare for he purpose of enabling the church to communicate
its gospel and salvation to men. The state no longer serves the
glory of God but its own. It becomes the all-consuming Levi-
athan, as Hobbes called it. In connection with modern nationalism and militarism it demands allegiance as the earthly god
of men.

As soon as the state ceased to have its purpose in the
church, it abandoned its interest for the inner life of the church
and for the conformity of faith. It became religiously neutral
and tolerant, permitting freedom of faith to Christians and
non-Christians. It merely required the churches and religious
groups not to undertake anything hostile to the interests of the
state! It furthered the ecclesiastical cause only in so far as
religious-moral forces might contribute to the health of the political system.

The policy described in these sentences was only gradually established. For a long time, only the United States of
America had a constitution which guaranteed the full separation between church and state. Even today, the separation is
completely actualized only in a few nations, although it is legally
in effect in the entire world.

The churches adjusted themselves to the new situation by
gradually formulating a new concept of the church in which
the independence of the church is asserted over against the independence of the state. It involves the abandonment of the
attempt to maintain a unified church and it also entails the
necessity that churches grant material recognition to each other.
Denominationalism thus became the answer of Protestantism
to the secularization of the state. In the work of the formulation of a church concept adequate to this change, the teachings
of Humanists, Spiritualists, Anabaptists and other sectarians

proved to be most effective. The modern churches ceased to define themselves as God-ordered institutions of salvation. To be sure, many of them continued the ecclesiological traditions of the ancient church, of Catholicism, and of classical Protestantism, but practically, these teachings lost their effectiveness. A church was defined as a religious corporation or association, represented first by local congregations and then by the combination of these in larger units. The theory of John Locke, definitely inspired by English Independentism, furnished the pattern. In his "Letter concerning Toleration," he wrote:[13]

"A church then I take to be a voluntary Society of Men, joining themselves together of their own accord, in order to the public worshipping of God, in such a manner as they judge acceptable to him, and effectual to the salvation of their souls."

Under the impact of the development of thus defined "free churches," the meaning of the article of the Apostles' Creed which speaks of the "one, holy, catholic church" was more and more transformed. Protestantism all over the world learned from America to refer to churches rather than to "the church." The concept of "the church" ceased to be the *norm* which is to be applied to the various responses to the *one* divine call through Jesus Christ. It became an *ideal* to which the various human historical manifestations of the Christian spirit in the world are to conform in the course of time.

The secularization of the state thus produced a humanization of the church. In the periods prior to the modern world, the state was confronted by a church which understood itself as an institution of supernatural origin set into the world by the divine revelation in Jesus Christ. Today, it is facing churches which interpret themselves as the social embodiment of the Christian spirit which, since the days of Jesus of Nazareth, has inspired men to higher living in accordance with the commandment of the love of God and fellowmen.

The transformation indicated in these sentences is of tremendous historical importance for the present and the future. For it suggests the question whether modern Protestantism will be able to act with authority when, in accordance with its modern all-sufficient character, the state assumes control also over the consciences of men.

Also, under the aspect of the problem "church and state,"

Chapter 9

The Character of Protestantism in the Light of the Idea of Revelation

NO HISTORICAL movement can be so interpreted that the character which distinguishes it as unique among other historical events is once for all fixed in the understanding. Just as the character of a person can be known only in connection with his acts in concrete situations, so the nature of a movement in human history can be comprehended only by a constantly fresh attention to the inner and outer circum- stances in which it has unfolded itself. And just as the char- acter of a person does not only impress itself upon concrete life situations but is also shaped by them, so the nature of a movement in history is conditioned by the living realities through which it proceeds. Thus Protestantism, which was born in the Reformation and then received the prophetic, dynamic character which set it in contrast to Roman Catholic- ism, can be fully understood only in terms of the transforma- tions and adaptations of its nature which it effected and under- went in the course of its development.

Moreover, in this case, the tension between character and concrete life situations which determines all human life, is of a particular complexity. For, from the beginning, Protestantism has displayed a dependence upon history and a freedom from it in such a way that both appear as simultaneous. It has always recognized itself as part of the Christian movement and never carried its protest against the Roman church to such an extreme that it disassociated itself from the historical Christian tradition of which, in the West at least, Roman Catholicism was the chief guardian. At the same time, however, it has been profoundly critical of any absolutization of historical achieve-

131

ments because there have always been Protestant believers who
were mindful of the absolute sovereignty of God, the only lord
of history. For this reason, Luther and his friends and followers were not revolutionaries or sectarians or schismatics, but reformers. In the name of God, the Lord of all and therefore
also of history, they claimed to speak from *within* the Christian
church against the papal church. Recognizing history, Roman
Catholic history included, as the realm in which God's creative
and redemptive will had been and was being done, they nevertheless rejected any absolutization of historical attainments as
blasphemy.

In the same way, Protestants have always acknowledged that
the concrete historical situation in which men find themselves
is the place where obedience is to be rendered to God, but, at
the same time, their prophetic spirit has moved them to criticize
in the name of God every attempt to render any historical attainment permanent and to regard it as sacred because of its
alleged permanence. On the one hand, they have displayed a
remarkable readiness to adjust the Christian religion to historical conditions and, on the other hand, they have shown a
great eagerness for religious reform whenever a historical tradition, particularly an ecclesiastical one, threatened to become
an end in itself.

When one searches for the source of this Protestant attitude,
he will ultimately find it in the Christian idea of revelation.
Now Protestantism has of course no special claim upon this
idea. It governs the life of all Christian churches. But it can
fairly be said that Protestantism has recognized the dynamic
character of this idea to an extraordinary extent.

The meaning of the idea of revelation is the togetherness of
hiddenness and disclosure. When we speak of an act of revelation, we refer to an event which discloses a mystery; renders
plain what is obscure; unveils what is veiled; brings into the
immanence of knowledge what transcends apprehension; makes
available what is unavailable. The light by which it illumi-
nates the human mind is "a light no man can approach unto."
The idea of revelation belongs to the realm of religion; it cir-
cumscribes the religious knowledge of God. Its meaning is
that the knowledge of God does not delimit the divine transcendence. It expresses graphically the insight of religious faith

that God's self-disclosure does not delimit his divinity.

The *Christian religion* stands and falls with the conviction that God has revealed himself to men in the historical person of Jesus of Nazareth. This means that God has made his character known in Jesus, although he is not confined in him. Even though he has disclosed himself in the historical Jesus, he still remains God in his unapproachable mystery. In ever new ways, the theologians have attempted to state these implications of the idea of God's revelation in Jesus. That is why the theories, the doctrines, of revelation have constantly changed.

While recognizing its indebtedness to ancient and medieval thinkers, Protestantism has paid special attention to the dynamic character of this idea of revelation. On the one hand, it has stressed the divine transcendence in all theological, liturgical and ethical thoughts of the presence of God in Jesus, and, on the other hand, it has given full freedom to the historical investigation of the figure of the Nazarene. It has not always escaped from the danger of dissolving the tension that is involved in the belief that God has made himself known in a historical person (Protestant theologians have been inclined either to minimize or to exaggerate the importance of the historicity of Jesus), but it has nevertheless injected the dynamic vitality of the Christian belief in revelation into all phases of its life.

II

Keeping these general observations in mind, I shall attempt in the following pages to view the nature of Protestantism in the light of the history of the Christian idea of revelation. It is not my purpose to offer a picture of the genetic development of the idea but to pay attention to those aspects of its history which may illumine the character of Protestantism.

The writers of the New Testament describe the power of life by which God had become a "God-for-them" through his self-disclosure in Jesus as the Holy Spirit. This concept "Holy Spirit" provides the most direct clue to the understanding of the Christian idea of revelation. It refers to man's personal participation in God's revelation and denotes that which man has received from the divine act of self-disclosure. It permits therefore an understanding of revelation in terms of human experience.

The original meanings of the Greek word for "spirit"
(πνευμα), namely "air," and of the Hebrew word for "spirit"
(ruakh), namely "wind," are preserved in the concept throughout the history of its use until our day. They indicate a primitive animistic metaphysical view of the nature of life. The
interpretation which the term received from the Hebrews of
the Old Testament has become the pattern of its Christian
understanding. They attributed certain manifestations in men,
but not only in men, of what was apparently a power not their
own, to the spirit (ruakh) of God. "This 'spirit of God' is not
Jehovah himself; it is the power of Jehovah working at a dis-
tance, a breath or wind, as it were, coming from Jehovah:
Jehovah abides in his holy heaven. The figure of a wind which
travels over vast spaces served admirably to convey the idea of
something coming from God which moved and controlled men.
. . . It is noteworthy, too, that even in this regard to the spirit,
it is not commonly spoken of as entering the prophet, but as
coming upon him. . . . He receives a power working from outside, felt by the man as essentially not himself. It is sometimes
described as a hand laid upon the man which he cannot resist.
This forms a signal contrast to all Greek and Indian ideas, according to which man looking into the center of his own being
can discover his fundamental identity with God."[1]

This Hebrew understanding of the Holy Spirit was employed by the early Christians. Their faith in Jesus, the revealer of God, manifested itself in the Holy Spirit in the sense
that a power not themselves, coming upon them from without,
so to speak, had taken possession of them. Thus their conception of the Holy Spirit reflects an understanding of the spiritual
life as based on a faith in God which is derived from revelation.
It depends upon the disclosure of a knowledge which man cannot derive from himself, and it is grounded upon the communication of gifts of insight and moral power which man cannot produce by his own initiative. Whenever Christians have
spoken of the Holy Spirit, they have had reference to the
transcendent power of God, the Father of Jesus Christ, at work
within their souls. And when the theologians dealt with the
problem of the Holy Spirit, they were concerned with the problem of the Christian's personal participation in God's revelation. This is the meaning of the Holy Spirit, the meaning also

of the Christian life in so far as it stands in God's revelation in Jesus.

For the purpose of this discussion, it is important to note that the conviction of the early Christians to have received from Jesus a power of spiritual life which transcended their own possibilities was described by them in terms which they had borrowed for an earlier religious tradition. But the traditional word-forms they used were given an entirely new meaning. To be sure, when they spoke of the "spirit" that dwelt in them, they had reference to a religious power which had been experienced by many generations of men before them and particularly by the Jews. Moreover, in their hearts, they felt this power as something absolutely new, because they related it to a new divine act of revelation through Jesus. A study of the writings of the New Testament will show that the almost ecstatic character of the early Christian faith in God's revelation in Christ was so immediate and so explosively spontaneous that it could only inadequately be expressed in forms of liturgical and theological speech and religious and social practice. Some of these forms were entirely new (the universal love ethic, for example); others were taken over from earlier traditions but transformed by the new Christian self-consciousness (the order of worship and the church idea, for example); still others were almost entirely transferred from non-Christian to Christian usage (the Old Testament, for example), but, in each case, the power of the awareness that God had disclosed himself in a new and final way in Christ and communicated through him a new life gave these forms a unique, dynamic content.

As Christianity became an historical social movement, the forms in which its faith was bound became more and more important. The forms of worship, thought, organization, and ethics which were developed related the Christian religion to the cultural life of its environment. At the same time, however, they were designed to preserve the uniqueness of the Christian faith in contradistinction from other religions and religious attitudes. There always remained a tension between the vitality of the faith as grounded in the divine revelation in Jesus and the necessity of conformity to the forms in which this faith was cast. The more institutional and traditional the Christian movement became, the more this tension relaxed. The dependence upon forms once developed then became more pronounced. But, nevertheless, even then the dynamic belief that God, who transcends time and space and history, had disclosed himself in the life and death of the historical person of Jesus of Nazareth in order to establish a community between himself and the believers, constantly threatened to break the forms of faith and order.

Thus we see that when Christianity became a historical social-religious movement, a seed of inner conflict was planted in its life: It required forms to enable its members as Christians to participate in the ongoing common life and yet these forms again and again proved insufficient to carry the effect of God's revelation in Christ. In a very profound way this conflict is a reflection of the event of revelation: In it God disclosed himself in history, yet remaining the lord of history, without entering history (in the sense that he confined himself to one historical person of definite time and place). The Christian church, which was the result of this revelation, was therefore compelled to understand itself in such a way that it represented neither a perpetuation or prolongation of a divine historical act nor a denial that God had really acted in history. All its life has been conditioned by this contrast. The togetherness of history and super-history which marks its "beginning" has forced it again and again to break the forms by which it has tended to become a participant in the movement of history and at the same time to create historical forms in order not to retire from history. To be sure, it happened frequently that, in thought and in life, one side of this contrast was overemphasized to the neglect of the other (the history of the interpretation of the figure of Jesus offers the best examples), but the contrast itself has always been the focus of Christianity's peculiar vitality.

III

The truth of these observations will be borne out by a further examination of the idea of revelation in Christian history. At a very early time the future history of Christianity was determined by the fact that the faith in God's revelation in Jesus which, from the beginning, had been proclaimed in Jewish and Hellenistic forms (built around such names and titles as the "Christ," the "Son of God," the "Lord," the "Saviour," the

"Word") were put in liturgical, ethical, doctrinal and organizational forms and concepts designed to maintain and preserve
its uniqueness. And nothing was more important than the fact
that when, in the first centuries, the Christian movement had
to preserve its identity against the Roman state and society and
especially against the syncretistic drive of Graeco-Roman religiousness, its leaders chose to preserve the faith in Christ's
revelation by an appropriation and re-interpretation of the
conceptual and sacred forms of the ideas of revelation as they
were held by Jews and Greeks. When by developing the Logos-
Christology the Apologists laid the foundation of the Christian
dogma and of the cultus of the sacramental-hierarchical church,
they formulated the Christian idea of revelation in such a way
that, although they appeared to be bound to the message of
the New Testament, they were actually dependent upon Jewish
and Greek concepts. Jesus Christ, the "Logos" incarnate, was
to them the realization of the Jewish messianic teaching about
the fulfillment of God's purposes for history in the revelation
of the Messiah as well as the realization of the Greek-Hellenistic
teaching about the ultimate disclosure of the one and unified
meaning of the diversities of the world in the revelation of
world-reason (Logos). By an extension and re-interpretation
of the Johannine teaching of Christ the Logos, they formulated a Christian concept of revelation in which the New Testament message was blended with the Jewish and Greek ideas
of revelation. The development of the hierarchical-sacramental
institution of salvation and of the trinitarian and christological
dogmas of the ancient church was the historical result of what
was thus begun. The Christian idea of revelation thus received
a form by which it was communicated to the peoples of the
ancient world and finally transferred to the European nations.

Harnack has described this process as the "chronic Helleni-
zation" of the Christian gospel. He and the modern historians
of Christian doctrine have shown that the formulation of the
doctrine of the Trinity, for example, must be attributed to the
effort of the ancient church to maintain the monotheism of the
Old Testament in conjunction with the characteristic Christian
faith in the lordship of Christ. They have explained further
how this effort had to be conditioned by Hellenistic philosophy
as soon as the Logos-speculation was employed as a means of

interpreting the Christian Christology. It is important to emphasize the fact that the trinitarian doctrine was developed in the concrete historical cultural environment of the ancient world, but the doctrine of the Trinity must not be explained in such a way that it appears merely as the expression of the historical effort of ancient Christians to interpret their faith in terms of the philosophy of their civilization. The doctrine is then seen as an inevitable by-product of the church's struggle for survival and consequently it is often suggested that, as part of past history, it should be returned to past history.

Accepting the partial soundness of the implications of this view, I must nevertheless insist upon an interpretation of the trinitarian controversies of the ancient world that recognizes the permanent Christian concern around which they arose. This concern was the exposition of the fundamental Christian belief in the revelation of God in Jesus of Nazareth. The theme of the trinitarian doctrine becomes plain in the arguments of ancient Christian "orthodoxy" against the denial of the actuality of God's revelation in the historical event of Jesus' life and death, represented by Arianism and Sabellianism. Together with the Christological heresies of Docetism and Ebionitism, of which the former denied Christ's historicity and the latter his eternity, these two trinitarian heresies show that in its opposition against them the ancient church had to preserve, to establish, and to define the togetherness of divine transcendence and immanence that was implied in its gospel of God's revelation in history through Jesus Christ. It had to distinguish its Christocentric theism from Jewish monotheism, Greek polytheism and Hellenistic-Oriental pantheism. The perennial meaning of the doctrine of the Trinity is therefore the exposition of the Christian doctrine of God in so far as it rests in the experience of God's revelation in Jesus. It expounds the immanent actuality of the transcendent meaning of life in history and in human experience on the basis of the presupposition that God is knowable only through Jesus the Christ.

It is not surprising that a full awareness of these theological implications of the Christian faith grew only gradually in the minds of the Christian thinkers of the ancient church. The theological defense of the Christian faith was naturally established only in accordance with the need for it, pressed upon the church by those who, from within or from without, challenged the validity of its message. Nor must the often-criticized and to us almost unintelligible artificiality of the terminology and the arguments employed in this defense astonish us. We should rather marvel at the restraint that was shown in the attempts to find forms of definition of what lay at the very heart of the mystery of faith. The trinitarian and christological doctrines are delimitations protecting the faith in revelation rather than descriptions of its content. The terminological difficulties of the ancient theologians should be slowly criticized by those who, in spite of the much more refined and complex philosophical and scientific instruments available in modern times, have not succeeded in interpreting the Christian God-idea as grounded in the divine revelation in Jesus in such a manner that what the ancients meant to achieve by their doctrines of the Trinity is effectively expressed for the modern church in modern terms.

The effectiveness of the form by which the Christian faith in revelation was expressed in the trinitarian and christological doctrines of the Incarnation was tremendously enhanced by the extension which they received in the cultic and organizational institutionalization of the Christian church. To this day the Catholic churches understand themselves as the concrete channels through which God's revelation in Jesus is spread into the lives of men. To what a degree the forms of the faith in revelation herein often obscured the vitality of the faith is known to every student of church history. These forms not only were often ends in themselves, but they easily became receptacles of ideas of revelation which cannot be called Christian. Moreover, the world-conformity of the institutional church, induced by the fact that by the circumstances of history it was called upon to exercise the function of world domination, often deprived the Christian faith of its prophetic and personal power. The dynamic character of Christianity, grounded in the belief in the initiative of God and in the confrontation with the person of Jesus of Nazareth, was for centuries hid in the forms which the Christian idea of revelation had assumed in theology, cultus, and ecclesiasticism. But as the inner life of the medieval Roman Catholic church reveals, this dynamic character nevertheless found ways of expressing

itself until it finally broke forth with revolutionary power in
the Reformation.

IV

The Protestant Reformation, long prepared for by the dissolution of the medieval feudalistic forms of life and the influence of this distintegration in the church, was caused by the
concern of the monk Luther for an existential realization in his
own life of the Christian religion of revelation. In his endeavors
to get a merciful God, i.e., a God who would be a God for him,
he tested the forms in which the church had cast the faith in
God's revelation in Jesus. By the direct impact of the Bible and
particularly of the Pauline epistles upon his profoundly, ter-
rifyingly sensitive, God-bound conscience, the full power of the
Christian gospel of the self-disclosure of God in Jesus was once
more rendered immediate to him and through his prophetic
personality to Christians of many lands. The new Christian
churches that came into being rejected the sacramental and
hierarchical forms of the Christian idea of revelation. They
put an end also to the encasement of the meaning of revelation
in ecclesiastical law and rendered impossible its superimposi-
tion upon the natural life.

The prophetic character of the faith in revelation, again
and again newly discovered in the directly accessible Bible, from
then on was expressed in numerous new forms of a theocentric
religiousness. The outstanding characteristics of Protestant
faith were the insistence upon the sovereignty of God and upon
the majesty of his grace. The early Protestants proclaimed the
faith by praising the freedom of the Christian man who, by
putting all his trust in God and none in himself, receives the
possibility to make a new beginning of life in deeds of unselfish love. Thus they intepreted the gospel of God's revelation in Jesus. John Calvin spoke for all of them when he
wrote: (Inst. III, 7, 1): "We are not our own; therefore neither
our reason nor *our* will should predominate in our deliberations and actions. We are not our own; therefore let us not
propose it as our end to seek what may be expedient for us
according to the flesh. We are not our own; therefore let us,
as far as possible, forget ourselves and all the things that are
ours. On the contrary, we are God's; to him therefore let us
live and die. We are God's; therefore let his wisdom and will

preside in all our actions. We are God's; towards him, there-fore, as our only legitimate end, let every part of our lives be directed. O, how great a proficiency has that man made, who, having been taught that he is not his own, has taken the sovereignty and government of himself from his own reason to surrender it to God!"

This prophetic religiousness which has remained character-istic of Protestant religion to this day was derived from the Bible. It need therefore cause us no great surprise that the form by which the reformers expressed the idea of revelation was determined by the place that the Bible occupied in their minds. They cast the rediscovery of the dynamic character of the Christian gospel in a doctrine of the "word." Henceforth the predominant Protestant form of the idea of revelation was the doctrine that the Bible was the means which God employs to make Christ known to man. This new doctrine of revelation was combined with the old doctrine of revelation in the form of the teaching concerning the incarnation. One is permitted, I think, to go so far as to say that thereby the reformers com-plicated the Christian conception of the idea of revelation de-spite the fact that they had broken the cumbersome medieval ecclesiastical apparatus of salvation in which the dynamic faith in revelation had been encased.

But nevertheless, what was begun by Luther's decisive dis-covery was to continue in a process of the gradual simplification and reduction of the forms of the Christian idea of revelation. Already in the sixteenth century, Anabaptists and Protestant spiritualists, mystics and humanists developed forms of an understanding of the divine revelation in Jesus that were free of the complexities of the old or new traditions. To be sure, the ancient Catholic Logos-Christology and the word-theology of the Reformation remained effective. The fact that God's dis-closure in Jesus could not be apprehended apart from the Bible made the continuance of a Bible-theology necessary. Further-more, the supernaturalist metaphysics that for centuries had been the philosophical theory presupposed by all Christians, theologians as well as laymen, when they explained their faith, remained intact. But the forms of public and private worship and the types of church organization, developed by the sec-tarian Protestant groups, signified that a tremendous process

of the simplification of the forms of Christianity had been begun by the Reformation. When, a little more than a hundred
years ago, Schleiermacher described the Protestant character
of his thinking by saying "The Reformation still continues,"
he made an observation which can well be adopted by anyone
who surveys the development of Protestantism.

V

Throughout the history of Protestantism, many interpreters
have insisted that the character of Protestantism can be properly
understood only by reference to the forms which it developed in
Lutheran, Calvinist, and even Anglican types. But there is no
classical expression of Protestantism which could serve as a
pattern for all its forms. Protestant Christianity must rather be
understood as a movement which is determined by a twofold
motivating power: the faith in the Father of Jesus Christ as the
only sovereign God and the ethos of love emanating therefrom.
This movement has never been enclosed in a definite, final
form. No ecclesiastical organization and no theological system
can claim to represent or express it fully. Neither Luther's
Biblicism and its doctrinal implications nor Calvin's Biblicism
and its ecclesiastical extensions could, even in the sixteenth century, hold in definite channels the impetus derived from the
direct encounter with the revelation-faith of the early Christians. The many so-called denominational forms of liturgy,
theology, church order, and ethics which Protestantism produced from the beginning of its history were the inevitable
expressions of its spirit. The claim which all Protestant groups
at some time in their history advanced, that their forms of
faith and order, life, and work were the final ones, has always
been refuted by the diversified vitality of Protestant religiousness. We may say, therefore, that there is no form of Protestantism that constitutes its ideal type. Protestantism is a spiritual attitude, grounded in the living faith that God has made
himself known in the person of Jesus of Nazareth and expressing itself ever anew in ways of life and thinking which reflect
this faith as a proclamation of the glory of God transcending
all human limitations and sufficiencies. The Protestant spirit
is a spirit of prophetic criticism. Its norm is the gospel of the
God of love who liveth in a light no man can approach unto

and yet is nearer to us than breathing, closer than hands or feet, and who has disclosed himself in Jesus who was born in a manger, had no place where to lay his head, and died on a cross.

No form can adequately express this content of the faith in revelation. No liturgical or ecclesiastical or theological form of this idea of revelation can be final.

In the light of this analysis, the actual development of Protestant thought in theological variety can cause no surprise. When, under the impact of modern civilization and its tools of philosophy, history and science, the old authorities and traditions of Western civilization were seen in the perspective of their historical growth, Protestantism inevitably had to apply the standards of critical interpretation to itself. To be sure, the principle of autonomy, which motivated modern man to free himself from the heteronomous forms of old traditions, was radically different from the principle of theonomy, which inspired the Protestant man to protest against the heteronomous forms of religious and ecclesiastical authority. Nevertheless, in order to obtain freedom from heteronomous traditions modern humanists and Protestants joined hands. Thus a new liberal Protestantism came into being. Its inner life was conditioned by an emancipation from the traditional forms of the idea of revelation and by ever fresh efforts to relate the idea of revelation, lifted from its historical forms, to the life of the modern autonomous man. It was constantly threatened by the danger that the formlessness of the Christian faith, which resulted from the criticism of the old traditions, would cause the absorption of Christianity by the general cultural stream, threatening it with the loss of its identity. But again and again the basic Christian message of the divine revelation in Jesus affirmed itself.

However, the more the emancipation of modern man from the medieval forms of life proceeded and the more the modern autonomous scientific technological civilization matured, the more difficult it became for Protestantism to make plain the central Christian message. And when the crisis of modern civilization became apparent because the forces of its expansion could find no outlet within the political and economic systems to which they were bound, when the World War and the world depression catastrophically revealed the sickness of the economic and political orders, Protestant religiousness was found to lack the forms which might protect it from being drawn into the crisis.

Throughout the nineteenth century, as an ever-increasing number of people left the organized churches, surrendering the theological forms in which the Protestant convictions were cast, an extra-ecclesistical Christian religiousness had developed. It expressed itself in philosophies of life that were moulded according to the patterns of modern philosophical, artistic, or scientific culture. Indeed, many of those who continued to identify themselves with the churches of the various denominational Protestant traditions had inwardly freed themselves in the same way from the old forms of the Christian life. In these circles, a clear understanding of the uniqueness of the Christian religion, in so far as it depends upon the belief in God's revelation in Jesus, was lost. The Christian religion was identified with a belief in the meaningfulness and purposefulness of life or a belief in the spiritual character of existence or a set of virtues more or less consciously derived from the historical Christian tradition.

Meanwhile, there spread in the proletarian masses, which had become the most immediate victims of the inner conflict of modern civilization, atheistic and secularist, gravely anti-Christian sentiments. When, on account of technological unemployment, the danger of dehumanization became highly acute among them, they and many members of the middle classes who were affected by the same fate, found themselves without protection against that final disillusionment which comes from the feeling of the meaninglessness of existence.

Protestantism reacted to this dissolution of religious power in various ways. While it largely remained bound to the traditional forms of its life, it became conscious of its own specific character in Christian history. Its interpreters began to understand it as that movement within Christianity which, inspired by an immediate confrontation with the person of Jesus of Nazareth as the revealer of God, endeavors to express the ethos of love derived from this experience in the actual circumstances of human life in such a way that the forms of this expression never assume any other importance but that of means and vehicles of the dynamic spontaneity of the act of faith.

VI

This insight into the fact that the spirit of the Christian religion is not bound to any historical form (an insight of the sixteenth century humanists and reformers which modern liberal Protestantism has fully made its own) has caused a frantic search for ways in which the Christian faith can become effective in the life situation of today. Exactly because we know that the superhistorical content of the Christian faith in God's revelation is apprehendable to the understanding without being forever bound to its biblical or any other church-historical form, we find it so difficult to give it a form which would communicate its life-transforming power to ourselves and our contemporaries. The endeavor of the liberal theologians and churchmen to render the faith contemporary by expressing it in terms of the cultural life and its ongoing stream was and is constantly beset by the danger that the faith loses its prophetic critical power. The revival of historical forms of the Christian faith, particularly of the Biblicism of the Reformers as the Barthians have undertaken it, is largely rendered ineffective because it makes the faith vital only to those who possess a highly sophisticated critical historical outlook so that when they speak in historical terms they are aware of the fact that they use these terms without necessarily adopting all the implications of worldview that were connected with them when they were first formulated. To others the return to historical forms of Christianity can easily become an escape from responsibility for the tasks of the present age. The possibility of stating the faith in forms that are not their own may easily cause them to identify "the word of God" with words of theology so that, in the last resort, they worship an idol and not the God of salvation.

The inner situation of contemporary Protestantism is thus characterized by a deep conflict of theological theses and practical programs. One group of leaders declares all historical forms of Christian faith and action relative and emphasizes the contemporaneous responsibility of Christianity. Another group of leaders advocates the return to historical forms as the only means of providing spiritual leadership to the present age. The first group faces the danger of so understanding the significance of the forms of the Christian faith that the Christian cause is easily associated with ideas and practices essentially hostile to it. The second group faces the danger of linking the spirituality of the Christian gospel to historical forms in such a way that its contemporaneous effect remains inaccessible to the theologically uninitiated. It is plain that that form of the Christian faith in revelation which would make it truly contemporaneous must include and overcome the contrast between modernism and fundamentalism, between liberalism and Barthianism, between theological formlessness and theological formality.

This form will never be found, if the Protestant movement should continue to be dominated by the tendencies toward religious individualism and toward an extra-ecclesiastical religiousness which now seem to determine its life. It will only be found if the two most promising trends in contemporary Protestantism win the loyal interest of an increasing number of devoted Christian people, namely the Christian social realism and the ecumenical movement. The future of Protestantism may therefore depend upon the work of those who try to discover a form for the Christian faith by applying it to the social-political problems of modern life, not failing, if necessary, to state the irreconcilability of the Christian ethos with the spirit which dominates the social, political, and cultural life of the present day. The church groups which may come into being under the effect of such endeavors will possibly demonstrate that, in the future that lies ahead, Christianity is again to be the concern of a minority.

But these new groups of a contemporaneous Christianity which proclaim the prophetic power of God's revelation in Jesus by releasing it in the midst of the crisis of modern civilization must co-operate with those who give themselves to the labor of accomplishing a united Christian movement, recognizing that the historical denominational churches have completed the work which their fathers assigned to them. The social realism of radical Protestantism and the ecumenical movement may therefore possibly be the means by which Protestantism will continue to break old forms and make new forms, so that also the history of the coming days will feel the impact of that revelation which, in the fate of Jesus, disclosed God's way of judging and redeeming human history.

Chapter 10

The Dynamics of Protestantism

A SK ALMOST any man who is not a clergyman to give you a definition of the nature of Protestantism. If he does not refuse to make a try at it, he will say something like the following: Protestantism lives of two sources: 1) the direct word of God to man in the Bible (this is the source of its *Biblicism* or *literalism*) and 2) of the direct judgment of man's own conscience (this is the source of its *individualism*). It rejects the authority of the church, especially in the form of the sacramental-hierarchical institutionalism of Roman Catholicism, as a barrier to men's direct approach to God. The authority of the individual conscience which is responsible to God is regarded as the guide to the truth by which men live. That is why Protestantism, Bible in hand, preached that individual effort was everything. By means of this attitude it acted first as an effective ally of capitalism and gradually as one of the chief motivating powers of the precedent-breaking aggressiveness of modern capitalistic democratic civilization. Protestantism thus became the religion of the modern middle classes, the religion of the bourgeois. In recent times its individualism has been made the target of many criticisms that are levelled at modern civilization as a whole: The atomization of Protestant Christianity, i.e. its sectarianism, is considered the chief reason why Christianity does not exercise a greater responsibility for the character of modern civilization. Indeed, the wide-spread belief that because religion is a private affair it has nothing to do with the political-economic affairs of society, has led to a practical abdication of religion from the affairs of the community.

This characterization of Protestantism is not an arbitrary invention. It is a paraphrase of what such a keen critic of our culture as Leslie Paul has to say of it in his book "The Annihilation of Man." I believe that his definitions are representative of the opinions of many of our contemporaries.

II

Can this description of the nature of Protestantism be effectively challenged? I believe that it can—but only under one condition: The historical effects and products of Protestantism must be distinguished from its spiritual dynamics. Protestantism cannot be identified with its historical development. It is more than the forms of faith and order, life and work which it has produced in the course of the four hundred years of its existence. This "more" I call its spiritual dynamics. Protestantism possesses resources that transcend its historical forms. This is proved by the fact that there are many movements in the Protestant churches of our times designed to combat the ailments not only of modern civilization but of Protestantism itself. These movements are reflected not only in the work of individual theologians and church-leaders but in the whole inner life of the denominations and particularly in the activities of the ecumenical organizations. What is happening is this: There are forces alive in modern Puritanism that point to a transformation of those of its features, particularly its individualism, which are recognized as inadequate, not merely from the point of view of the needs of civilization but of religion itself. These forces are no less Protestant than the ways of historical Protestantism which they tend to criticize. They articulate the spiritual dynamics of Protestantism in the new historical situation of our own day just as the older Protestantism, many of whose forms and attitudes of life have been carried over into our times, tried to express them in relation to the historical exigencies it confronted. What many of us now criticize, in the name of Protestant faith, e.g. Biblical literalism or the alliance between the Protestant ethic and the spirit of capitalism, was, in its time, a genuine expression of the dynamics of Protestant faith within a concrete historical situation. By our act of criticism, we are under the impact of these dynamics, criticizing historical Protestantism in the name of the Protestant faith. In this sense, it can be said that the dynamics of Protestantism are not identical with the historical forms of Protestantism.

It should be understood, however, that this denial of the identity between spirit and form does in no way imply that the spirit (or the dynamics) ever lives apart from the historical form. What we affirm is that the Protestant spirit is not dependent upon a particular historical form of expression—of past, present or future, but that it dynamically articulates itself in ever new historical manifestations, turning even against that which in some past time was its own form. Thus conceived, Protestantism stands in a true continuity with the Reformation. For the Reformers never claimed to be innovators or revolutionaries as if they intended either to introduce a new religion or to destroy Christianity. They labored for the *reformation* of Christianity by rejecting its Roman Catholic form in the name of the Christian faith. In order to keep alive the spirit of the Reformation, Protestantism must continually reform itself. Inspired by the dynamics of its faith, the Reformation must continue within its own body.

III

Now we can proceed to describe the spirit of Protestantism, defining at the same time the dynamics which have activated it in the past and which will determine its course in the present and in the future.

1. The central affirmation of Protestant Christianity concerns not man but God. It proclaims the sovereignty of God. God, the Creator and Redeemer, is not bound. He is not confined to limited forms of life, i.e., to historically relative, man-made institutions, for example Roman Catholic hierarchalism. Protestant faith and life arise from the hearing of the speaking God who discloses himself when and how he chooses, and calls men into fellowship with himself. The church, therefore, is a communion of believers, a *people* committed to God because he has chosen them. It is *not an institution* of a super-personal character.

The spirit of this people is prophetic. In the name of the sovereign creative Lord of history who must be acknowledged ever anew as the sole course of all good, it protests against all absolutizations of the historically relative and against all tendencies toward the self-sufficiency of man. Whenever the natural and the historical are deified, the Protestant jealousy for the lordship of God is aroused. For the Protestant faith is: God is alive in history but nothing historical can capture him.

Here lies the *religious* secret of Protestant divisiveness. By binding themselves to God, who alone is sovereign and free, Protestants were made non-conformists, dissenters from all ways of life, also the religious and Christian ones, which tended to confine God's spirit to restrictive forms. To be sure, much of Protestant denominationalism is an expression of human selfishness, arrogance and cantankerous conceit. In such cases, sectarianism has been and is mistaken for prophetism. But because God in his sovereign freedom ever transcends even the true apprehensions of him, it is always difficult for men to distinguish the prophet of holiness from the sectarian crank. Moreover, the followers of prophets and cranks are always a minority. Yet God affirms his lordship in such a way that even in history the prophetic flocks are established and the sects are doomed to failure, for he makes the word of the prophet come to life again and again but he lets the shrill voice of the crank die with him.

2. Protestantism believes then in the *living* word of God. It hears it in Jesus Christ in whom all prophetism culminates and is fulfilled and from whose martyrdom all witnessing to God derives its power. Jesus Christ *is* the Word of God. It is strange that, under the influence of modern historicism, the isolated personality of Jesus was made the center of attention. The Christological dogma, which the modern concern for the "life of Jesus" was to replace, expressed much more adequately (though, to be sure, in mythical and philosophical language no longer directly intelligible) what the Christian community affirms in its Christ-faith: Jesus is the meaning of history. Being so strongly imbued with the spirit of modern culture, Protestantism should have translated the old Logos-Christology into historical terms. Instead of centering its attention upon the solitary, quasi superhistorical figure of Jesus, it should have seen him in connection with the life of history. For behind him stands Israel, from which he arose, and before him lies the church, the new Israel, which he called into being. But the old Israel and the new Israel are complex bodies and movements of historical life. Because Jesus is the "clue" to this history, he

is the Christ. As the "king" of both Israels, he is the living Christ, ever present with his people.

In a way, Protestantism has always treasured this understanding of Christ in its Biblicism. It has read the message of the Old and the New Testaments as the Word of God and has thereby kept alive the faith in Christ who is alive in history. Neither the extremely artificial doctrine of the literal inspiration of the Bible nor the apparently so natural historicistic interpretation of the Biblical books by modern criticism have consciously cultivated the faith in Christ as the Lord of history, but they have preserved it, nevertheless. Both have threatened to deprive the Christian faith of its aliveness—Orthodoxy, by confining the living Christ and the living God to the letters of the Book; Modernism, by relegating them to a historical past. Both have maintained the Christian faith as the Bible faith—literalism by its high esteem of every single word and sentence of the Bible, and criticism by the unheard-of diligence of its historical interpretation of the whole and the details of the Biblical books. Thus the Bible has been maintained as the chief clue to the understanding of the ways of God with men. Whatever the errors and extremisms of the theological schools, Protestantism today still lives of the Bible and its Biblicism guarantees its Christocentrism.

3. The sovereignty of God which manifests itself through Christ in the life of the people who believe themselves to be God's people is actualized, so Protestantism holds, by faith. Faith is the act by which God becomes the God of every believer. It is a commitment by virtue of which every one of us is enabled to say: "God is *my* Lord" and "Christ is within *me*." Thus understood, faith is a personal event. As such, it has often been misinterpreted, even by Protestants, as subjectivistic and individualistic. But the actualization of faith which is as personal as the experience of dying (Luther used to say: "Every one must do his own believing as he will have to do his own dying.") is not subjectivistic because it links man to God, the lord of life and history, and the source of all good. Thus he is not thrown back upon his own resources, even though they be religious, but he is made to rely upon the fountain of life.

Nor is faith individualistic. For by faith in Christ, God is shown as the forgiving father, in whose presence every man must acknowledge himself a sinner who precisely by confessing himself with a repenting heart to be such, is given the promise of divine mercy. In receiving the divine love, he experiences himself as one transformed who transmits the love from which he lives to his fellowmen. Faith is intensely personal, but it is the source of a relationship of unselfish love with all men. It is therefore never individualistic but always social.

Protestantism has permitted itself to be drawn into an individualistic misinterpretation of its life of faith, first by Pietism and then by its alliance with humanistic modern civilization (whose roots lie in the Renaissance rather than in the Reformation), but it always has preserved sufficient spiritual resources to recover its heritage.

The chief cause of the misunderstanding of faith in terms either of subjectivism or of individualism is probably religious in character. For the faith in the divine forgiveness involves an unconditional surrender of all human security and sufficiency to God. Against this demand man rebels primarily in the name of that religiousness by which he tries to preserve an inner poise in the midst of life's turmoil. It is this religiousness which is the source of all humanism. The Christian gospel of forgiveness cannot be truly heard if one receives it in support of this attitude. This has been the predicament of "modern man."

From this rebellion against faith there follows another misunderstanding of the Christian faith: Moralism. Whosoever tries to preserve himself, even in the presence of God, in the end turns out to be a moralist, i.e. one who stands in his own innate goodness and thus attributes to himself an absolute quality. But the Protestant faith in the forgiving grace of God is radically antimoralistic. Luther's protest against salvation by "good works" is indelibly imprinted upon the Protestant conscience. Yet the truth of the sentence: "Good works do not make a man good, but a good man does good works," is most difficult to affirm, even for a Protestant, for at heart every man is a Pharisee. Nevertheless, the spiritual dynamic of Protestantism—a dynamic which it has turned even against itself—is its antimoralistic and anti-pharisaic message that man lives by grace through faith alone.

4. Closely connected with faith is the principle of the universal priesthood of believers. Again, it is indicative of the way in which Protestantism is misunderstood (even by Protestants themselves) that this principle is often interpreted as if it meant that every believer is to be his own priest. If this were right, Roman Catholic critics of Protestantism would be justified in their criticism of the essential individualism of Protestantism. But, as a matter of fact, the teaching of the universal priesthood of believers is a call to the exercise of social responsibility by everyone who believes himself to be a Christian. Insofar as it is built into the very texture of Protestantism, it has inspired Protestantism not only to anti-clericalism but also to the free and full exercise of Christian responsibility for the character of civilization. By the cry "No popery" which has again and again been sounded in history, Protestantism has manifested itself as a lay-movement, intent not only upon the restriction and even the elimination of all clerical aspirations to dominate and shape the Christian life but also upon the penetration of all spheres of human endeavor with the spirit of Christian love.

To be sure, clericalism has not entirely disappeared even from Protestant life; Anglicanism in particular has preserved it and, in the Anglo-Catholic movement, especially emphasized it. But even the Episcopalian esteem of "holy orders" discourages clericalism. Indeed, whenever Protestantism stresses the role of the clergy in Christian life, it does so with an awareness that clergymen are not Christians of a different status before God than laymen. The Methodist bishop, who is not a hierarch but a servant of the churches under his leadership, can perhaps be regarded as the symbol of the way in which Protestantism as a lay-movement has dealt with the clerical forms of organization which it too inherited from ancient and medieval history.

The really important aspect of this anti-clericalism in the doctrine of the universal priesthood of believers is that while it denies hierarchical domination, it affirms the duty of all Christians (by the priesthood of their faith) to serve one another in love in all stations of life. Here is the source of what has often been called the "Protestant activism." It has shaped Protestant life from the days of the early Lutheran and especially Calvinist vocationalism to the modern times of the "social gospel" and the work of the denominational "councils for social action." When one criticizes Protestantism for its too close identification with modern civilization, one must not forget to what an extent it has endeavored to penetrate all cultural spheres with the ethos of Christian service and love.

5. By the practice of the universal priesthood of all believers, the church comes into being. For, according to the Protestant understanding, the church is the people of God who, believing under the headship of Christ in the renewal of life by the forgiveness of sins, actualize this faith in love for one another within the concrete circumstances of human existence in the world. In other words, the church is the fellowship of believers in Christ. The limits of this fellowship are not fixed by externals of any sort, for wherever men bind themselves to one another by the love that springs from faith they manifest their citizenship in the kingdom of Christ which is God's messianic people. This "city of God" is universal because it is not limited to any time or place. It is this universalism of the Kingdom of love which the cherished Protestant teaching of the invisibility of the church means to express. For the realization of the fellowship of believers in deeds of love is not dependent upon conformity to visible, i.e. concrete historical orders of polity and social constitution. At any rate, it is the Protestant conviction that membership in an ecclesiastical organization does not guarantee citizenship in the Kingdom of Christ. This conviction has come to forceful expression in Protestant history ever since the Reformation, for it inspired not only the Reformers to their protest against papal ecclesiasticism, but also ever new groups of Protestant believers to an antagonism against Protestant denominational demands for conformity with certain creeds and orders as a condition of membership in the church of Christ. Thus Protestantism is nonconformist in the name of the universalism of the fellowship of love, which it believes to be the Kingdom of Christ. Here again the Christian root of its denominationalism is laid bare. It should be understood, however, that this denominationalism can never be an end in itself. It must be seen as the result of the protest against the particularization of the universal church and against binding it to limited conditions and forms. We may say, therefore, that only that denominationalism is truly Pro-

testant which is a passing product of the spiritual will that all denominations should die if they obstruct the realization of the Kingdom of Christ. It is this will which, in our day, comes to the fore in the Protestant concern for the world church and for inter-denominational fellowship. But let no one assume that, if a united Protestant church ever should come into being, the universalism of the Kingdom of Christ would thereby be realized. For if the conditions of union and unity would limit the universalism of love, the prophetic Protestant spirit would be led to dissent from such a church.

It may be asked: Does, then, the universalism of the Kingdom of Christ never come to historical realization? The answer is: It is actualized in all concrete particular acts of Christian faith and love by which a fellowship of believers is built. The people of God becomes visible in little groups—where two or three are together in Christ's name! That is why Protestantism, whatever its historical denominational forms, has always regarded the local congregations as the cells of the universal church. For where by the worship of God in Christ a fellowship of love is produced, there the rule of God in the hearts of men is manifested—there he has chosen his people. This, then, is the Protestant conviction: Where people of a particular time and place hear the word of God and do it, there is the church, God's holy nation, for only in the concrete historical circumstances of life can the church manifest itself; but these circumstances, even though they are of a "religious" nature (e.g., forms of worship, creeds and confessions) are never of the essence of the church itself, but merely means and instruments by which it is made real.

IV.

The nature of Protestantism, we conclude, is a spiritual dynamism which can never rest with anything that has been attained. If the Protestant church, the products of the Protestant spirit in the life particularly of the western nations of modern times, should choose to be loyal to their faith by preserving and perpetuating merely their historical inheritance, they would deny their lord. Responding to the source of spiritual power from which they profess to live: the sovereign, free, unbound Word of God, the living Christ, they must act in the

CHAPTER 11

Roman Catholicism and Protestantism

R OMAN Catholicism and Protestantism are the two major
historical channels of Christianity in western civilization.
Since the sixteenth century, they have been engaged in a continuous rivalry with one another. They fulfill the Christian
responsibility for the character of civilization only in terms of
this rivalry. In countries where one of them predominates, the
influence which the other exercises upon the whole cultural life
is sometimes forgotten or at least disregarded. In those parts
of the world, where Roman Catholic and Protestant churches
exist next to each other, all Christian work is marked by the
Catholic-Protestant tension. Whenever either Roman Catholicism or Protestantism interpret themselves as bearers of the
Christian gospel, they must necessarily take account of each
other and, by means of a mutual comparison, define their
respective right to represent Christianity.

Roman Catholicism, believing to rest upon an unbroken
tradition that dates back to the beginnings of Christianity,
indeed to Jesus Christ himself, occasionally acts as if it could
afford to avoid an encounter with the claim of the Protestant
churches that they are the true stewards of the gospel. But,
actually, the Roman Church has found itself compelled to make
reference to Protestant teachings whenever it interprets the
Christian faith and life through its spokesmen. Indeed, in a
way, it was the Reformation which forced the Roman Church
to define specifically the nature of Catholicity and the bases of
its authority (in the decrees of the Council of Trent). Modern
Roman Catholic dogmatic work is, at least partly, determined
by an awareness of the rival doctrines of Protestantism.

Protestantism on its part has never been able to circumvent a confrontation with Roman Catholicism. From its be-

ginnings until the present, it has been compelled to justify
its own interpretation of the gospel by setting it in contrast
to the teachings and practices of the Roman Church.

The Christian movement within western civilization is therefore marked by the continuous presence of the Catholic-Protestant conflict. If we were all not so definitely accustomed to it,
we should regard it more consciously than we actually do as
the most tragic and most decisive hindrance which prevents the
full flow of the powers of the Christian faith into the common
life.

Roman Catholicism awaits the day when the Protestant
churches, which it now anthematizes as heretical and schismatic,
will repentantly effect a reunion with the mother church.

Protestantism hopes for the time when the Roman Church
will be willing to join the churches which directly or indirectly
have sprung from the Reformation in a penitent, mutual examination of all historical forms of faith and life and in an
ecumenical search for the meaning of the Christian gospel for
mankind and its changing needs.

These expectations looking toward a settlement of the Catholic-Protestant conflict are so different that an abatement of
the rivalry between the two Christian churches cannot be anticipated in the foreseeable future. Therefore it will be inevitable for a long time that Protestants must express their
faith by contrasting it with that of Roman Catholic Christianity and that the Roman Church will have to reckon with the
criticism of the Protestant dissenters.

In the following we shall undertake a comparison between
the two types of Christianity primarily for the purpose of eluci-
dating the character of Protestant religiousness in so far as it
differs from the spirit of Roman Catholicism. By being treated
in this way both will appear simplified, for the historical complexity of their life will have to be neglected. We shall disregard in particular the variety of religious forms which both
Roman Catholicism and Protestantism embody in themselves.
Both are undoubtedly syncretistic. Indeed, Christianity as an
historical religion is syncretistic. Therefore Roman Catholicism
is just as little explained in its special nature by being described
as a *"complexio oppositorum"*[1] as Protestantism is adequately
interpreted by an emphasis upon its diversity.

I.

Let us begin with a comparison of very simple aspects of worship. It is customary that Roman Catholic church buildings are kept open at all times. The faithful enter them at all hours of the day. They go to pray there—but not because they could not say their prayers anywhere in the world wherever they happen to be, but because only in the church house (in the cathedral, the parish church, the chapel) they can go into the immediate, objective presence of Christ, their God and savior. For wherever the host of the Holy Sacrament of the Altar is reserved, Christ himself is present. When the holy wafer is placed in the tabernacle of the high altar, Christ himself is there, bound so to speak, to the visible, ocular signs of the bread, so remain in it as long as it will last. The church is really the house of God. Christ lives in it and can be visited by all who yearn to meet him. That is why Catholic churches are filled with the splendor of beauty. The artistic magnificence of the altars, the colors of the windows, the warmth of the candlelight, the symbolism of the innumerable decorations of carved stone and wood, of hand-wrought metal, of tapestries and carpets are designed to celebrate the presence of the Lord.

Protestants do not habitually go to the church-houses to pray except at stated hours of worship. To be sure, in recent times, some Protestant churches have been kept open throughout the days of the week just as Roman Catholic churches are, and the people have been encouraged to enter them for periods of quietness and meditation. But this practice is suggested by the needs of modern human existence, particularly its haste and rush, and not by essential convictions of Protestant Christianity. For the Protestant house of worship is not a house of God but a meeting house where the regular divine services are held. It is kept sacred and it is not profaned because it serves the congregation for its gatherings in worship, but God is no more really present in it and no less than he is in any other place. The Protestant does not experience the objectivisation of the divine in the same way as the Roman Catholic does. He does not identify it with a place or with an institution and its practices.

For the Roman Catholic, however, "the worship of the Church is . . . . a continual participation by visible, mysterious signs in Jesus and his redemptive might, a refreshing touching

of the hem of his garment, a liberating handling of his sacred
wounds. This is the deepest purpose of the liturgy, namely to
make the redeeming grace of Christ present, visible and fruitful
as a sacred and potent reality that fills the whole life of the
Christian."[2] His faith is bound to the invisible by visible
things. His commitment to God is made real by the sensual
perception of the divine. He grasps the holy reality of God
in a devotion that is enlivened by the seeing and hearing, feeling and touching of the material, sensuous signs. This is so
because according to Roman Catholic conviction, God has
chosen to communicate with men by means of the visible mysteries of the church. Having disclosed himself once for all in
the incarnation of Jesus Christ, he is henceforth accessible to
all in the sacraments which Christ left to the church. In them
Christ has extended his existence among men in a visible way
apprehendable by the senses. The spirit by which he enlivens
and sanctifies all who belong to him as his people does not
operate apart from these signs. The life of the Christian is a
sacramental life, for the Holy Spirit, the spirit of Christ, does
not become efficacious in men apart from the sacraments. The
most fundamental of them is Baptism because it initiates man
in the church and makes him a participant of the life and grace
of Christ. But the most vivid of the sacraments is the Eucharist,
the Sacrament of the Altar, for in its dramatic miracle Christ
becomes physically and locally present. In it, so the Roman
Catholic Christian believes, "Jesus shares with his disciples
his most intimate possessions, the most precious thing He has,
His own self, His personality as the God-man. We eat His flesh
and we drink His blood. So greatly does Jesus love His community that He permeates it, not merely with His blessing and
His might, but with His real Self, God and Man."[3] No wonder
then, that the Mass is the most elaborate and splendid rite of
the church, conceived, celebrated and surrounded with all the
skills and refinements of liturgical art. It is that part of the
cultus from which the awareness of the divine presence is extended throughout the whole life of the church!

This objectivization of the divine cannot happen without
sacramental persons, the priests. Their actions render the material signs of the sacraments efficacious. Only through their
office the living power of Christ inherent in the matter of the

sacraments is made real and active. Claiming that Jesus Christ
himself instituted the priesthood by the bestowal of priestly
power upon his apostles and by extending it through them to
their successors, Roman Catholics see in the persons and actions
of the hierarchy of the church "a visible attestation of the continual living and working of Christ in the world."[4] Christ, the
revelation of God, is bound not only to the sacraments but also
to the priesthood. Indeed, he becomes livingly real only through
the hierarchical office which administers the sacraments. In
view of this fact, the following statement by one of the cardinals
of the Roman Church cannot be regarded as an exaggeration.
"Where in heaven is such power as that of the Catholic priest.
. . . One time only Mary brought the heavenly child into
the world, but lo, the priest does this not once, but a hundred
and a thousand times, as often as he celebrates (the mass). . . .
To the priests he transferred the right to dispose of his holy
humanity, to them he gave, so to speak, power over his body.
The Catholic priest is able . . . to make him present at the altar,
to lock him up in the tabernacle and to take him out again in
order to give him to the faithful for their nourishment . . .
in all this, Christ, the only begotten Son of God the Father, is
yielding to his will."[5]

Sacraments and priesthood, and what they represent and
signify are the "mystical body of Christ." No one is a member
of this body, unless he partakes of the sacraments and submits
to the administration of the priests. Man becomes acceptable to
God as a believer in Christ only through the justification represented in baptism. He is cleansed of his sins only when, ab-
solved by the priest in the sacrament of penance, he participates
in the passion and resurrection of Christ by means of the
Eucharist. He is assured of his salvation only if the blessings
also of the other sacraments—confirmation, marriage, extreme
unction and, most of all, priestly ordination are available to
him. He has no communion with God and he cannot live the
Christian life unless he becomes identified with the life of
Christ in a mystical way by means of the sacramental-hierarchical institution in which the divine operates as a living, active
reality.

The characteristic feature of Roman Catholic religiousness
is then that it is grounded in the objective performance of the

priestly-sacramental cult. According to Roman Catholic theology, the sacraments work *ex opere operato* and not *ex opere operantis;* that is to say the sacramental grace by which the Christian religious life becomes a possibility is produced solely through the priestly administration of the sacrament, quite apart from personal, moral and religious, efforts or qualities of the recipient or of the administrator. "A sacrament is not fulfilled by the fact that one believes in it but by the fact that it is performed." This statement, which pervades all Roman Catholic liturgical literature, must not be so understood as if it meant that sacraments are to be used without an inward participation of him who partakes of them. The distinction between the *"opus operatum"* (the sacramental event) and the *"opus operantis"* (the believer's response to the sacrament) is made primarily in order to stress the objective, all-sufficient supra-human givenness of the miraculous, healing divine presence made real in the sacrament; it does not imply that the divine gift is not to be received in the spirit of a devout religious commitment. But, nevertheless, it is important to note that when Roman Catholic teachers describe the cult by which man is related to God as objective, they emphatically stress its "non-subjective" character. This suggests that the religious encounter between God and man is understood by them in such a manner that it is deprived of the feature of a personal relationship.

Hierarchy and sacraments, indeed the whole cultus, manifest the supra-personal and supra-natural order which God has established in, by and through Jesus Christ and the Holy Spirit for the salvation of man. Whosoever submits to this order, and comes under its sway as a believer, finds himself in the *immediate* presence of God. An authoritative spokesman of Roman Catholicism puts the matter in the following way: "Thus through the sacraments the divine wins tangible reality and becomes a tangible and present value. Therefore, the Catholic has an immediate experience of the divine, an experience as immediate and objective as is the child's experience of the love of his mother. In the sacrifice of the Mass, we are not merely reminded of the Sacrifice of the Cross in a symbolical form. On the contrary, the Sacrifice of Calvary, as a great supra-temporal reality, enters into the immediate present. Space and time are abolished. The same Jesus is here present who died on the Cross. . . . So Holy Mass is a tremendous real experience . . . of the reality of God, etc."[6] These words show how the Roman Catholic experiences the Christian faith essentially as a supernatural miracle in which God has made himself accessible to man. The divine reality thus understood is objectively given. Religious belief is in its foremost nature the acceptance and acknowledgment of this miracle. To him who does acknowledge it, Christ, the God-Man, is immediately and directly present.

The church as a sacramental-hierarchical institution is the embodiment of this miracle. The sacraments are the prolongation of God's incarnation in Jesus, which is the basic miraculous event of the divine self-manifestation in history. The hierarchy, represented in the papacy, also continues the incarnation: the pope, and through him every bishop, and through the bishop every priest, is Christ's vicar on earth. Therefore, when Roman Catholics define the church as "Christ's mystical body," they think of it primarily as a sacramental-priestly order and only secondarily as a society and a community. *"Ecclesia, id est fides et fidei sacramenta"*[7] and only as such it is also a *"congregatio hominum fidelium."*[8] The persons who constitute the community of the church are as the congregation of believers the participants in the supra-personal mystical body of Christ. When they take part in cultic prayer, they share in a sacral act which loses none of its reality, value or effectiveness when they fail to concentrate upon the petitions with personal attention. When the Lord's Prayer is recited in Roman Catholic worship and devotion, it is not necessarily spoken as a personal prayer. "The Pater Noster," so says an interpreter of the Roman Catholic liturgy, " is the voice of Christ which echoes through history until the end of time. When we say it, it is as if the divine voice were reproduced by our own voice organs."[9]

The community life of the Roman Catholic Church, in so far as it is expressed in the liturgy and the cultus, absorbs the personal being of the members of the church. It implies a surrender of individual existence and all its potentialities and wants to the holy "organism" that comes alive and breathes in the cultus. The Roman Church is only derivatively a fellowship of people who mutually share with one another what they possess, in the name of their common faith. This judgment is con-

firmed by the following statement of a priest who, interpreting what he calls the "socializing powers" (*Gestaltungskraft*)
of the Roman Catholic cultus, emphasizes the community character of the church by insisting upon depersonalization and
de-individualization: "Sacramental acts are according to their
nature liturgical acts (even when they are performed by single
individuals) and as such they are intended not for individuals,
but for the totality, the whole body. . . . From this it follows
that the cultus as a whole is essentially a community-act and
that the individual person who participates in it must first of
all assume the spiritual attitude of membership, of solidarity in
order to be concerned only with the good of the whole: (it follows further) that he must become *depersonalized* in a certain
way in order to be a living member of Christ in the church."[10]
"We must renounce our exaggerated personalism,. our egocen-
tric individuality, we must come out of our spiritual isolation,
out of the exclusiveness of our inwardness, in order to form
a community and to become members of a commonalty, of a
"family" which as such lives in union with Christ and of Him,
which in his name performs the cultus we owe to God. We
must therefore *de-individualize* ourselves in order to become
perfect members who receive their life from the life of the
whole body, from the life of Christ. Then our real and whole
personal being and its integral supernatural fullness will be
restored to us in Christ through the church."[11]

These sentences confirm with distinct clarity the impression which the non-Catholic often has occasion to form when
he tries to understand the Roman Catholic assertion that only
in the Roman Church the true common life in the organic
body of Christ is realized. It is the impression of a religious
community which is not formed by the sharing and interchange of the spiritual goods of individual persons, but by the
abnegation of the personal individualities of the members in
order that they may be integrated in the supra-personal body
of the sacramental-hierarchical church. When one has once
understood the meaning of the need of de-personalization which
the Roman Catholic emphasizes in speaking of the common life
of the "mystical body of Christ," one comprehends many of
the prominent public features of Roman Catholicism: the
sameness of the liturgical order in all churches all over the

world; the use of Latin as the ecclesiastical language and the refusal to employ the variety of tongues which the people of the church speak in their daily lives; the subjection of the clergy all over the world to the same routine and rule of education and discipline; the de-individualization of the theological thought of the church by the establishment of the Thomistic system as the theological norm; the perpetuation of contingent historical usages of ceremonials, rituals and vestments after they have been deprived of their singular uniqueness, etc.

The conception of the divine reality embodied in the sacramental- hierarchial church as something supra-personally objective which implies a depersonalization of the members of the church is consistent also with the interpretation of the grace of God as a supernatural "quiddity," a substance, which through the sacraments is infused into the metaphysical substance of the soul of the believer. It is a "medicine" which has power to heal and make whole the defects of his nature due to sin. It transforms his being in an impersonal way when it is miraculously operating in him. Its reception is an event taking place in his person, an event in which to his inmost human nature something supra-natural is added, but it is not a personal encounter or meeting between himself and God which can be described in terms of a personal relationship. Because this is so, the whole religious life is a commerce with objectively given holy things.

In the light of the description of the character of Roman Catholicism which we have thus far given, the following judgment of the lack of personal fellowship relations in Roman Catholic church practice appears to be justified. Canon Wedel, an ecumenically minded Episcopalian, writes of the Roman Church: "There is here little reading of the Bible. Ritual action has replaced words. There is no preaching, or very little, and that not thought essential. There is no confession of faith. The worshipper's presence at the Church's cult-act takes its place. Communion is not thought of in communal terms. Individuals go to the altar for the sacred host if properly shriven in the Confessional, but of the Mass as a Holy Supper of a people-Church there is no hint. The Church as the Body of Christ, a mystery of fellowship, a life of *agape* is strangely absent. Catholic churchmanship means membership in a world-

wide organization, but the membership is atomistic, each Christian largely for himself. Horizontal fellowship is scarcely to be
found. It is unity in a cult, not a localized social reality. . . .
The congregation is missing—the parish, *the Gemeinde.* Catholicism has, in a sense, the Great Church, a Church in history.
It has lost, to a large extent, the Little Church, the local family of God.''[12]

This criticism of the Roman Church is guided by a Protestant understanding of the Christian life. Bible-reading,
preaching, confession of faith, personal fellowship, the communal life of the local congregation, all of which Roman Catholicism is said to lack, are practices or values which Protestantism deems essential to the Christian religion.

II.

It may seem arbitrary when, in order now to explain the
spirit of Protestantism in contrast to that of Roman Catholicism,
we begin with a description of the church service as it was and
is still held in Calvinistic churches, particularly in Scotland
and Holland. It may be objected that the practices of these
churches are not representative of Protestantism as a whole.
Yet they give an insight into the secret of Protestant worship
which cannot be had anywhere else with the same clarity.

The services in these churches take place in plain halls.
There are no pictures hanging on the white-washed walls. The
high windows let the light of day pass into the meeting house
but do not permit a view of what is outside. There are no
permanent decorative designs anywhere. The rows of the
wooden pews face the pulpit before which stands a table. During the service all that takes place in such a hall is centered in
the pulpit and on the Bible which is placed on it. The minister reads the Biblical lesson; he leads in the singing or the
responsive reading of the Psalms; he speaks a prayer—extem-
poraneously and without using prescribed liturgical forms; and
he preaches on a Biblical text. Except when participating in
the singing or reading of the Psalms, the congregation listens.
There is nothing in the outward arrangement of the whole
proceedings which could induce the people to avoid hearing
the words spoken to them. (The hard, uncomfortable benches
make it difficult for anyone to fall asleep!) Yet here the church

is meeting and comes into being. What all major Protestant Reformers affirm concerning the nature of the church is here put into effect: "Where the Word is rightly preached and heard, there is the church."

Here too the worshipper is brought up against the divine as an objective reality, namely in the Gospel. He hears the gospel of God in the words of the preacher who in preaching makes real the incarnate Word of God, Jesus Christ, by relying for the content of his message upon the Bible and its testimony concerning Christ. Here too Christ is present and his "invisibility" is rendered "visible," but he is not bound to the means by which he is there. For though he is there through the medium of the word, namely the preaching of the Biblical message, he transcends this medium. He becomes a living reality only by breaking through the words of Bible and preacher. For the Bible is not the Word itself—it merely bears witness to it through its own frail words which can always be subjected to the critical questions of historical uncertainty. Nor is the sermon the Word itself—the preacher is only the minister of the Word and his ministry is often marked by his piecemeal, faulty and perhaps confused understanding of the Biblical message; sometimes it is even voided by his intellectual, moral and religious failure to make the sermon a witness to the Word. All this suggests a divine presence which is strangely intangible and indirect, not only because it is actualized through the least verifiable and most evanescent of all human means of communication, written and spoken words, but also because it can manifest itself only in meaning, spiritual understanding, feeling or impulse—whatever it is that is carried in the context of words.

Protestants themselves have often felt the frailty of the means by which the divine becomes present among them. Finding this frailty intolerable and desirous of having a firm medium of the word of God, some have identified the divine with the **Scriptures**: God himself, so they say, speaks out of them; as they stand they are inviolable; they are the very words of God himself, literally inspired by his Holy Spirit. Even the Reformers, Luther, Zwingli, Calvin, sometimes took recourse to this objectivisation. Thus whole generations of Protestants were able to point to the authoritativeness of their great teachers when they did likewise. Yet wherever men effected this identification of God and the Bible they found that it did not make it immediately available. The meaning and the message of the Bible had still to be discovered; the words of the text and the words of the exegete still remained words. Christ was still the "Lord of the Scripture"—as Luther once formulated the supremacy of the revelation over the means of revelation—it still transcended the arbitrary absolutization of historical documents even though its livingness was blocked by the idolatrous human act of rendering dead words divine by declaring them authoritatively definitive in their literalness.

Sometimes Protestants have identified the divine also with the sermon. It has to be admitted, however, that they choose this method of avoiding the indirectness of God's manifestation only in comparatively rare cases. The people listening to sermons are less inclined to commit this sin than the preachers and theologians have been (though they too have been known to yield to the temptation to do so!) In order to understand how inviting it may seem for a minister to identify the sermon with the Word of God itself, one must consider how narrow the way is he must travel in order to fulfill his task rightly, and how broad the road is on which he can go to failure. If in preaching he does not dare to assume the authority which voices in his speaking the affirmation "Thus says the Lord," his sermon is no true witness to the Word; yet when he directly identifies the words of his sermon with the Word of God, thus failing to place himself and his thinking and speaking in the service, only the service, of God, his preaching becomes idolatrous and a sin against the Holy Ghost.

In view of these difficulties rightly to use the means by which the invisible God makes men to see his presence, it happens sometimes—nay, it happens often—that people who stand in the Protestant tradition try to apprehend the divine reality without *any* means. Then they circumvent sermons and Scripture and everything else that may be regarded as equivalent to them and they seek God in an experience of immediacy. But they can never be certain whether what they find by searching in their immediate inwardness or outwardness is really the divine. It may be a mysterious something or nothing, the abyss of the self or the depth of the world, the spark of their own life or the creativeness of the universe—they may call it God, but whether it is really he, they can never know. When they tell of what they have found, they sometimes try to speak a new language, but generally they use words which have the meaning of the Christian tradition in which they have been brought up. They are the words of Scripture and of the theological exposition of Scripture undertaken in connection with preaching. Thus it turns out that what was to be avoided asserts itself after all and what was to be immediate is bound to means, indeed the very means that were to be disregarded, namely Scripture and the ideas which it inspires.

"Where the Word is rightly preached, there is the church" —this is only one aspect of the way in which the Protestant experiences the reality of God.[13] The complete definition of the Christian church according to the Protestant tradition must read: "Where the Word is rightly preached *and heard,* there is the Church."[14] The hearing which is here meant is, of course, an inward listening and a response of mind and heart. It is the personal answer of him who listens to the preaching of the Word—an answer that is nothing else than the awareness that what is spoken concerns him in his innermost being because it is addressed to his conscience. Only when the external words of the sermon and the Bible are inwardly received, only when their own internal meaning—the gospel, Christ—is appropriated in faith by the listener, only then God becomes real. Indeed, the hearing of the Word is complete only when the Christ of whom the Bible speaks and of whom the sermon, on the basis of the Bible, bears witness, is an inward Christ. The confrontation with him which the words of Bible and sermon effect must become a commitment. Christ, too, must cease to be an external reality, one who is faced as an opposite one, who is encountered as an historical figure or as the subject of someone else's testimony, *Christus pro me, Christus in me.* The Word of God which he is must be appropriated by me so that it becomes part of my life. The Gospel which he brings must become the fountain of life *for me.*

The Reformers and following them Protestant leaders generally described this inward hearing of the Word as the working of the Holy Spirit. What they and particularly Calvin and the Calvinists with their doctrine of the "inner testimony of the Holy Spirit" had in mind was the safeguarding of the inner experience of the Word as a divine act. It is God himself, so they meant to say, who by means of the Bible and of Biblical preaching, touches the understanding of the listener in such a way that he applies the message to himself and appropriates it for his own living. In experiencing Christ as his own and adopting his truth as a truth for himself, he thus does not make an arbitrary, subjective decision but Christ who is the objective reality that imbues the Biblical message with its peculiar meaning and life, communicates himself to him from without, so to speak. In becoming a believer, he does not choose to accept the truth of the Word as if he could claim to possess criteria of his own by which to judge its validity, but the truth of the Word affirms itself in his mind by its own power of persuasiveness. He does not grasp it by adding it to convictions of truth which he already possesses and which he enlarges by the truth of the Word, but he is being laid hold of by a power, a life, a verity not his own, i.e. not of his own producing.

Luther gave forceful expression to this Christian experience which comes about by the inward hearing of the Word, i.e. by the inner testimony of the Holy Spirit, when he said: "Our theology (our knowledge of God) is certain, because it puts us outside of ourselves; I do not need to rely upon my conscience, my senses, and my doing, but I rely upon the divine promise and truth which never deceive."[15] He was persuaded that the certainty of the Word of God was different in kind from the certainty that inheres in sense-perception, in the knowledge of conscience or in moral decision. When he judged the certainty of the Holy Spirit (the certainty of salvation) with respect to its content, namely communion with God through the forgiveness of sins in Christ, and when he compared it with the certainty which is the object of man's usual search for knowledge, faith appeared to him as a blindly trusting audacity. "For this is the nature of faith," he once wrote, "that it dares trust in God's grace . . . faith does not require information, knowledge or security (i.e. the criteria ordinarily required for certainty), "but a free surrender to and a joyful daring upon an unfelt, untried, unknown goddess."[15]

And yet, he never left any doubt about his conviction that in order to be valid, faith must be a personal experience. A Christian, he taught with tireless insistence, must have the certainty of the Word by a personal act of commitment. "You yourself must decide"; he said in a sermon, "your neck is at stake. Therefore unless God says to your own heart: This is God's word, you cannot comprehend it. . . .If you do not feel it, you do not have faith, but the word merely hangs in your ears and floats on your tongue as foam lies on the waters."[17] In his own life, he was well acquainted with the fact that in so far as faith had to be his own act, the deed of his own believing, it was beset with all the doubts, vagaries, confusions and waverings that lie upon all human knowledge, but he was persuaded that this insecurity of his own believing would never shake the certainty, reliability and trust-worthiness of the Word of God nor undo its objective truth and reality. Therefore, he was sure that if he would but let the Word speak for itself, it would affirm itself by its own persuasive power.

Indeed, as he saw the work of the reformation of the church, which he had unwillingly begun, he conceived of it as the task of clearing a path in the world for the freedom of the Word, so that by means of the Bible and a faithful and unprejudiced interpretation of it, it might capture the faith and the loyalty of men. As he saw it, the Roman Church had put arbitrary obstacles in the way of the Word, primarily by declaring its own historically developed institutions (and particularly the office of the papacy) as of the essence of the gospel and thus necessary to salvation. He was also aware of the fact that what Roman Catholicism had done, namely to confine the gospel within arbitrarily determined limits, was in every man's range of possibilities. He dreaded in particular that it might happen that the authority of his own interpretation of the gospel would become a hindrance to its free course in the world. For he was persuaded that he, Luther, could add as little to the truth of the Word of God as Paul and Peter and even an angel from heaven could have added. God's truth, he was sure, requires the guarantee of no man or creature. Yet it cannot be spread and published abroad without the means of human communication, nor can it be known anywhere unless it is appropriated by individual acts of faith resulting in commitment to its truth.

In the perspective of history, we must now say that what Luther feared has actually come to pass: many aspects of his own interpretation of the Word which he developed in the course of his own tempestuous career and not without much unenlightened stubbornness on his own part, have been perpetrated as essential features of the truth of God. Moreover, many of his own followers among the Protestants refuse to set the Word free. Yet, the spirit of his Reformation is still alive: Because of Luther and in spite of Luther, there are Protestants who can see that the objective reality of God cannot establish itself among men except by its own cogency and that, though none of the modes and circumstances of its apprehension must be permitted to delimit its free sovereignty, it is impotent among men if it is not apprehended in personal faith.

Indeed, it is because Protestants of all generations since the Reformation have had this spirit that the Christian church is alive among men in another form than that of Roman Catholicism. It is a free, dynamic social movement of believers who by a personal act of faith apprehend the divine reality which in the writings of the New Testament is declared to be the gospel of Jesus Christ, and who render it visible in their own actions. Whatever their specific doctrines and traditions, Protestants of all types agree in this that because the church comes into being by the preaching and the hearing of the Word, its nature is not realized unless the hearing of the word is manifested in deeds. The motivation of these deeds is the personal response to the gospel that occurs in the secrecy of the heart of each individual who hears it in faith. The deeds themselves are the words of love motivated by personal faith in Christ which link each believer to his fellowmen in a spiritual communion. The church as Protestants understand it is therefore primarily a fellowship of believers. It consists of all those who having heard the Word, each for himself in his own particular inward and outward situation, relate themselves to their fellow-believers and to all men in the spirit of faith and love which the Word induces in them. This church originates only when men congregate (gather as listeners) around the Word, commonly as it is expounded by preaching on the basis of the testimony of the Bible, but it is realized fully only in the believers' fellowship of love. It is no sacral institution, no supra-personal miraculous entity made visible in holy signs and liturgical offices, but a living communion of people who holding in earthen vessels the heavenly treasure of the knowledge of God in Christ manifest their faith in fellowship with one another. The foundation of this church is the Word of God accessible only in and through the insecure testimony of historical men, first the writers of the New Testament and then all those who stand in their succession. The structure of this church is the faith of the Word, obtainable only by individuals in concrete, unrepeatable situations and realizable only through actions in the contingent historical circumstances of human society. This church is continuously beset by the danger that its life of faith, order and work may become statically fixed. For it is the tendency of men to perpetuate what is precious to them, in arbitrarily absolutized traditions, usages and practices. This danger to which preeminently Roman Catholicism has fallen prey, has also tempted the Protestants. It has become apparent especially in the way in which Protestants have interpreted the division of churches that resulted from the Reformation.

The understanding of the Christian religion which Luther and his fellow-reformers accomplished, can not entail uniformity of any kind in outward Christian behavior. For as soon as it was established as a principle of Christian life that each person or group of persons must receive the Word by a commitment to it within the concrete and individual conditions of historical circumstances, all spiritual compulsion to conform to certain rules of faith, polity or ethics were rendered impossible. It was therefore unavoidable by reasons of faith that a variety of Protestant forms of Christianity came into being. From the beginning, Protestantism could not but express man's response to the Christian gospel in individualized ways. These were dictated by motives and forces not only of individual but also of common life. The peril threatening the freedom and sovereignty of the Christian gospel lay not in the variety of these concrete forms of piety, doctrine, church-order and morality, but in the tendency of the spokesmen and representatives of specific ones of these forms to establish what they had developed or what had developed among them as absolute as if their own historical form had to be regarded as of the essence of the Christian gospel itself. Such attitudes were in part induced by considerations of the public law then universally in force, namely, that concord within a civic community rested on the uniformity of the religious confession of all citizens or political subjects. But they were also due to the stubborn unwillingness even of the spiritual leaders of the Reformation to live up to their own often declared principle, that among Christians all matters of faith have to be adjudged before the tribunal of the Word of God alone.

This principle implied that differences in Christian faith and order should be conscientiously discussed and compared (the German term used at the time of the Reformation was *"vergleichen"*) in the light of the common desire of all Christians to be loyal to the lordship of Christ, in order either to cause corrections to be made if the need for them was recognized in the course of conference, or to declare varieties and differences possible of mutual toleration if their pragmatic historical necessity and character was mutually acknowledged. It has to be said in honor of some of the Reformers, particularly Martin Butzer and Philip Melanchthon, that they were mindful of this rule and vowed to obey it, in order that Christian unity might be actualized. But their successors, the representatives of Protestant Orthodoxy, almost entirely lost the will to seek unity and understanding with those who differed from them. Thus it came about that Protestant Christianity was divided into many exclusive churches and groups which perpetuated their individual historical creeds, liturgies and polities as if they were part of the Christian gospel and not mere products of historical Christian generations.

This arbitrary objectivisation of Christian believing in normative traditions and norms of faith caused those Protestants in whom the original Protestant spirit was alive to become separatists and dissenters in the name of the Word and the Spirit. Though they too often came to bind the Word of God which in the beginning they hailed as unbound, they proved to be the true successors of the Reformers and the true children of the Spirit. They were the real channels of Protestant dynamism. Because they were non-conformists, they were often discredited as individualists. But actually they were not individualists in the sense in which this word is commonly understood, but prophetic spirits who knew that the church of Christ is founded in a free preaching and hearing of the Word and that neither the Word nor the believer can be forced into arbitrary forms. They became the founders of new Christian groups and churches and thus increased the variety of Protestantism. Yet the fact that they set themselves apart made it possible for the gospel to run a free course through the lives of men. To be sure, not all secessions that happened in Protestant history were inspired by a prophetic concern for the freedom of the gospel. Many were caused by considerations of Biblical legalism and of Pharisaic moralism. This was the price that had to be paid in order that the Protestant form of Christianity might live—a personal fellowship of individual believers responding freely to the sovereign Word of God in the midst of the everchanging concrete conditions of human life: a church whose ground of unity is the Word of God which can never be exhaustively identified with any of its historical witnesses, including the Bible, and which cannot be known apart from historical testimonies, especially not apart from the Bible; a church whose structure of unity can only be the fellowship of faith and love which is ever newly to be attained by men who respond to this Word in personal commitment to it and by mutual service to one another in its name.

III.

The spirit of Protestant Christianity, so we may state by way of summing up the results of our analysis, is dynamic. The Protestant believer interprets the divine-human relationship which men are promised in the gospel of Jesus Christ as a living religion. His faith in God is trust and reliance in the divine love revealed to him in Jesus and in the spirit of those who belong to him as his messianic people. He knows God as the living fountain of all good which shattering all pride and selfishness by forgiving love is ever renewing the life of believing men. He knows him as a free sovereign whose livingness is never confined in an objective spatial presence, because it manifests itself only in the living words and deeds that testify of the spirit of Christ. Therefore the Protestant understands the Christian religion as a personal life: As the living God discloses himself in the life of persons in such a way that in the light that lightens them his light can be seen, so all who believe in him, knowing him in the individual secrecy of their hearts as their own Father, bear witness to him in personal fellowship with their fellowmen, particularly with their fellow-believers, thus constituting the church, the people of God.

The spirit of Roman Catholic Christianity is static. The Roman Catholic believer interprets the Christian religion as the participation in the supernatural reality of God, the Being of beings, who having once for all become man in Jesus of Nazareth is incarnate also in Christ's mystical body, the church. This faith in God is the partaking of the divine grace which through Christ is made available to all men in the sacraments of the church and its priesthood. He knows God as the creator and redeemer who through the holy institution of the church heals all imperfections of nature, particularly man's loss of original righteousness caused by Adam's disobedience of the divine commandments, and thus makes it possible for them to see him as he is. He knows him as the supreme reality, the cause of all being, the source of all life, the light that lightens the world, made accessible to all men in Christ, who until the end of the world is objectively present in the sacramental-hierarchical institution of the church. Therefore the Roman Catholic understands the Christian religion as a sacramental life. God is present among men in the supernatural reality of Christ's mystical body, the church; all who let themselves be nourished by grace through the church and are obedient to its order, become members of Christ's body, being mystically and supra-personally united with one another through him as sharers of his divine life.

CHAPTER 12

The Roman Catholic Critique
of Protestantism

THE DIFFERENCE between Protestantism and Roman Catholicism is so profound that it seems almost impossible to recognize them as two forms of one Christianity. Yet because both are part of the one historical religious movement that issued from Jesus of Nazareth and his disciples, they must relate themselves to one another seeking to justify their particular interpretation of the meaning of the Christian faith.

To Roman Catholics the Reformation and the whole movement of Protestantism appear as a "revolt from the church." They interpret this revolt as caused by the individual desire of men to be emancipated from the ecclesiastical institutions and the divine authority embodied in them. In their eyes, Protestantism is inspired by individualism. Expressing an opinion which is common to the Roman Catholic critics of Protestantism, Professor Adam writes: "The sixteenth century revolt from the Church led inevitably to the revolt from Christ in the eighteenth century and thus to the revolt from God in the nineteenth century. And thus the modern spirit has been torn loose from the deepest and strongest support of its life, from its foundation in the Absolute, in the self-existent Being, in the Value of values. . . . Instead of the man who is rooted in the Absolute, hidden in God, strong and rich, we have the man who rests upon himself, the autonomous man. Moreover, this man because he has renounced the fellowship of the Church, the communio fidelium, the interrelation and correlation of the faithful, has severed the second root of his life, that is to say, his fellowship with other men. He has lost that closely-

177

knitted union of self and others, that communion with the supra-personal whole, which proves itself in joy and sorrow, in prayer and in love, and by means of which the individual can ever renew and regulate his strength . . . nowhere else, in no other society, is the idea of community, of fellowship in doing and suffering, in prayer and love . . . so strongly imbedded in doctrines, morals and worship, as in the Catholic Church. And so the rupture of Church unity has of itself loosened the bonds of social fellowship and thereby destroyed the deep source and basis of . . . a complete humanity. The autonomous man has become a solitary man, an individual".[1]

In this statement four major criticisms of Protestantism are implied: 1) Because the Reformers revolted from the church and broke its unity, modern man, the Protestant man, has lost the sense of the Christian verities; 2) Protestantism is responsible for the crisis of modern civilization, especially in view of 3) its individualistic spirit and 4) its loss of membership in the community of the church. By discussing these criticisms in order, we shall be able further to clarify the basic religious differences between Protestantism and Roman Catholicism.

I

The argument that, if the Protestant Reformers had not broken the unity of the church, modern man would not have lost Christ and God and the fellowship of the Holy Spirit and the sense of belonging to an all-embracing community is not sound or convincing. For the Protestant Christian movement has always lived of the divine revelation in Jesus Christ and it has been inspired by the mission to unite men all over the world in the community of the Christian faith. To be sure, the Protestant interpretation of the meaning of the Christian gospel has been different from that of Roman Catholicism since the days of the Reformation and, in the course of the centuries since then, this intepretation has undergone a development which has deepened the estrangement of Protestantism from Roman Catholicism. For Protestants have opened their minds more fully to the cultural achievements of modern man than Catholics were ever permitted to do. Protestant thought has become "modernized" and as long as its vitality lasts, it will continue to be modernized. This has not been brought about without difficulties and errors, for the task of the modern Protestant theologians was an intricate one: the uniqueness of the Christian faith had to be maintained over against the readiness of some to adjust it to temporary needs and fashions of the world and over against the unwillingness of others to recognize the involvement also of the Christian life in historical change.

What all this amounts to is not that Protestants have lost the sense of Christian verities but that they have learned to interpret them in a way fundamentally different from that of the ancient and medieval dogmas to which Roman Catholicism still clings. The charge that Protestantism has caused the emancipation of modern man from Christ and God and the church has therefore only this meaning: Protestantism has broken radically with Catholic dogma; it does not maintain it in its ancient and medieval form as Roman Catholicism does but it interprets it by means of historical criticism. In the eyes of the theologians of the Roman Church this fact means that Protestants have no Christian truth at all or that they have it at best only in a much perverted form. This judgment again implies the opinion that, because Protestants helped to alienate modern men from Roman Catholic Christianity, their conviction that they have kept the Christian gospel alive in the midst of modern civilization is an illusion, for, according to Roman Catholic teaching, there is only one Christian church, namely the Church of Rome, and nothing that exists apart from it deserves the Christian name.[2]

Protestants reject this verdict as arbitrary. It appears to them inspired by an unwarranted absolutization of dogmas and institutions that were developed in the Middle Ages. They see in the assertion that only the Roman Church possesses true Christianity nothing but an unhistorical perpetuation of norms of truth which fitted medieval thinking but which have been disproved by religious, philosophical, scientific and historical knowledge. The following examples will illustrate this criticism of fundamental Roman Catholic tenets: It cannot be historically proved that Jesus founded the hierarchical order of the Roman Church and that he gave it authority to speak in his name. It is an arbitrary, historically undemonstrable dogma that the popes are the successors of Peter and that by virtue

of this succession they are endowed with apostolic authority.
It is untrue that the seven sacraments of the Roman Church
can be derived from Biblical injunctions and that they can
thus be attributed to the authority of Christ. From scientific,
metaphysical and religious points of view, it seems fantastic
to explain the presence of Christ in the Eucharist by the dogma
of transsubstantiation. Indeed, the whole basis of Catholic
religion in the supernaturally miraculous is insecure and uncertain. Moreover, the dogma that the Roman Church possesses an inerrant sense of religious truth and that it is possible
for the popes by virtue of the authority of their office to articulate this sense infallibly in conformity with a "tradition" that
has been "one" since apostolic times is a colossal fiction.

No Protestant can deny that the Roman Church has preserved ancient and medieval traditions. Indeed, he cannot but
marvel at the ability of Roman Catholicism to maintain so
many historical dogmas, rites, customs and practices. He
should also not hesitate to admit that in many of the Roman
traditions a religious symbolism is preserved the loss of which
would impoverish the souls of Christian men. Yet he cannot
grant that the fact of this accomplishment constitutes a claim to
truth.

The Protestant is horrified when he considers the cost
which Roman Catholic Christians must pay in order to preserve their treasure of tradition and dogma: that they must
absolutely refuse to submit their church's authoritarianism to
investigation and debate in which anyone may share who is
open to be convinced by evidence of fact and value. The Protestant cannot but shudder at the fact that the many millions
of Catholic believers are able to accept the decree of the men
of the Vatican Council who allegated to themselves the right
to declare it as a "divinely revealed dogma" that "when the
Roman Pontiff speaks from his chair, i.e., when exercising his
office as the shepherd and teacher of all Christians, he defines
by virtue of his supreme apostolic authority a doctrine of faith
and morals, he acts under divine assistance by that infallibility
by which the divine redeemer wishes his church to be instructed" and that such definitions are "in and from themselves unchangeable" *(ex sese irreformabiles)*.[3] Even if one
recognizes that this dogma does not mean that the Pope can

"like a Delphic oracle give dogmatic decisions at his own discretion" but that he is bound in conscience to proclaim and interpret that revelation which is contained in the written and unwritten mind of the Church, in the twin sources of . . . . . Scripture and tradition,"[4] the attribution to one man of such absolute authority to define religious truth, must be regarded as an almost blasphemous presumption.

The promulgation and acceptance of this extravagant dogma is consistent with the Roman Catholic conviction that divine truth is objectively and supra-personally given in the sacramental-hierarchical institutions and that its nature can therefore be defined quite apart from personal faith. As, according to Roman Catholic teaching, the personal religious faith of the pope is not involved in the infallible dogmas which he may proclaim, so also the personal faith of individual Christians is irrelevant to the validity of the religious substance of the church. It is this separation of the religious object from the religious subject which the Protestant Christian deplores most in Roman Catholic Christianity, for to him God is not real apart from faith and faith is not real apart from God. That it is at all possible for the Roman Catholic to believe that there is an objectively given supra-personal substance of divine truth and life which can be disassociated from personal faith, the Protestants can explain only by assuming that Roman Catholicism has arbitrarily come to regard a historical human tradition of religious rites and traditions as a living divine reality which is declared to be sustained by a super-personal ground of life, without any dependence upon the personal conviction and judgment of those who carry this tradition. This is, so the Protestant concludes, what has happened and is happening in Roman Catholicism.

The Roman Catholic Church has taken the historical faith of ancient and medieval Christian believers out of human history by depersonalizing it and by perpetuating it as if it were a superhistorical entity. This depersonalization and preservation of the historical product, called the "tradition," is in itself a human historical act. It cannot be and could not have been accomplished except by the decision and volition of men to absolutize a certain body of human religious culture and to objectivize it as if it could be separated from the persons who

produced it. The "objectively given tradition" of the Roman
Catholic Church is therefore nothing divine; it is the human
product of the Roman Catholic community acting through its
hierarchical leaders. It was they, believing to act by virtue of
apostolic authority speaking through them, who elected to iso-
late certain Christian institutions, rites, laws and doctrines of
medieval origin and to set them apart from the living, changing context of Christian history. This "tradition" is connected
arbitrarily (i.e., in disregard of reliable historical investigation)
with the beginnings of Christianity in the periods of the New
Testament and the ancient church and it is extended into the
present by way of a specific explication of contents that had
remained unexpressed but were implied in the doctrines and
teachings of the medieval Roman Church. This is the way in
which the establishment of the Roman Catholic "tradition"
has come about.

It is even possible to state at what time in the history of
the Roman Catholic Church the decisive beginnings of the
interpretation of the Christian life in the light of this "tradition" was made: at the time of the Reformation! When Luther
arose to demand a dogmatic clarification of the meaning of
indulgences, an authoritative definition of what was to be regarded as "Catholic" was not yet in existence. To be sure, the
medieval popes had established hierarchical authority in terms
of Canon Law and the Scholastics had set the pattern for the
interpretation of Christian doctrine and practice by means of
the "authority" of the Bible and the "Fathers," but neither
papal nor scholastic authority governed absolutely the definition of "Catholicity." The question, for example, whether the
Occamist theology (called the *via moderna*) was truly Catholic
was not seriously raised at the beginning of the sixteenth century, but, in modern times, it has proved troublesome to Roman Catholic theologians, because they cannot regard it as Catholic in the light of the tradition as they now define it.[5] The
definition of "Catholicity" which determines modern Roman
Catholicism was given only by the Council of Trent which
was unwillingly convened by the popes in a half-hearted response to the demands of the Holy Roman Emperor and which
(fortunately for Roman Catholicism) was dominated by the
leaders of the "Counter Reformation" that had come about

in reaction to the Protestant Reformation. Only since this time (and after Luther, responding to the accusation of heresy, had defined as Catholic that which was in accord with Scripture!), the norm of "tradition" has been known as an authoritative rule. In establishing this "tradition," the "fathers" of Trent affirmed as normative that part of ancient and medieval Christianity which could be read in the light of the teachings of Thomas Aquinas. Their own predominant theological position was Thomistic. Thus it happened that in modern Roman Catholicism nothing is regarded as normatively "Catholic" which cannot be explicated in terms of the Thomistic system. It was in conformity with these tenets and in the expectation that they would and could be held for all times that the Vatican Council of 1870 proclaimed the pope as the infallible guardian of the "tradition." It was also consistent with the doctrinal spirit which, since the Council of Trent, had come to determine Roman Catholic Christianity that, at the end of the nineteenth century, Leo XIII specifically ordered that all theological training in the church should be based on the teachings of the "angelic doctor."

In the light of these facts, it is no exaggeration to say that the definition of Catholic tradition which guides all modern Roman Catholic thought and action was made only in reaction to the Reformation. The judgment of the Roman Catholic critics of Protestantism that the Reformers broke up the unity of the church is therefore open to question. Without denying that the effect of the Reformation caused the break-up of ecclesiastical unity, one can say with considerable justice to the actual historical events that the Roman Catholic authorities who refused to deal with Luther by acknowledging the seriousness, if not the validity, of his concern for an adequate interpretation of penance, were really responsible for the Protestant break with Roman Catholicism. It is entirely conceivable that if Luther had not been abruptly opposed after he published his Ninety-Five Theses and if he had been treated as one who had the welfare of the church at heart, the Reformation would not have happened by way of a Protestant separation from Roman Catholicism. It is also not correct to assert, as modern Catholics habitually and generally do, that Luther defied authoritative Catholic teachings when he first came to the fore as a critic of religious practices in the church. For neither the popes or any theological school were then endowed with absolute authority to define what was Christian. Such authority was then still widely believed to inhere in a General Council. The appeal of Luther and his sympathizers to such a council was therefore not unjustified. It was not his fault that he was banned before he had received a fair hearing and that, later, the Council of Trent was convened only when neither he nor the Protestants generally were able to recognize it as impartial, in view of the fact that in the eyes of the conveners and members of the Council they were heretics.

In summing up this discussion of the Roman Catholic criticism that the Reformation and Protestantism resulted from a revolt against the church, we conclude that the Roman Catholic leaders of the sixteenth century are not without responsibility for the break-up of Christian unity and that the Roman Catholic conception of this unity is based on an arbitrary definition of the nature of Christianity. Protestantism, therefore, cannot be justly accused of having become amancipated from true Christianity. What it has done is that it has set itself against the Roman Catholic delimitation and distortion of Christianity that is embodied in the super-personal and super-historical "tradition."

II

Turning now to the charge which Roman Catholic publicists have made so popular in recent times, that on account of its "individualism" and lack of social cohesiveness, Protestantism is in part responsible for the crisis of modern civilization, we suspect that, when Roman Catholics make this accusation, they minimize their own involvement in the development of modern cultural life. The Roman Church certainly would not want to concede that Protestantism was the decisive Christian movement that shaped the cultural motives of modern men or that Protestantism so eliminated Roman Catholicism from the common life as to make it impossible for it to influence modern civilization. As a matter of fact, Roman Catholics have always outnumbered Protestants and the institutions of Roman Catholicism have at all times been more powerful than those of Protestantism. Why then should one not ask why

Roman Catholicism was not able to prevent modern man from getting into the predicament of humanist isolation? When Protestants are made directly or indirectly responsible for the crisis of modern civilization, it is therefore entirely justified, if they in turn ask why Roman Catholicism did not do more to make the development of this crisis impossible. This question can in part be answered by pointing to the fact that Roman Catholicism can adopt only with great difficulty the modern scientific and historical world-view which no one who has ever come under its sway will voluntarily surrender. By failing to relate the Christian religion openly to the spirit of the modern generations who succeeded in devising a new conception of man's place in nature and the universe, Roman Catholicism has estranged itself from innumerable modern men. Also large sections of Protestantism must be charged with this failure and this is the reason why Protestantism too has lost the adherence of many who by tradition and upbringing should belong to it. But Roman Catholicism is at this point undoubtedly in the greater predicament.

III

As to the point that by virtue of its individualistic spirit, Protestantism has encouraged the tendency of modern men to conceive of themselves as autonomous, it must be stated first of all that Roman Catholics tend to attribute to the Reformation the spirit which was characteristic of the Renaissance and to Protestantism as a whole attitudes which were those of the children of the Renaissance. The inner development of modern civilization is not properly understood if one fails to distinguish between the two movements of the Reformation and the Renaissance. Both have moulded the mind of modern man in a decisive way, but the two movements were never inspired by the same spirit. As a matter of fact, the Renaissance which was indeed a cultural revolt from the medieval church and laid the foundation of the individualistic character of modern civilization blossomed first on Roman Catholic soil, the popes being among its most influential furtherers. Its spirit spread in civilizations in which Roman Catholicism was the determining religious factor before it came to influence the cultural areas dominated by Protestantism. The intellectual movement of the Enlightenment, which brought to full fruition what had first unfolded in the Renaissance, was furthered by Roman Catholics as well as by Protestants. To be sure, the Protestants reacted to its achievements differently than Roman Catholics did. They (or at least an influential minority among their leaders) saw allies in the modern humanists who emancipated human reason from the bondage to a heteronomous authoritarianism but they were not concerned to enhance the cause of human autonomy for its own sake. They were interested in the achievement of human liberty because they knew that the freedom of the Christian man is realizable only in personal acts of individual decision. It must be acknowledged that many modern Protestants got into great mental and spiritual difficulties because they did not sufficiently distinguish modern humanist liberty from Christian freedom. But in any case, it happened only rarely that Protestants went so far as to affirm openly and bluntly that the human autonomy accomplished in modern cultural life was identical with the freedom of the Christian man. One should not deny that Protestant religious liberalism had some kinship with secular liberalism which flourished in the eighteenth and nineteenth centuries and that Pietism and Rationalism encouraged individualistic tendencies in Protestant life which could easily be blended with the cultural individualism of the Enlighteners who fought for the autonomy of human reason.

But Protestantism was able to extricate itself from an alliance which, if continued, would have entailed the loss of the theonomous spirit which had guided the Reformers in their protest against Roman Catholic heteronomy as well as against the humanistic autonomy of the Renaissance. Today, Protestant thought is filled with a deep awareness of the irreconcilability of humanistic individualism with the prophetic religiousness which the Reformers first discovered as the true mark of the Christian faith. All over the Protestant world, religious and theological leaders are engaged in the task to effect a new reformation. So there is hope that the crisis may be overcome into which modern civilization has fallen chiefly on account of its individualism. In these efforts they are motivated by a deep awareness of the fundamental difference between the Renaissance and the Reformation, especially in so

far as they try to avoid an interpretation of Protestant Christianity which could be called individualistic.

Roman Catholics are convinced that such an undertaking
can never be successful because they are certain that as long
as Protestantism permits itself to be guided by the spirit of the
Reformers it must necessarily cultivate individualistic habits.
This judgment is largely due to the inability of Roman Catholics properly to understand Protestant personalism. Because
their churchmanship encourages depersonalization, they suspect that the Protestant cultivation of a personal Christian life
is individualistic. This attitude is excellently illustrated in
the recent work by the Roman Catholic church-historian Joseph
Lortz on the Protestant Reformation. The author is an irenic
interpreter of Protestantism. Fully acquainted with the extensive modern research of Protestant scholars in the beginnings of Protestantism, he is not primarily concerned to defend
Roman Catholicism against the Reformers. In noteworthy difference from his predecessors among Roman Catholic historians
of the Reformation, he endeavors to draw an objective picture
of the events that led to the break-up of the medieval church.
He is even able to write of Luther in the spirit of sympathy
and admiration. Precisely on account of these accomplishments, his judgment of Luther must be regarded as a characteristic expression of the inability of Roman Catholics fully to
understand the Protestant spirit. The features of Luther's
faith which he feels compelled to criticize are those which all
Protestants, including many who refuse to attribute any normativeness to Luther's teachings, will be inclined to regard as
essential aspects of their own religiousness.

Professor Lortz is fully aware of the fact that the Christian
religion cannot be adequately interpreted unless it is viewed
in terms of a relationship of man with God. He suspects that
Protestants understand this relationship in such a way that
undue emphasis is placed upon man's part in it. He writes:
"The Christian spirit can be rightly interpreted only if objective events of salvation are seen in correlation with subjective
attitudes. The wholeness of Christianity is not safeguarded
unless these two elements are connected with one another.
But this must be done in such a way that the inner attitudes
of man are made to appear as less important than the objective

power and the objective life of the mystical body of Christ.
Yet, it is undeniable that for man the decisive factor in this
relationship is . . . . the better, inward righteousness of a new
heart and conscience. Whenever this obligation is taken singly
by itself, the Protestant attitude is produced, ... for an exaggeration of personal religious earnestness signifies the danger
of heresy.[6]

In the light of this fundamental conception of the Christian
religion, Professor Lortz attributes to Luther the error of an
exaggerated concern for personal religiousness involving a
denial, or at least a foreshortening of the primacy of the divine
as it is objectively set before man in the authoritative institutions of the church. Indeed, Luther's emphasis upon personal
faith and his rejection of ecclesiastical authoritarianism appear
to him as proofs of a religious subjectivism. He describes
therefore the religion of the Reformation as a "revolt against
the church in so far as it is anchored in the objective teaching
office and in the sacramental office of the priesthood" and as "a
religion of conscience based on individual judgments concerning the meaning of the Bible."[7] Roman Catholicism is seen
as marked by objectivism, traditionalism and clericalism, and
Protestantism by subjectivism, spiritualism and laicism. Professor Lortz admits that the protests of Luther against the
exaggerated clericalism of the medieval church were in part
justified, but he regards the abolition of the clerical authority
and the destruction of historical sacramentalism, which the
Reformation effected, as an "emptying" of Christianity's "objective source of power" resulting in the dissolution of Christianity and its replacement by a personal religion of conscience.[8]

Professor Lortz's most telling criticism of Luther is expressed in the following sentence: "With all his powers, Luther
seeks only the one God and he desires to submit wholly to
him; having found God in the word of the Bible, he submits
to the authority of the word . . . . yet, nevertheless, from the
very beginning, his submissiveness is sometimes totally different from the simple receptiveness of the plain Christian. It is
at all times an act of appropriation by Luther, the seeker, the
fighter, the gigantic wrestler. And this is the decisive point:
He who wished to surrender unconditionally to God's word,

never succeeded in being a listener. In the roots of his being, Luther is inclined toward subjectiveness."[9]

That Luther was no "listener" is a very curious statement. For nothing seems to be so characteristic of Luther's interpretation of the Christian faith than his ceaselessly repeated insistence that a man cannot become a Christian until he hears God's word and, having heard it, acts according to its promise. Indeed, all Protestants have learned from Luther to understand the Christian religion as the faith of responsive and responsible listeners. What Professor Lortz desires to suggest by this oddly formulated criticism is that in emphasizing the influence of becoming a "hearer of the word" Luther made the personal appropriation of the message of the word too important. This personalism of Luther appears to the Roman Catholic interpreter as a subjectivistic defiance to the impersonal objective order of the church. That Luther was no "listener" means therefore that he was not seriously enough concerned about the task "to take care that the traditional substance of the 'deposit of faith' was not endangered."[10] Professor Lortz is willing to admit that Luther wished to be and was a servant of the word, but he adds that Luther was such a servant "in a very personal sense." By absolutizing and isolating the word, he caused religious objectivism to become an illusion for a religious objectivism is impossible unless it is assured again and again by a living interpreter, i.e., by an infallible, living, teaching office.[11] Luther could therefore not really serve the word because he understood it in terms of personal insight and not on the basis of an authoritative super-personal interpretation. His reading of the Bible was subjectivistic because he "read it outside of the organism of the church to which it properly belongs."[12] He lacked the consciousness of being in the church as an order which was set before and above him and to which he was expected to submit. "Relying upon his own individual knowledge and interpretation of the Bible, he sovereignly passed by the church."[13] "The weak point of Luther's theology," as Professor Lortz sees it, is therefore "that he based his thinking not upon the given reality of the church but upon his own singular, individual, and personal reading of the Bible."[14] Thus he put man, the religious subject, "in a

grandiose way in the center of the acts and events of salvation."[15]

"How close Luther seems to be to Catholicism," Professor
Lortz exclaims when he chooses to recognize also Luther's objectivism. "But he failed on account of his one-sidedness or, to
put the case differently, because of the Catholic synthesis. To
be sure, he had recognized the enormous difficulty of this synthesis in trying to take very seriously one of its parts, namely
the affirmation that nothing can stand independently next to
God because there is nothing that does noc come from him.
But this is only one part of the Catholic doctrine. It has
to be admitted that Luther taught it with a great religious
profundity and with an awareness of the great wealth of the
mysteries, symbols and powers of the word of God. But he
was of the persuasion that this one part was the whole of the
Christian faith. Luther's Catholic thesis therefore became
untenable; he understood it one-sidedly, for he failed to supplement it in the proper way by relating it to nature, will,
priest, pope."[16]

The significance of these criticisms is that because Luther's
faith was nothing else but a personal commitment to the divine
promise of salvation apprehended in the Word and because it
was independent of the intermediate instrumentalities of the
sacramental-hierarchical institutions of the church, it must be
regarded as individualistic and subjectivistic.

What is here attacked is that feature of Protestantism which
is commonly referred to as the right of private judgment in
religion. While it is undeniable that the exercise of this right
by Protestants has sometimes led to religious individualism, it
cannot be granted to the Roman Catholic critics that this is
the inevitable consequence of the Protestant understanding
of the Christian faith. As it cannot be proved in the case of
Luther that he failed to be a "listener," so it cannot be convincingly shown that Protestant religiousness as a whole lacks
attentiveness to the objective reality and primacy of the divine
revelation. The Roman Catholic interpreters of Protestantism
identify all Christianity with their own ecclesiasticism to such
a degree that Protestant personalism appears to them as determined by an arbitrary unwillingness to submit to the divine
order. Thus they judge Protestantism to be nothing else but

an individualistic revolt against an authoritative divine order. They fail to do justice to the spirit of Protestantism which the English Congregationalist Dale well expressed in the following words: "The right of private judgment in religion, as the Reformers understood it, was not the right of every man to form a religion according to his own fancy, but the right of every man to listen for himself to the voice of God. In the Scriptures, which contain the record of divine revelation, there is an appeal to the whole human race. It is every man's right, it is every man's duty to consider that appeal for himself. . . . . It is to him that God speaks and neither bishop nor pope has the right to stand between him and God."[17] He concludes therefore: "The appeal which God makes is to me—directly to me; and if priests, or bishops, or synods, or councils, or popes, are guilty of thrusting themselves between me and my God, I revolt against their blasphemous pretensions. In Christ, God speaks to me, for myself I must listen to him. To listen to them instead of to *him* is a crime."[18]

The lines between Protestantism and Roman Catholicism are thus sharply drawn. What to Roman Catholics appears as a diminution of the fullness of Christianity, namely the Protestant rejection of priestly authority for the sake of a personal encounter between man and God, is for Protestants the guarantee of the freedom of Christian faith. The Roman Catholic suspicion that Protestant religiousness is individualistic is not justified. Upon closer examination, it turns out to be nothing else than an expression of their inability to understand the religious reasons for the Protestant opposition against clericalism and ecclesiastical authoritarianism.

IV

Another feature of the Roman Catholic charge that Protestantism is individualistic is the opinion, widely spread in Catholic literature, that while Roman Catholic Christianity is carried by the community of the church, Protestant Christianity lacks a dynamic communal character. Also this criticism does not do justice to the spirit of Protestantism. It, too, appears to be merely a biased statement of the fundamental difference between the two types of Christianity. For, from the beginning, Protestantism has interpreted the church preferably as the "fellowship of believers." Indeed, its greatest strength has been at all times that the local congregations which constitute the real church have been encouraged to develop their own communal life. Moreover, the vitality of this common life of Protestants has always been inspired by those motives to which Luther gave classical expression in his teaching of the universal priesthood of believers. This great doctrine that every believer is called upon by virtue of the faith that relates him to Christ to become a mediator of Christ, even a Christ, to his fellowmen has been actualized in personal Christian fellowships in all Protestant groups throughout the history of Protestantism. Indeed it is of the essence of Protestant Christianity that because it is impossible to be a Christian in solitariness, although becoming a Christian is an event taking place in the secrecy of the individual soul, the true mark of the Christian life is the fellowship of service and of mutual sharing.

Roman Catholics too like to speak of the priestly character of the Christian life. The Christian church is to them a community, a society, the members of which share in the priesthood of Christ and stand in a special relation to one another by virtue of this participation. But this doctrine cannot be regarded as the equivalent of the Protestant conception of the universal priesthood of believers. The priestly mutuality which Protestants are encouraged to practice is direct and immediate; every Christian relates himself personally to his fellow-believers and fellow-men. But the priestly mutuality as Roman Catholics conceive of it is indirect in so far as it cannot be actualized apart from dependence upon sacramental-hierarchical offices. The Protestant actualizes the priesthood of Christ by his own personal participation in the fellowship of love with his fellowmen, but the Roman Catholic cannot render the priesthood of Christ real except by submission to the authority of the hierarchical office through which he believes Christ's priesthood to function. For him the church is a priestly community, a universal priesthood, not because everyone of its members is called upon to be a priest to his fellows, but because no one can be a member of the church, unless he shares in the priesthood of Christ through the sacraments administered by the vicars of Christ. Professor Adam writes as follows: "The Church is the Kingdom of God thoroughly leavening all mankind in slow but irresistible process, the Body of Christ embracing the whole of fallen humanity in a supra-personal unity. Therefore of her nature, she rests upon faith in the divine Redeemer, in Christ. As the supra-personal unity of mankind, reunited to God, she obtains in Peter's office the perfect expression of this unity and its guarantee, while her inward life, with the living commerce which characterizes it, is realized in the Communion of Saints."[19] It is important to notice that the unity of the church is here characterized as of a "supra-personal" character brought to a focus in the papacy. The communal nature of the Roman Catholic Church is therefore of a special sort: it is that of a society in which some are set over others so that universal mutuality in the full sense can never really take place. This is well expressed in an Encyclical of Pope Pius X. He said: "The Church is the mystical Body of Christ, a body ruled by Pastors and Teachers, a society of men headed by rulers having full and perfect powers of governing, instructing and judging. It follows that this church is essentially an unequal society (!), that is to say, a society composed of two categories of persons; pastors and the flock; those who rank in the different degrees of the hierarchy and the multitude of the faithful; and these categories are so distinct in themselves that in the pastoral body alone reside the necessary right and authority to guide and direct all the members towards the goal of society. As for the multitude, it has no other right than that of allowing itself to be led, and, as a docile flock to follow its shepherds."[20]

In view of such a definition of the church, offered by the most authoritative spokesman of Roman Catholicism, the judgment of a Protestant that "in the Roman Communion, the Church vanishes and only a priesthood is left",[21] seems only slightly exaggerated. The following Protestant opinion, however, appears to be amply justified: "The trouble with traditional Catholicism in practice . . . is that the ordinary member has little opportunity of expressing his membership of the Church except through his attendance at Divine Service and his obedience to his pastors. Indeed, he is not so much a member of the Church through whom the lifeblood of the Church flows, as a person who derives his physical sustenance from the Church which appears to exist in some way independently of him."[22]

We conclude that the Roman Catholic judgment that the Protestant faith is unable to inspire a true communal life cannot be sustained. Indeed, by comparing Protestantism with Roman Catholicism we find that the nature of Protestantism is much more definitely social than that of Roman Catholicism. That Roman Catholics are at all able to characterize Protestantism as lacking a true drive toward community must be attributed again to their inability to conceive of any other form of the church but their own as a valid expression of the Christian life. Because of this tendency of theirs, they cannot see that Protestantism can actualize the communal nature of Christianity in a much better way than they can, in spite of the fact that they claim perfection for their own sacramental hierarchical society.

One might wish that this analysis of the difference between Roman Catholic and Protestant Christianity could be concluded by a discussion of the ways by which Roman Catholics and Protestants could become reconciled with one another. But it is not possible to suggest such ways. The spirit which moulds the life of each of these groups is not one and the same, although both bear the Christian name. Roman Catholics cannot but regard the Protestants as revolters from the divine institution of the sacramental hierarchical church, and Protestants must consider Roman Catholicism as a sect that sets itself apart from the rest of Christendom by demanding conformity with its own arbitrary absolutizations of certain historical Christian practices. The religiousness of Protestants is essentially dynamic because it is centralized only in ever new encounters of individual believers with the free, unbound work of God. The religiousness of Roman Catholics is essentially static, because it lives by the divine substance embodied in the sacred organism of the institutional church which is believed to be of divine origin and character. In so far as both Roman Catholics and Protestants are persuaded to depend upon the divine life made available to men in Jesus Christ, they seem to be related to one and the same source of religious inspiration. But the difference of their religious apprehension of Christ is so great that it is almost impossible to believe that it is the same lord whom they endeavor to worship. Yet because both Roman Catholics and Protestants profess that, in the last resort, they worship only God as he has revealed himself in Jesus Christ, there is hope that, at some time, the chasm that now separates them from one another may be closed. For it may happen that the lordship of Christ may so assert itself over them that they will surrender the historical practices and traditions which they now regard as essential to the proper service of Christ. The time when this will happen may never come. But Protestants and Roman Catholics may be certain that it will come at all only if as Christians they are willing continuously to re-examine all their faith, order, life and work in the light of the lordship of Christ. A mere preservation of Catholic traditions for the sake of avoiding the Protestant heresy and a mere continuation of the Protestant attitude for the sake of remaining undefiled by Roman Catholic sectarianism will only perpetuate the Catholic-Protestant conflict and prevent men who desire to be Christian from being true disciples of Jesus Christ.

Chapter 13

Protestant Faith and Religious Tolerance

O NE OF the greatest achievements of the democratic state is the establishment of religious tolerance or the freedom of religion. This fact confronts the church with an opportunity that it has not yet fully realized. It still has to perform important tasks in connection with religious liberty. This is due mainly to the fact that it was by political and not by ecclesiastical action that the practice of tolerance was secured. To be sure, the fathers of American democracy were influenced by Christian ideas and movements when they provided for the freedom of religion, but these represented radical minorities within Christendom and not the larger churches. Indeed, the major impetus toward tolerance came as a reaction against the practice of persecution of religious minorities by majorities and it was inspired by a view of religion that was critical of the traditional religious and social reasons for intolerance.

For centuries, political thinkers had been accustomed to the principle that no peace and concord could prevail in a state or commonwealth unless there existed among the people uniformity particularly in matters of faith. Until the end of the eighteenth century and the beginning of the nineteenth century all states were organized according to this requirement.

I

The Romans permitted a variety of religions to exist in their Empire, but they did not grant religious liberty. They required all their citizens and subjects to demonstrate the religious uniformity of the state by participation in the emperor-worship. Such groups as the Jews who on account of their monotheism were unable and unwilling to bow before the altars of the Roman deity, were given the privilege of being excused from the observance of the general rule. But this was not because their faith was regarded as universally valid, but because it was deemed to be the national religion of the Jewish race. The fact that the Jews were non-conformists and that as such they occupied a special place in society, led to the rise of popular mistrust of them. Because they were religiously set apart, they became the victims of prejudice.

The Christians, who were religious universalists and professed a faith that transcended all religions by a claim to truth that rendered other faiths untrue, were not recognized in the same way as the Jews were. When they refused to worship both Christ and Caesar, they were persecuted as enemies of the human race. From the reign of the Emperor Decius (which began in 248 when the millenial anniversary of the founding of Rome was celebrated), they were treated as outlaws who were said to endanger the very existence of the Roman state. But, after Constantine's "conversion," Christianity became the privileged religion of the Empire and, by the decree of the Emperor Theodosius in 380 it was made the official religion of the state. From then on, the insistence upon religious uniformity with the Christians was just as rigorous as it had been when the Christians were persecuted because of their non-conformity.

The founders of the medieval European national states followed the example of the ancients. They adopted Christianity as the official religion of their realms with the expectation thus to secure political unity. The Roman Catholic Church, which was organized according to the pattern of the Roman Empire and regarded itself—not without justification—as the heir and successor of Christian Roman imperialism, encouraged these tendencies. By the coronation of Charlemagne at the hands of Pope Leo III on Christmas Day, 800, the Holy Roman Empire was founded and the Roman Catholic uniformity of the German Empire was thus established. Throughout the Middle Ages, church and state co-operated in the maintenance of this uniformity, despite the fact that the popes and emperors were often in conflict with one another about their respective authority in Christendom and about the control of the church. Nonconformists were ruthlessly oppressed by ecclesiastical and political action. The Jews were tolerated as a non-Christian minority, but they were ostracised by being compelled to live apart from the Christians and did not enjoy political and civil privileges. When the towns and cities came into being, they were restricted to the ghettos. Popular resentment was easily aroused against them. Again and again they were the victims of persecution and of forcible conversion.

One of the greatest crimes was the doubt of the fundamental Christian dogmas. Such heresy was punishable by the severest of all penalties inflicted upon criminals—execution by being burned alive. When, in the late Middle Ages, anti-Trinitarianism made its appearance, it was regarded as atheism. As such, it was held to be the most dangerous of public crimes, because it implied that the foundation of the Christian religion and therefore the basis of the unity of Christian society and of its moral law and order were untrue. This opinion has exerted its influence even upon modern society. A wide-spread prejudice against the Unitarians is attributable to it. Moreover, the profession of atheism is still widely regarded as an act not only of religious but also of civil significance. Until comparatively recent times, an atheist could not serve as a witness in the courts because he could not swear an oath to God. The background of all this is the old tradition that religion, and specifically the Christian religion, is the guarantee of social unity. It is for the same reason, that anti-Semitism can again and again become a threat to the peace of society. In its modern form, it is fed by many springs of prejudice originating in historical, cultural and particularly economic judgments and attitudes of a great variety, but its deepest source is still the tradition that Christian uniformity is the basis of public concord. This tradition has long lost its actual validity, but its authority nevertheless persists in the subconsciousness of society.

Medieval religious uniformity received its death blow at the time of the Reformation. Although it was not the intention of the Reformers to destroy the unity of Christendom, they actually did so. A variety of Christian churches came into being. Even then the practice of religious intolerance persisted and primarily for social and political reasons. Because they themselves had to suffer persecution and public condemnation of various kinds and because they represented minorities in Christendom, the Reformers re-asserted the principle (which had never been absent from the Christian consciousness but had

never been made the basis of social action) that faith cannot be
coerced. Thus they came to advocate religious tolerance. But,
actually, they found no way of practicing it. For the conviction
still generally persisted that a state must be ordered in religious
uniformity. The states and communities in which the Reformation had been introduced were therefore unified by means of
the Protestant creeds and by the principle *"cuius regio, eius
religio,"* according to which the confession of the ruler determined the religious and creedal allegiance of his subjects. Non-
conformity was not tolerated. Those who found themselves
unable to accept the faith of the commonwealth were given the
privilege of emigration (this was the only method of granting
tolerance then deemed practicable). If they refused to avail
themselves of it and persisted in the open and public profession
of their non-conformist faith, they were treated as disturbers
of the peace and seditionists. Political considerations demanded
the adherence to the laws of religious uniformity and conformity.

But the fact that the terms of the Peace of Augsburg which
concluded the conflicts of the German Evangelical estates with
the Holy Roman Emperor and his Roman Catholic allies, provided for legal parity between the Roman Catholic and Evangelical territories of the German Empire, demonstrated the impossibility of absolute religious uniformity. A wedge had been
driven into the old tradition. It was inevitable that it would
break down more and more. One after the other of the European states was forced to acknowledge the actually prevailing
variety of different Christian confessions by the proclamation
of Acts of Tolerance and other laws. Efforts to restore the old
order caused the international conflict of the Thirty Years' War
or plunged individual states into civil wars; but the confessional
multiformity of Europe as a whole and of its individual states
could not be undone. Where economic prosperity assured political peace and allowed for a magnanimous treatment of individual tastes and opinions (in seventeenth century Holland, for
example), or where economic interests were foremost (in the
founding of the colony of Maryland by the Roman Catholic
Lord Calvert, for instance), the practice of tolerance was frankly
discouraged.

In the meantime, the advocacy of tolerance by non-con-

formist minorities and by Protestant radicals who developed a
new understanding of the religious life under the influence of
the Reformation, Humanism, and mysticism began to work a
change in the general atmosphere of religion. Their point of
view was supported by the mood of fatigue that followed upon
the religious wars of the seventeenth century. Soon thereafter,
the traditions of theological orthodoxy as they had been fostered by the various church groups, were criticized with ever
increasing effectiveness by the rationalist and empirical philosophies which arose under the impact of the humanistic and scientific impetus of the Renaissance. Ecclesiastical authoritarianism
in all forms was more and more discredited. The application of
reason and experiment to human experience resulted in the
new understanding of the world by natural science and history.
The Age of the Enlightenment dawned. Men declared their
emancipation from the authorities and traditions of the past
in the name of reason. They desired to accomplish rational
autonomy in all cultural endeavors. In the American and
French Revolutions these tendencies came to a dramatic expression. The political independence which was then achieved
entailed also religious freedom. The influence of these revolutions upon the whole Western world led gradually to the
abolition of the historical traditions of uniformity everywhere.

The Constitution of the United States declared religious
liberty primarily on the basis of the humanistic faith which inspired the making of American democracy. The fundamental
human rights which were established in the founding of the
republic implied that no religious test or profession should be
made the conditions of citizenship. This principle led also to
the separation of church and state. In some colonies it had
already been established previously to the Revolution, but in
other states of the new union, notably in New England, it was
introduced only in the nineteenth century and, indirectly at
least, under the impact of the Constitution.

Nevertheless, the founding fathers recognized that the republic of the United States was a Christian nation and they did
not intend to change this character. One reason why they specifically provided for the separation between church and state was
that only by such a separation they could deal justly with the
many Christian denominations organized in America, as none

could be given legal preference to another. Thus the fact of
Christian multiformity was officially acknowledged and the old
principle of religious uniformity was abolished.

In the course of the nineteenth century, constitutional government was established in all major states of the West. Many
of the principles of freedom, first realized in the American Constitution, were then introduced into practice. Foremost among
them was the principle of religious freedom. Conformity with
Christian creeds and confessions and religious conformity ceased
to be political requirements. Some churches continued to enjoy
a privileged status, largely on account of the power of the historical national traditions which they represented, but the citizens were granted religious freedom. The Jews were finally
emancipated and received civil rights.

What happened was that the modern state declared itself
religiously neutral. The importance of this event cannot be
overestimated. For it meant that the basis of political unity
ceased to be religious. To be sure, in most nations the older
tradition did not cease to be effective. Most western countries
continued to regard themselves as Christian nations—and they
still do. But ever increasingly they tended to maintain unity
by the appeal to non-religious principles. The outstanding one
was the purely political one of preserving the sovereignty of the
state, i.e., to maintain and, if possible, to increase its internal
and external power. In practice, appeal to this principle had the
effect that the state granted freedom to all activities of the citizens which did not interfere or conflict with the *raison d'état*.
In its relation to the churches and the religious groups, the state
tended to encourage them to contribute to the stability of public
morale, but it brooked no disregard of its sovereignity for religious reasons. In effect, therefore, its religious neutrality
amounted to the abandonment of the traditional principle of
securing political unity by religious conformity.

The need of social unity as the basis of political action continued to prevail, of course. It had to be met by new means. In
most cases, nationalism took the place of religious uniformity
and became a very potent force of social control. It was developed by a subtle cultivation of national history. The historical traditions of a nation or people, brought to light and kept

alive by modern historical research, were blended with the political ambitions of the rulers and the dominating political parties. Thus linked to history and constantly fed by historical study and writing as well as by the public celebration of the anniversaries of the great events of national history, western nationalism took the place of the older religious basis of social solidarity. It absorbed a great part of the Christian tradition. In fact, in most countries a "Christian nationalism" was permitted to develop. In the debates which accompanied the rivalry of the modern nations, the claims made in the name of this Christian nationalism were often challenged, but in the life of the individual nations the incongruity of the combination of Christian traditions and nationalist ambitions was seldom found to be disturbing. It is significant that this form of nationalism developed particularly in the predominantly Protestant countries. It found an entrance also into the life of the United States, although here it derived its strength from the "democratic faith," in which Christian and secular beliefs were blended, rather than from the Christian churches and their particular tradition. By virtue of this fact, American nationalism is strongly inbred with the spirit of democratic universalism and humanistic idealism.

At the present moment, the phenomenon of nationalism and of "Christian nationalism" in particular is found to be very disturbing all over the western world. For, in Germany, the Nazis fostered a nationalism for the purpose of sanctioning their aims of conquest and domination which they declared to be an end in itself. They endeavored to transform German nationalism into a religiousness which was to challenge all other religious faiths. They absolutized the nation and demanded that it be worshipped as a divine reality. Thereby they brought to the surface the ultimate implications of the modern principle of the sovereignty of the national state. Although, at first, they expected to deceive the churches concerning their true intentions, even hoping that the Christian forces of Germany could be made subservient to National-Socialist totalitarianism, they were finally forced (mostly by the resistance of the churches to the idolatry which the Nazi party imposed upon the German nation) to declare openly the irreconcilability of National Socialism and Christianity. Thus they compelled their opponents, not only in Germany but everywhere in the world, to a reconsideration of the nature of the social unity that must be presupposed in political action. The war against the Nazis was undertaken primarily in national self-defense and in the name of universal democratic rights. It aroused the nationalism of the various nations to a new pitch, thus forcing them into an absolutism of national sovereignty which, although different in kind from Nazi totalitarianism, was very similar to it in spirit. In the case of Great Britain and the United States, this nationalism was greatly tempered by the devotion to the cause of democracy and the defense of its freedoms. According to frequent statements of their leaders, they fought the war as "Christian" nations. This appeal to "Christian nationalism" was intended to arouse the memory of the Christian foundations of all national cultures in contrast to the Nazis' denial of them, but it referred primarily to the democratic faith which was largely identified with Christianity. The churches responded to this appeal only reluctantly. In the British countries and in America, they did not hesitate to declare that the defense of democracy was indeed their major concern, but they refused to admit that the public spirit on which the governments relied for the successful pursuit of the war-effort should be identified with the Christian faith. Thus they have been brought face to face with the question what part they must play in public life in view of the fact that Christian uniformity is no longer a requirement of citizenship and the basis of the exercise of political responsibility, while at the same time the drive for social unity in every political community is stronger than it ever was. This question cannot be answered without a consideration of the churches' reaction to the establishment of religious freedom (or tolerance) in the modern political world.

II

We have seen that the separation of the church from the state was primarily due to the initiative of the modern state and not of the church. To be sure, it could not have been effected without the strong influence of tendencies in the church that pointed to such a separation. Furthermore, the actual conditions of divisiveness within the churches made it inevitable that the freedom of religion was declared in connection

with the establishment of the democratic state. But the major
churches themselves did not exercise any really significant
leadership in order to bring all this about. Only the Protestant
minority groups greeted and hailed the establishment of religious tolerance because it ended the long struggle for freedom in which they had been engaged either in defense of
religious principles or on account of their minority position.

Thus it came about that the churches were compelled to
adjust themselves to the accomplished fact of the freedom of
religion. They were drawn into a complicated process of
change and reinterpretation which has been going on for almost
two centuries and is still shaping their lives.

Generally speaking, the churches related themselves to the
new situation by a new concept of the church in which the
independence of the church is asserted over against the independence of the state. It involves the abandonment of the
attempt to maintain a unified church and it also entails the mutual recognition by the churches of one another's rights to
exist. Denominationalism thus became the answer of Protestantism to the secularization of the state. In the work of the
formulation of a church concept adequate to this change, the
teachings of Humanists, Spiritualists, Anabaptists, and other
sectarians proved to be most effective. These groups which had
been exposed to the intolerance of the major church bodies
thus were given an influence upon the mind of modern Christianity of which their founders could never have dreamed.
The modern churches ceased to define themselves as God-ordered institutions of salvation. To be sure, many of them preserved the theological-ecclesiological traditions of the ancient
church, of Catholicism, and of classical Protestantism. But,
practically, these teachings lost their effectiveness. In agreement with the practice which the churches came to follow in
the exercise of their function within the modern political and
social community, a church was defined as a "religious corporation or association," represented first by local congregations and then by the organization of these in larger units.
The theory of John Locke, definitely inspired by English Independentism, furnished the pattern—not in the sense that
Locke directly determined the new interpretation of the church
but rather in the sense that the principle which he was one of

the first to articulate was actually adopted as the point of departure by all who concerned themselves with the formulation and the enactment of the new concept of the church. In his "Letters Concerning Toleration," he had defined the church as a "voluntary society of men" gathered for the purpose of worship and concerned for the salvation of their souls.

This conception of the church was to become increasingly effective. Although most church groups continued to adhere to ecclesiological doctrines based on the idea of the "one, holy, catholic church," they were compelled to recognize themselves in practice as churches ordered according to sociological principles. They began to understand themselves as products of historical forces and circumstances. The expansion of Protestantism in the United States of America and the rapidly growing influence of the American denominations upon world Protestantism produced a rapidly growing awareness of the actual divisiveness of the "church" and of its causes in relative human conditions.

When the modern state abandoned the principle of religious uniformity, it forced the church to reconsider its nature. One may say that when the churches learned to assess the significance of the fact that the state had declared itself neutral in the affairs of religion, they began to interpret the idea of the church in new terms. Instead of viewing themselves as embodiments of the catholic church, entitled to claim universal authority for themselves, they came to see themselves as historical societies of Christians who have still to accomplish the task of establishing a unity among themselves in common loyalty to the one Lord in whom they all believe. Catholicity which once had been the basis of ecclesiology, thus became the goal toward which ecclesiastical practices must be aimed.

The development of this church idea was very gradual and also very complicated, for it occurred in the context of the formation of so-called liberal theology. Indeed, it was one part of that radical re-thinking of the nature and truth of religion which was undertaken by the theological liberalism. Under the influence of modern philosophy and science and, generally, of the spirit of modern civilization, the theologians were led to criticize the norms by which the truth of Christianity had been traditionally affirmed. They showed that the absolute normativeness of the authority of Scripture, creeds, and ecclesiastical institutions could no longer be maintained in the light of the new philosophical and scientific criteria of knowledge. Furthermore, they undertook a historical, psychological, and sociological interpretation of the Christian tradition, thereby proving that what formerly had been regarded as supernatural, divine (and therefore indubitable) revelations had to be understood in terms of a historical development subject to changing and relative human decisions. Theological orthodoxy together with all its claims for authority was thus rendered untenable.

The acceptance of the tenets of liberal theology by the churches and their people was very slow and even in this day it is by no means general, although the influence of liberalism upon the life of the churches is much deeper than is commonly acknowledged. The main reasons for the gradualness of the growth of liberalism were the conservative character of most churches and the problematical nature of liberalism itself. The faith and order of the churches depended upon old traditions which could not be undone without destroying the ecclesiastical institutions themselves. Roman Catholicism most clearly exemplifies this fear of modernism. It has consistently barred it from its life in order to preserve the pre-liberal character of its faith and order. The Protestant churches did not possess the means for such a total exclusion of the spirit of liberalism, but many of them, particularly the older ones, endeavored to keep themselves immune from its influences. They were motivated not merely by traditionalism but also by a well-founded suspicion of the validity of the liberal interpretation of Christianity. This suspicion was often directed to the critical methods of liberal theology and to the historical understanding of Christianity which resulted therefrom. But this achievement of modern theology cannot be discredited. It must be regarded as final, although it is, of course, to be expected that, in the years to come, the historical character of the Christian religion will be further illuminated. However, the doubts that were cast upon the reinterpretation of the Christian message which liberalism claimed to derive from its treatment of Christian history were, as we now know, to a large extent justified. For liberalism tended to understand the Christian faith primarily in terms of human experience, either individual or social. On the basis of this assumption, it proceeded to relate it to the cultural ideals of modern man. Because these ideals were humanistic and inspired by the concern for freedom which had led modern man to emancipate himself from the authorities which he believed had been superimposed upon the life of his predecessors, Christianity was seen as an ally of the cause of human autonomy. But the fact is that while the heteronomous character of medieval Catholicism and of orthodox Protestantism cannat be defended as of the essence of the Christian faith itself, the interpretation of the Christian gospel in terms of human autonomy is also untenable. For the Christian gospel is not reconcilable either with a heteronomous authoritarianism or with an autonomous liberalism. It is truly received only by a prophetic apprehension which sees that the fulfilment of human life and the release of its true possibilities originate in the grace of God. This prophetic understanding of Christianity, according to which the freedom of man is grounded in obedience to God, may be called theonomous. As history shows, this prophetic Christian faith is capable of an alliance with the autonomous criticisms of all heteronomous authoritarianism but it is also able to align itself with those movements and tendencies that resist the interpretations of religion in terms of human autonomy. By virtue of this character of Christianity, the churches were able, in modern times, both to permit the criticism of their orthodox, authoritarian traditions in the name of liberalism and to preserve these traditions in self-defense against a humanistic misinterpretation of their faith.

With the help of this orientation, they may best be able to come to terms with the situation that is provided for them by the freedom of religion. For they may be enabled by it to avoid the practice of intolerance, which is quite irreconcilable with the spirit of democracy and, at the same time, they can steer clear of an attitude of tolerance which would render the demand for obedience to the lordship of God irrelevant. For a prophetic Christianity does not need to bind itself to certain historical forms of faith and order—to this extent it encourages the liberal criticism of historical traditions; but it must remain subject to the word of God—to this extent it must be bound to an authority which transcends all human apprehensions of it and is therefore not open to the change of human opinions.

III

In a society to whose members freedom of religion is guaranteed, there is no room for religious and ecclesiastical intolerance. If it is nevertheless practiced, either religious liberty or the religious body will ultimately be destroyed.

Roman Catholicism still preserves its old traditions and is therefore, in principle, intolerant. In countries where it possesses the following of a clear majority of the citizens (as for example, in some South American republics) it therefore prevents the full observance of religious liberty. In states where it represents a minority of the citizens, it is exposed to forces which constantly threaten its authoritarian claims. There it endeavors to protect itself from the pressures of change that inhere in democratic life by avoiding in the name of religion co-operation with other religious bodies. But this religious isolationism is impossibe in the long run. Various Protestant groups have had this experience. They tried to keep themselves immune from the impact of religious liberty upon their life by holding tenaciously to their traditions and by avoiding a co-operative encounter with other denominations. But they have found that it is impossible to stay aloof from the democratic environment in which religious liberty thrives. They were compelled not merely to claim the benefits of the freedom of religion for themselves but to acknowledge that these benefits belong also to other groups. Thus they were led to relate themselves to them.

The establishment of religious liberty makes for denominationalism but also for interdenominationalism. On the one hand, it encourages religious divisiveness, because every religious group is given the opportunity freely to develop itself. Yet on the other hand, it puts the various religious movements into such a proximity to one another that an exchange, not only of members but also of work in a common cause, become inevitable.

Such has been the experience of the Protestant churches in the United States. Religious liberty has fostered the divisiveness of American Protestantism. There now exists among us a pluralism of churches each pursuing its own course and engaging in a rivalry with other churches. Many of them are on principle intolerant toward one another and only live up to the

rules of religious liberty by reducing the tendencies of intolerance to such an extent that their relationship with other groups
is that of a truce between combatants. But, at the same time,
there has grown up a spirit of co-operation between American
churches which has found very concrete expression in common
enterprises. The Federal Council of the Churches of Christ in
America, to which most large denominations belong, is the
chief exponent of this interdenominationalism. It encourages
a constant collaboration of the churches in practical church
work. Moreover its influence upon the common life is such
that it represents the unity of Protestantism in the very midst
of its divisiveness. Its power will grow in the years that lie
ahead. The churches will more and more relate themselves to
one another not only in co-operative enterprises but also in
mutual interpenetration. During the past decades, many unions
of church bodies have taken place. Old divisions of denominational families have been healed by reunion and new bodies
of churches have been created by the merger of denominations
of similar background and outlook. This process will probably
grow in extent. However, one must recognize that the historical
differences between the major church groups are such that they
cannot all be united with one another. It is not even desirable
that they should form one single body. But under the power
of the interrelationship which religious liberty makes possible
they will increasingly learn not to absolutize their respective
historical differences but to expose themselves to one another
out of the awareness that each in its own way bears witness to
the same religious message of salvation. Thus they will come
to recognize the relative nature of the differences that separate
them from each other. In this connection the spirit of liberalism
will determine their lives and the modernization which has
taken place in the whole of western civilization and which
already has been effected in those sections of Christendom that
have opened themselves to liberalism will envelop all of its
parts. At this moment it is inconceivable that Roman Catholicism can be drawn into this process, but we may expect Protestantism to be shaped by it more and more thoroughly.

If this anticipation is correct, it will be of utmost importance that the spirit of prophetic Christianity be kept alive.
For the danger will arise that the reduction or the relativization

of the differences between the Protestant groups will promote an attitude of indifference toward the distinctive character of the Christian faith. Such an attitude is now already widespread among the large number of those who have become alienated from the churches, chiefly under the influence of modern secular education and of modern secular philosophies of life. Many church members, particularly those of the so-called intelligentsia, have been affected by the same mood.

Indifference and religious faith exclude each other. If, therefore, the broadening of outlook which the practice of tolerance induces, because it stimulates the desire of mutual understanding, should lead to religious indifference, the churches would die. They would not only lose their identity, but they would also be deprived of the strength that alone can keep them alive, namely a faith that knows what it is committed to. A commitment to God involving an absolute allegiance which nevertheless allows for the recognition of the relative character of religious practices, is implied in that Christian faith which we have called prophetic or theonomous. Such a faith is aware of the fragmentary nature and the inadequacy of all human apprehensions of God, but is upheld by a power that is derived from the divine itself. It expresses itself in the spirit of repentance, i.e., in the willingness of the believer not only to seek renewal from God but also to rethink and to reform all the ways by which he is obedient to God's will. Prophetic Christianity relativizes the forms of the Christian life out of the concern for the lordship, the sovereignty of God. It, therefore, calls for a religious reformation inspired by the concern for the purity of the gospel.

The norms by which this purity can be achieved are out of the reach of human decisions or decrees. They have to be furnished by the divine inspiration which breaks and shatters all arbitrary human absolutizations and which possesses only the men of humility.

We thus come to the conclusion that the establishment of religious liberty in modern democracy is offering to the churches the opportunity to realize what the Reformation movements of Christian history intended: the liberation of the gospel of God from the incrustations of human traditions. As long as religious uniformity was regarded as the precondition of social political unity, a full religious reformation in this sense was actually impossible. But freedom of religion has opened the doors not only to tolerance of men toward one another but also to the work of a reformation of the churches by an unencumbered obedience to the word of God.

If the churches will learn to respond to this challenge of prophetic Christianity, they will experience an increase in spiritual power that will exceed the strength they once enjoyed by virtue of the practice of religious conformity and uniformity. It will also enable them to inspire democracy with the resources by means of which a true community of free men can be built.

The opportunity that is offered to the American churches is tremendous. If they avail themselves of the benefits which democracy has bestowed upon them and if they fulfil the obligations toward democracy which the Christian gospel imposes upon them, they will be able to open to European Christendom the vision toward a Christian social order for which it longs, and they will deepen the American democratic faith—perhaps with the help of the Christian spirit which the Europeans have rediscovered during the war years, so that the freedom of democracy may be extended into all realms of human endeavor.

CHAPTER 14

Protestantism and Democracy

MODERN *political democracy* is that system of government in which those who fulfill the duties and responsibilities of government are elected to their offices by the free vote of the citizens of the republic, remaining always subject to the consent of the governed. All decisions of national policy are reached by free discussion in which all citizens of the country are represented. This representation is secured by universal suffrage, protected by the secret ballot and kept flexible by freedom of speech, press and assembly. Parliamentary debate clarifies the issues and the divergent wishes of the several elements of the citizenry, thus providing a basis for national policy.[1]

In the United States of America, the operation of democracy in politics is dependent not only upon the Constitution as the fundamental law of the land but also upon the practice of *social democracy*. On the basis of the principle that all men are entitled to the inalienable rights of life, liberty and the pursuit of happiness, because they are created equal, equality of opportunity is extended to all not only in political matters, but also in the cultural and economic spheres. By means of universal education, every member of the community is given the opportunity to share in the cultural life; and social legislation is such that all have an equal opportunity, according to their abilities, to make economic advancement.

I

This democracy is the result of a long historical tradition. It is rooted in Graeco-Roman civilization, in Hebrew prophetism, and in early Christian universalism. From Stoic philosophy and ethics, it has learned a view of human life based on moral individualism and humanistic universalism. From the Hebrew

212

prophets, it has derived its passion for universal justice and for the rights of the downtrodden and the underprivileged. By early Christianity it has been inspired with the faith in the dignity of each individual human soul and in the unity of all men in the love of God.

These roots were kept alive in the long history of western Christian civilization in ancient and medieval times, although they were embedded in social and political orders that were far from being democratic. As a matter of fact, modern democracy is the expression of a reaction against the feudalist-ecclesiastical civilization of the Middle Ages and against the absolutism of the modern political state which took the place of medieval feudalist imperialism. It is the political phase of the destruction of the sacramental-hierarchical authoritarianism of the medieval papacy by the Reformation, and it is the chief expression of the achievement of the autonomy of man in the civilization of the so-called Enlightenment, in which the cultural beginnings made by the Renaissance were fulfilled.

From the Reformation and from Protestant Christianity democracy derived many a major impetus. The *Lutheran* doctrine of the universal priesthood of all believers resulted not only in a Christian morality which encouraged every individual Christian to practice the virtues of faith and love in the concrete circumstances of life, but also in an ecclesiastical polity of congregationalism. Indeed, the democratic principle of church organization according to which each local congregation has the right, under the headship of Christ, to organize its own affairs by autonomous decision is one of the chief fruits of the Reformation. By the *Congregationalists* and other like-minded groups, particularly the *Baptists,* it was realized first in England and then fully in America. The congregational church polity of New England Puritans served as the pattern for the New England town-meetings and became thus one of the chief sources of American democracy. It also contributed much to the realization of freedom of local church congregations in the life of most protestant denominations and thus to the actualization of democracy in church life.

To *Calvinism* democracy is especially indebted primarily because the Calvinist form of Protestantism, begun in the republican environment of Geneva, was developed by way of reaction against political and religious tyranny in France, Holland, Scotland and also England.

It was of equal significance for democracy that Calvin inspired all his followers with the conviction that the sovereign God, the glorification of whose name is the chief end of man, rules the universe by the instrument of his law and that he governs the affairs of men by the law which is revealed in the Bible. This teaching (followed by Presbyterians and Puritans and introduced, though somewhat modified, also into Anglicanism by Richard Hooker, the author of "The Laws of Ecclesiastical Polity") served as a guide for the regulation of church affairs wherever Calvinism prospered. It also became the principle which the fathers of modern constitutional law and the first protagonists of the idea of the social contract (e.g. Althusius, Grotius, and Locke) transmitted to democratic thought and practice.

To the *Anabaptists* and the sectarians of the Reformation democracy owes the passion for freedom of faith and thought. They suffered persecution at the hands of Protestants and Catholics, because their faith did not permit them to conform to the principle of religious uniformity without which, according to common belief, no state could preserve the peace. Their testimony has been confirmed by the practice of modern democracy, especially in America, where most of the descendants of the Anabaptists, still true to the faith of their fathers, finally found refuge and also the opportunity to make their religion count in the common life.

Thus we see that the major movements of the Reformation made decisive contributions to modern democracy. We can go farther and assert that American democracy in particular is inconceivable without the impact of the various Protestant groups and denominations upon it. The Congregationalists have stood for social freedom and education for all; the Quakers have demonstrated the sanctity of conscience and the service of love; the Baptists have been intrepid defenders of the liberty of the individual and of tolerance; the Presbyterians have developed procedures of freedom by their emphasis upon law and order; the Methodists, grown strong on the frontier, have proclaimed the doctrine of the free individual in conjunction with the preaching of the universalism of the forgiveness of sins. Thus they have all added to the strength of the democratic life.

II

It can therefore not be doubted that democracy has Christian roots. Yet its greatest strength was derived from sources which, although they were fed by the Christian religion, are not primarily Christian. The most vital mainsprings of modern democracy are the teachings of the Rationalists of the 17th and 18th centuries. The founding fathers of American democracy were led by the persuasion (classically expressed in the writings of John Locke and Thomas Jefferson) that because men as reasonable beings are created free and equal, they must have the right to determine the nature of the political government and the society in which they live. This persuasion was derived from the philosophy of rationalism according to which man's life will be fulfilled if his reasonable capacities are set free, so that they can determine all human enterprises. Because the universe operates according to a pre-established harmony of reason, the release and unfettered practice of human autonomy on the basis of reason will demonstrate in the end the attainment of a perfect human life. For, within the limits of reason, the perfectibility of man can be actualized and freedom in the name of reason must therefore be made the basis of human progress.

This philosophy was used to justify the American and French revolutions and it has furnished the principles for all realizations of democracy accomplished since then. It was particularly significant that the creative power of this view of man and the universe was demonstrated not only in the abolition of political tyranny, but also in man's conquest of nature by science and in the development of the capitalistic economy of free enterprise. Indeed, the extension of the scientific method to all phases of life and the production of economic wealth by the capitalistic exploitation of natural resources have been the chief contributors to the democratic process. These rationalistic principles were understood by their advocates in such a way that they were seen to embody the long humanistic tradition which had been begun by the ancients and had been sheltered by

Christianity throughout its history. The philosophy of democracy could therefore also be stated in moral and religious terms. It was then presented as the expression of the belief in the spiritual equality and brotherhood of all men. Its spokesmen have always claimed that everyone shall share in its processes regardless of creed, race, social position or circumstances.

Thus interpreted, democracy as it actually developed in America could be related to the democratic tendencies that had been fostered by the various Protestant groups. As American democracy gradually took its form under definite political, social and economic circumstances, that do not need to be discussed here, it could not claim to be the product of the dynamics of the Christian religion or any of its churches, but it could—and was—held to be reconcilable with the tenets of the Christian faith and particularly with the social ideals of the Protestant groups that dominated the early American scene. As a matter of fact, American democracy and American Protestantism grew up together and mutually influenced each other. In consequence of this fact, American democracy has today a character of its own that sets it apart from other democratic systems and forms of life, and American Protestantism too is marked by traits characteristically American that distinguish it from Protestant groups in other lands.

The proof of this "Americanism" is furnished by the "democratic faith" that pervades all American life. It is the chief result of the syncretism of the various forces that have played upon American democracy in the course of its history. It is marked by an awareness of the many historical roots from which democracy, as it is known today, has grown. It is the faith that holds Americans together whether they are believers or unbelievers; Christians or humanists; Protestants, Catholics or Jews. Whether they are of European or African descent, it binds them to one another. It is proclaimed to the world in the political pronouncements of our leaders; it is presupposed in political speeches; it is taught in the schools and in the forums of adult education; it is preached from the pulpits of the churches, particularly on national holidays. Its greatest symbol, revered by all—statesmen, politicians, teachers, preachers—is Abraham Lincoln.

The basic affirmation of this democratic faith is that all

human existence is ordered in a moral law and that man is endowed with a conscience with which to apprehend it. Human society and government must therefore be organized according to the demands of universal justice and right and all persons must be treated as moral agents who can be held responsible for their acts, having the dignity of moral sovereignty. It is the trust of this faith that if in all human affairs room is given to the sway of the moral law, the "law of nature," or the "law of reason," the life of society will be filled with the harmony of cooperation and good will. It believes in a kind of cosmic constitutionalism of the golden rule and it finds support for this belief in the age-old human concern for equality and fairness. Emerson gave expression to this faith in the following statement in which the moral spirit of Graeco-Roman humanism, Hebrew prophetism and Christian love is summed up for the believer and practitioner of democracy: "Whenever a man has come to this state of mind that there is no church for him but his believing prayer; no Constitution but his dealing well and justly with his neighbor; no Constitution but his invincible will to do right—then certain aids and allies will promptly appear; for the constitution of the Universe is on his side."[2]

This sentiment points to the second doctrine of the democratic faith: life is good and right, if it is freed from the fetters of conformity to institutional authority; the individual must be given freedom. Then he will yield to the demands of his moral conscience and secure his human dignity in social responsibility. By developing the virtue of neighborliness, he will preserve his own independence and at the same time concern himself for the rights of his fellow-men. He will constantly improve himself intellectually and morally and by thus seeking education and civilization, he will not only reach maturity for himself, but share in the life of his fellows and together with them advance toward a better world.

This democratic faith imbues all Americans who have made it their own, with a sense of mission. The "American spirit," which takes the place of the nationalism of the European nations, must be made to pervade the whole life of the United States and it must willingly come to the rescue of human aspirations toward liberty and justice everywhere in the world. For the destiny of Americans is to make their own nation a strong and mighty citadel of the good life and to lead all mankind to that freedom which by divine providence was first planted on the American continent.

It cannot be doubted that this democratic faith has been the deepest concern of responsible Americans throughout the history of the nation. It was the chief spiritual issue of the Revolutionary War; it was confirmed by the abolition of slavery as the outcome of the Civil War; it inspired American fighting men to participation in the First World War; it has been the chief reason for the entry of the United States into the Second World War.

I am not trying to make the point that every phase of American life has been guided by the moral idealism of the democratic faith. The pages of American history are filled with records of the inhumanity of men toward men. America has grown to be what it is today not primarily because Americans have always defended the cause of right and justice, but because they engaged in a mighty struggle to exploit the riches of a virgin continent endowed with seemingly inexhaustible national resources. The search for profit and economic advantage and power has so determined Americans that the wealth which they have gathered and which is now the chief support of their power in the world has been paid for with the suppression of the weak by the strong, with the selfish maintenance of advantage and privilege to the detriment of the poor and the disinherited, with the injustice of the ruling classes toward the economically dependent. Tyranny, graft, cruelty and violence and all other social vices have moulded American life as they have determined other societies. But, nevertheless, American democracy in its political and social form would not be what it is today, if the struggle for power, which undoubtedly has shaped American life, had not always been opposed and hampered by the loyalty of believing Americans to the tenets of the democratic faith.

What I have said about the great American wars and the moral idealism that inspired men to make the great sacrifices that war always entails, is true in spite of the fact that those wars were caused by motives that were not identical with the moral issues which were secured by the victories. The War of Independence was a revolt of the American colonists against the English crown, unleashed by the desire of the colonists to reap and hold the products of their land for their own advantage. The Civil War was a conflict of the industrial North against the agrarian South and its issues were primarily economic on both sides. America became involved in the First World War when her economic advantage demanded it. The Second World War became America's conflict when the balance of power in the world was threatened with the possibility of a change to her political and economic disadvantage. The triumphs which America achieved at each occasion were exploited for the sake of the increase of selfish political and economic power. And yet they also procured the advancement of liberty, justice and good in the world, because the spokesmen and advocates of American democratic faith saw to it that their cause was not suppressed but kept high as a challenge to the attainment of ends greater than mere success of selfish will and strength.

The actualization of democracy never took place except in the presence of forces that, if left unchecked, could have destroyed the cause of human freedom. The historical process in which democracy has developed was never determined merely by factors friendly to democratic good. Indeed, the very allies of democracy, without whose help it would not have triumphed, were often undemocratic powers, and they threaten democracy even today. American democracy would not be what it is without the wars in which it has been engaged—yet war is the greatest social evil; its weapons are so terrible that they can engulf the victor and the vanquished in destruction. Modern democracy would not have developed if the drive of capitalism had not given it strength—yet the profit motive makes for economic inequalities that prevent the freedom and equality of all men. Democracy is the accomplishment of white men of Northern European stock and particularly the Anglo-Saxons—yet the supremacy of white over colored men and the imperialistic desires of Anglo-Saxons threaten to destroy not only the inter-racial and inter-national democratic community of the United States but also the confidence in democracy in lands abroad. American democracy is the product and privilege of pioneers who conquered, tamed and civilized a continent, making it the land of the free, while transplanting to it the mores of their home lands all over the earth—yet it is beset with the danger of selfish isolationism and exclusive nationalism.

In view of these facts the cynic is inclined to regard democratic faith merely as the trappings of the quest for political and economic power. Selfish men have often acted in terms of such cynicism. It is also possible to accuse the defenders of democracy of hypocrisy and cant, because they claim to fight for moral right while they actually seek domination over others for themselves. Skeptical men have often judged democracy in this way. Furthermore, the moralism of democratic faith can be understood as the weakness of unrealism. The foes of democracy have dealth with it according to this view. But democracy has never actually turned out to be merely dishonest, hypocritical or weak, despite the fact that in the course of its history and in the present it has existed and does exist under conditions that it rejects on principle.

The fact is that democracy as it prevails today is not perfect and that, in actual performance, it lags far behind the professions made by the 'democratic faith' and the hopes entertained by it. It is the danger of the democratic faith as it is held by many of its proponents, that it identifies the ideal with fact and, particularly, that it permits itself by moral enthusiasm and passion to be driven into a moralism which is belied by the actual attainments of men as well as by their moral possibilities.

III

It is in this connection that the relationship between democracy and the Christian faith becomes important. For the Christian faith is of such a character that it does not identify human accomplishment or fortune with the truth or untruth of what it believes in. It makes a distinction between believer and belief, between human devotion to truth and truth itself, between man and God. To be sure, this distinction must not be understood as a separation as if believing were irrelevant for what is believed and as if what man does or fails to do in the name of God were irrelevant for God. No human love is without the spark of divine love, but divine love so far transcends human love, that no human love can really be the proof of divine love. For this reason, Christianity is not moralistic or humanistic despite the fact that it is the source of human striving for moral goodness. It is an ethical religion but it does not identify the moral life with salvation. That is why it is not moralistic.

In this respect, it is superior to the democratic faith. It is historically closely connected with democracy, as we have seen, but it is not identical with it. Christianity and democracy are not the same, although democracy must be judged to be that social-political order which is most akin to the spirit of the Christian religion. The historical connection between Christianity and the development of democracy must not be absolutized, as if Christianity had fulfilled itself in contributing to the making of democracy or as if democracy could usher in the kingdom of God.

Christians have often spoken in that vein. Mark Hopkins was so sure of the moral progress of mankind under the banner of democracy that he was persuaded of the proximity of the fulfillment of life which the seers of the Bible had prophesied for the end of the world. "Sooner or late," he said,[3] "the time must come, when the evils which now provoke the vengeance of heaven and curse humanity shall come to an end. Wars and intemperance, and licentiousness and fraud and slavery and all oppression shall cease." Such a conviction, so we must judge, could not but inspire the democratic faith and action, but it was absolutist and therefore unrealistic. Yet it identified Christian and democratic faith.

The following statement of Bishop Lawrence is still more emphatic in its identification of the ways of democracy with the Christian religion, and it is open to the criticism that it interprets Christianity as a gospel of wealth. He wrote: "In the long run, it is only to the man of morality that wealth comes. We believe in the harmony of God's universe. We know that it is only by working along His laws natural and spiritual that we can work with efficiency. Only by working along the lines of right thinking and right living can the secrets and wealth of nature be revealed. . . . Godliness is in league with riches. . . . Material prosperity is helping to make the national character sweeter, more joyous, more unselfish, more Christlike."[4]

Even Walter Rauschenbusch thought that Christianity and democracy were the same. He believed that the "social gospel" of which he was one of the chief advocates, would bring about the realization of the Kingdom of God by democratic action.

"The social gospel," he wrote, "is the religious reaction to the advent of democracy. It seeks to put the democratic spirit, which the church inherited from Jesus and the prophets, once more in control of the institutions and teachings of the church."[5]

These statements, which may be regarded as representative of many others by Christian spokesmen of all denominations, are characteristic of the democratic faith rather than of Christianity. They must be criticized in the light of the judgment that while the Christian religion encourages the democratic faith, it is not identical with it.

Christianity believes in the goodness of life. Its faith in God the Creator testifies to that. For by worshipping God as the creator it gives expression to the confidence that what ought to be—beauty, truth, goodness, love—can be made real in the circumstances of life, for God, the source of all goodness, has made "the heaven and the earth!" Christianity also believes in the ultimate victory of goodness. Its faith in God the Savior bears witness to that. For by worshipping God as the savior it gives expression to the sure hope that what ought to be—beauty, truth, goodness, love—will be fulfilled in the concrete conditions of existence, for God, the giver of every good and perfect gift, has been incarnate in Jesus Christ, his "Word," and all who believe in him have the "holy Spirit" and "sanctifier."

This faith, that life is created good and that goodness will triumph in it, is not the same as that held by the democratic faith, for it presupposes and implies that life as it now is, between creation and salvation, is marred and disturbed—by sin and evil. The Christian faith holds that the world, which by the will of God is full of potential good, is a fallen world and that, even by the will of God, it will be redeemed from imperfection, if the sin as the cause of its fallenness will be acknowledged and overcome. By thus recognizing the reality of sin in the world, Christianity is prevented from sharing the immediate and direct optimistic confidence in the goodness of life which is characteristic of the democratic faith. It too is ultimately optimistic, but its understanding of man is such that it sees him as a sinner who violates the laws of the good God and is in need of redemption. So great is its persuasion of the reality of sin and of the power of sin in human life, that it regards even the Christian, who believes that his sins are forgiven and that he has the promise of divine forgiveness, as one who is still a sinner, a man not yet perfect but, by the grace of God, set on the road to perfection. The Christian understanding of life can be summed up in this sentence: No man is so good that there is no evil in him; and no man is so bad that there is no hope for him.

Christianity reckons with evil, although it believes in the victory of good. For this reason, it is critical of the humanistic faith which attributes to man an innate goodness. It professes that life will be sanctified only through the forgiveness of God. It rejects therefore the humanistic faith which affirms that life grows into goodness by evolution, development and nurture. It interprets life as a conflict between man and God, a battle that begins in man's ever new rebellion against God caused by his aspirations to Godlikeness and that ends in God's victory over man by humbling him. For this reason, it cannot hold the "cosmic constitutionalism" of an Emerson who proclaimed the support of the universe of men's every expression of good will.

Christianity is suspicious of human autonomy. Its view is that man is free, i.e. that he is able to make decisions concerning his life and that he is responsible for his actions, but that he is not the master of his fate nor the captain of his soul. He is free to determine himself according to the determination of God but not according to himself, or even according to the dictates of his reason and his conscience. In order to be able to realize his freedom under the determination of God, he must be reborn. Only by the Holy Spirit, by which he is made a new creature through repentance, forgiveness and sanctification, can he live according to God's will. There is no immediate continuity between man and God. The true goodness of life must be released through the crisis of rebirth; it cannot be realized by the cultivation of man's natural capacities. The view that goodness will be made to reign in human existence, if the restraints of heteronomous authority are removed from individual persons, is too simple. To be sure, human experience is warped, if it is enslaved to tyranny or any arbitrary authority, but neither is it truly free if it is liberated from such subjection. For what appears to be true liberty because it is liberty from tyranny is not really the liberty of realizable good. Whenever man is thrown upon himself, he is bound to be himself. His major concern then is self-maintenance. Even though he may be willing to grant to others what he desires for himself, he is not able to break the shackles of his egocentricity.

If he believes that a "law of nature" is operative in all free beings which enables them to maintain their individual freedom and to live in the mutuality of equity, he deceives himself. The "natural law" which in its highest form prescribes the golden rule that one should do unto others what he would have them do unto him, is not fulfilled by the recognition of its validity or even its desirability. As a matter of fact, the free, autonomous man who acknowledges his obligation to this law of equity, is compelled to admit that he does actually not conform to it. Man is such that he does not do what he knows he ought to do. The Kantian slogan *"Du kannst was du sollst"* is not borne out by experience, although the view of human nature which it expresses has guided the humanists of all history. Their affirmation of the validity of the morality of "natural law" has led them to attack and to destroy tyrannies and other forms of domination by arbitrary authority, but it has not really enabled them to actualize the good life of equity and mutuality. The spokesmen of "natural law" have been the revolutionaries who have unbound the human quest for the good life. This has been their great contribution to civilization, but it has not brought about the actualization of the good life.

The history of "natural law" also shows that the universal acknowledgment of its validity has often been used in order to justify conditions of power which actually perpetuated inequity. Again and again, power and privilege, slavery, the inequality of races, the superiority of the male over the female sex, etc. have been defended in the name of "natural law." This was an abuse of its sanctity, but this abuse shows that allegiance to "natural law" is not necessarily the same as its actualization. Furthermore, it can be shown that what men of different times and circumstances conceived this law to be is as diverse as the historical conditions under which they lived. Although the meaning of "natural law" was always seen to consist in granting everyone his own in equity, mutuality, benevolence and good will, the actions performed in its name have been of such a variety that these definitions must be considered as generalizations which have no consistency in fact. Men use the freedom which they have achieved by the defense of the goodness of all, in order to acquire power for themselves. That is why "natural law" does not guarantee the realization of the good life. It is, at best, an instrument of criticism by which the inequalities of society can be laid bare. It is a road-sign but not the power to travel the road.

In all this, the strength and the weakness of democracy is indicated. For democracy, and particularly the democratic faith which supports the democracy of the United States, bears all the characteristics of "natural law." In so far as it is grounded in the claim of universal human capacities for goodness, it is subject to the criticism which must be directed against "natural law." Democracy, even if it is inspired by "democratic faith," has actually never accomplished what it professes to aim at. It too is, at best, a society that criticizes itself in the name of what it ought to be and thus opens itself to the possibilities of reconstruction that inhere in critical thinking. But the power for the deed of reconstruction must be derived from sources which democracy as we know it probably takes for granted but does not actually acknowledge in its basic philosophy, constitution, or faith.

This power is proclaimed in the Christian gospel. It offers the good news of the divine forgiveness of sins which implies not only the possibility of a new start in life for the sinner and a break with his past, but also the bestowal upon him of the renewal by grace. Faith in the forgiving love of God expresses itself in the forgiving love of man. Wherever it is actualized, a new community comes into being: the church, the communion of believers, the fellowship of love. This communion becomes the divine instrument by which goodness is made an event. The goodness realized in the fellowship of love is born of the transformation of the self, of unselfish giving and self-sacrifice. It is derived from a power that transcends the "natural" possibilities of man. It is of the Holy Spirit not of his own spirit. It makes man truly free, because it liberates him from the bonds of selfishness and self-sufficiency, thus really enabling him to do the good for its own sake.

Yet this never becomes the experience of anyone apart from a concern for the moral law. The law and the gospel are related to one another. What is demanded by the law is fulfilled by the gospel. The law is the call to the good life; the gospel opens the door to it. What morality envisages becomes an event in the deeds of love. For the gospel transcends the law but it does not suspend it.

The law to which the Christian gospel is related is the morality of the Decalogue, of the prophets, of the Golden Rule, of the universal humanism of Stoic "natural law." Indeed, it is the morality of that law by which democracy is constituted and the life of that humanism which the spokesmen of the "democratic faith' proclaim. It is that moral law which is addressed to the "free" man of individual responsibility, the law of the man who has attained to human dignity by living according to his own conscience. It is to this man that this Christian gospel directs the judgment that he is actually unable to realize the good life by the moralism of his freedom, because he is a sinner. It is to this man, who has accomplished "humanity" by binding himself to the universal moral law, that it shows the better way of the grace of divine love.

Democracy is then related to Christianity, the fellowship of love, in the same way in which the law is related to the gospel. Or, we can also say, what the Old Testament means for the New Testament, democracy means for Christianity. The freedom of the gospel is given to him who has sought in vain to find freedom by the law; salvation by grace is not the same as salvation by works.

Democracy as the system of government and the society of morally free men who acknowledge no higher law than that of the universal morality of men held together by the bonds of equality, liberty and fraternity cannot bring about the fulfillment of the good life. It is the highest achievement of the humanity of man. But it is still subject to the power of evil that inheres in the selfishness of men. Democrats who believe in the innate goodness of man are liable to have a great disillusionment. The only power of goodness by which democracy can live is the love that the Christian gospel proclaims. For the Christian religion contains not only an understanding of the tensions in which the highest human morality becomes involved (an understanding of which the moralist himself is incapable),

but it also knows a way by which these tensions can be overcome, so that the good life may be fulfilled.

Christianity is a higher order of life than democracy. It is
as much higher than democracy as the fellowship of love is a
better way than the moral community of free men.

It is probable that the power of the Christian life in democracy is much greater than is commonly acknowledged.
The strength given to democracy from its Christian roots will be
found to be much greater than the power that is bestowed upon
it by the rationalistic humanism which is primarily affirmed in
the "democratic faith." However this may be, Christianity is
not irrelevant for demoracy, for it furnishes it not only with a
criticism really competent to judge the moral life, but also with
the power by which its true intentions can be realized.

In order to render this service to democracy, it is necessary
for Christianity to be loyal to its own faith. The Christian gospel of forgiveness in which the morality of law is transcended
must be kept pure, and the fellowship of love must be actualized by Christian believers. This is a task which must ever
anew be set before the eyes of Christians and which they must
fulfill with ever fresh devotion. For the Christian churches and
instiutions as they actually are have permitted the gospel and
its fellowship to become deformed by many lesser concerns and
considerations. As we have seen, their tendency in America
is to identify the way of the gospel with that of the law, to
embrace a moralism which refuses to be humbled and trans-
figured by the mercy of God, and to propound as Christian
the salvation by good words which the humanism of the democratic faith has written upon its banner. If the Christian church
would listen to the gospel and make room for it in its own life,
it would assume fully the mission which, despite its imperfections, it has at least partially always undertaken—the mission
of calling upon democracy to live up to its own program, of
judging its failures, and of transforming its moral aspirations
by bringing them under the sway of the sovereignty of God.
Thus Christianity would lead mankind through democracy to
the good life of God.

Part III

Liberalism

CHAPTER 15

The Central Question in the Mind of Contemporary Protestants

T HE temper of contemporary Protestantism is characterized by the predominance of theological questions. All over the world people are inquiring for the meaning of human existence in the light of their religious inheritance. The reasons for this orientation of Protestant thinking are not far to seek. They are inherent in the human situation in the present world. The World Wars and the continuous political and social-economic unrest that have followed in their train have laid bare a deep crisis in Western civilization. The threat of war, which has arisen again and again over the common life; the economic insecurity which has shattered the foundations of human existence everywhere; and the horrible explosion of the new war, can no longer be understood as more or less regular events in the cycle of political and economic life, as such disturbances were formerly interpreted, but they must be taken as signs of the fact that cultural principles, upon which Western civilization has rested, have lost their binding power. All over the world people have therefore been driven to ask for the meaning of human life. Such questioning is essentially religious in character.

The concentration upon theological issues which has resulted from this demand is further enhanced by the fact that the church itself is drawn into the maelstrom of uncertainty and skepticism that marks the crisis of civilization. Movements and attitudes generally described under the name of secularism are attacking not only the church as the organized form of Christianity but the Christian religion as such. Social-political movements like Communism and National-Socialism have pursued a policy of religious persecution, and large and powerful groups within Western culture have shown an indifference to the church, sometimes to the point of hostility. These attacks have forced the church into a position of defense, compelling it to examine its inner character and the validity of its message.

The present discussion of the nature of the Christian faith is thus distinguished from similar discussions in the history of modern Christianity by the fact that it is based upon a realization of Christianity's precarious position in the modern world. The church has become aware of the fact that Christianity can no longer be considered as the universally recognized and accepted religious attitude of Western men. While Christian ideas are woven into the fabric of Western civilization so that they dominate the life of every one of its members, whether he knows it or not, they are no longer consciously regarded as authoritative by all. The position of Christianity in the Western world is still strong enough to prevent the rise of a new religion that might demand universal recognition, but the Christian churches know that they represent one group and not the whole of the common life. Every day the possibility becomes plainer that, as in the era of its beginning, Christianity may again become the religious concern of a minority group within civilization.

Such a possibility does not necessarily imply that Christianity may have to maintain itself over against religious indifference or even irreligiousness. It may rather be that the Christian church will become one among several religious concerns of Western man. For already today large groups in the populations of all lands have declared their independence from the church not on account of non-religiousness but because they have been attracted to other forms of religious life. These may not be unchristian, but in organization, manner of worship, and even thought, they are different from the forms which have developed within the Christian movement. There is a widespread extra-ecclesiastical Christian religiousness that is characterized by considerable instability because of its formlessness and inarticulateness. But the ways of religious life that attract men outside of the church are chiefly (1) a religious individualism, which carves its thought and practice out of the variety of religious notions and traditions, preferably mysticism, and (2) Humanism, which, dependent upon its ancestors since the era of ancient civilization, confines its religious interest to ideals of human living apart from a concern for ultimate and universal questions of a metaphysical sort. The types of Humanism which have proved attractive to the contemporaries of our era assume many forms. Their range extends from the bourgeois philosophy of life, which consists of an abstraction of moral ideals from the Jewish-Christian tradition and is represented by the mores of the "Babbits" of all capitalistic-commercial social orders, to the various ways of reviving the human ideal of Graeco-Roman classicism, particularly Stoicism. But also the partly sceptical, partly religious, ideals that are expressed in the nationalist-racial world-views of National Socialism and Fascism and in the class-conscious social-revolutionary philosophy of Marxism and Communism are forms of Humanism.

The re-thinking of the Christian faith which is demanded today of Christian leaders, clergymen and laymen alike, must be oriented to this remarkable defection of innumerable modern men from the tenets of Christianity. At any rate, it must be given on the basis of the questions addressed to Christianity which are implied in these various forms of more or less intentionally non-Christian, or at least unecclesiastical, attitudes.

Such a task is tremendously complicated by the fact that the Christian church itself and particularly Protestantism have contributed to the cultural development out of which this dilemma has emerged. Many of the conflicts which beset the life of modern society and many of the attitudes of its members which cause anguish and difficulty to the churches could not have come into being without the changes which Protestantism effected in Western civilization. It is therefore impossible to achieve a clarification of the Christian faith without a full awareness of the historical participation of Protestantism in the growth of modern civilization.

Some salient aspects of this interdependence of Protestantism and modern civilization may be described as follows:

(1) The Reformation is rightfully regarded not only as the beginning of Protestantism but also of modern civilization. It not only produced those forms of Christian life, worship, and thought by which the evangelical churches set themselves apart from and in contrast to the sacramental-hierarchical institutionalism of Roman Catholicism, but it also liberated the cultural

life from the domination of the unifying "Christian" control, represented and symbolized throughout the Middle Ages by the papacy.

It never was the intention of the reformers to emancipate the secular life from the Christian church. On the contrary, they strove to build a Christian social order which was to fulfil what, in their opinion, the medieval church had failed to achieve. But actually their defiance of papal authority made the beginning of the emancipation of the secular cultural life from the church and Christian guidance which today is so largely an accomplished fact. The Reformation had little in common with the movement of the Renaissance, of which it was a contemporary. Indeed it was hostile to its ardent and enthusiastic "this-worldliness." But as the reformers could not but make use of its humanistic learning, their descendants could not prevent its secular cultural forces from spreading throughout the Western world on the basis of the breakdown of the medieval religious authority which the Reformation had effected.

The classical example of this strange affinity between the secularism of the Renaissance and the prophetic spiritualism of early Protestantism is the development of the commercial profit-system. There is no *inner* connection between the growth of Protestantism and the rise of Capitalism. As a matter of fact, the reformers were opposed to the new commercialism for religious-moral reasons. But it is nevertheless an indubitable fact, not only that capitalism spread primarily in those countries that had embraced Protestantism, but also that as soon as the Protestant moral virtues became separated from their religious basis, they began to enhance the spirit of capitalism. This early unintentional alliance has been perpetuated throughout the modern centuries with the result that, today, in the minds of many, Protestant Christianity and capitalistic economy are inseparable from each other.

Or, to give another example, which shows the same paradoxical relationship between the Reformation and the spirit of modern civilization emanating from the Renaissance: It was far from Luther's mind to assert a subjective religious experience over against the authority of the Roman Catholic church. He became a reformer, because he put the authority of the biblical word against the authority of the pope. That a subjective religious individualism was not his chief concern is indicated by his hostility toward the evangelical spiritualists and enthusiasts of his day who derived from his movement the right to interpret the Christian religion in terms of personal religious experience apart from the primacy of Scriptural authority. But nevertheless, the relentless dependence upon the voice of conscience which had caused him to grow dissatisfied with the means of salvation offered by the sacramental-hierarchical church and which enabled him to defy the thrones of empire and papacy clearly exhibits a reliance upon inner human resources that is not foreign to the autonomous humanistic spirit of the Renaissance. It is not surprising that it has inspired many forms of individualism which have marked the progress of modern civilization.

The Reformation, by which Protestantism has been guided throughout its history, thus injected into modern life many of those features which today challenge Protestantism and cause it to participate in the cultural crisis.

(2) The Reformation caused the division of the Christian movement in many ecclesiastical groups. To be sure, the creeds and orders of the early Protestant churches, particularly Lutheranism, Calvinism, and Anglicanism, were devised with the claim that they represented the only true expression of the Christian faith. But their common contrast to Roman Catholicism and their understanding of the Christian religion as a free encounter of the believing man with the gospel inspired them, from the beginning, with the ideals of the freedom of conscience and of tolerance. Although the inner and outer condition of early Protestantism rendered a realization of these ideals impossible, they were ineradicably infused in the Protestant mind. After the confessional wars and conflicts of the sixteenth and seventeenth centuries, they asserted themselves with full force. While in the interests of self-preservation, the major groups of Protestantism closed themselves as much as possible to the effects of tolerance, new denominations and sects opened themselves fully to them. However, the most important step in this direction was taken by the political governments, when, since the eighteenth century, they began to separate the state from the church, rendering impossible the domination of the political and social life by one church to the exclusion of another.

The rivalry of the Christian groups against one another

continued, indeed it prevails to this day, but they became inevitably imbued with the effects of practiced religious tolerance. Not only the observation that good citizenship does not depend upon membership in a certain religious group but also the inevitable interpenetration of various Christian denominations and other religious groups within the social-political community have caused the rise of the feeling that the creeds and orders of the various Christian groups are not absolute but historically selective embodiments of the Christian faith.

The economic and cultural interdependence of recent times has entailed the abandonment of religious uniformity in all social orders. Christianity has thus definitely become one among many religious possibilities for modern man. The task of defining the Christian gospel for our times can therefore be pursued only with the recognition of the actuality of religious multiformity. For Protestantism this task is of special concern because it has vitally contributed to the rise of tolerance.

(3) The most significant aspect of the inter-relationship between Protestantism and modern civilization is represented by the effect of modern intellectual culture upon the Christian religion. The development of modern scientific and historical knowledge and the practical application thereof in technological industrialism have completely transformed the environment in which the Christian religion has to live. Not only man's relation to nature and the universe but also his position in society have been so rapidly changed that, in many respects, the historical church has lost touch with the times. To many a citizen of the metropolitan mass who, often beyond the limits of individual decision and personal choice, stands in a largely depersonalized, vast system of technological economics and legalistic politics, subject to an economic and political fate over which he can exercise only a minimum of control, the church has become a historical relic. If he does not ignore it, he considers it as a source of consolation and inspiration, from which, in times of crisis, he may derive a spiritual comfort for the solace of his soul, often without the possibility, however, of welding the religious insight that he has obtained into his actions within the world of struggle for economic survival. He comes to depend more and more upon the leadership provided by political and economic authorities, even in his needs for relaxation and spiritual edification.

The change of living, most directly expressed by the spread of mechanical devices in all areas of human existence, has been so fast that the church has been unable to measure the effect upon itself. Particularly its form of worship has not been adequate to the mood of modern living. Adjustments and reforms have been attempted, to be sure, but the full depth of the realm of life that is represented by the connection between religion and technics, has hardly been fathomed. No less difficult are the problems of social ethics which await the church's solution. Although it has become aware of them, as is indicated by the "social gospel" movement, it has not grappled with the issues of the modern social order except by efforts to extend the traditional Christian morality into the sphere of modern social living.

The full weight of the impact of modern civilization upon the church has been felt by theology. As the theologians began to subject the traditions of the church, and particularly the theological ones, to the scrutiny of historical critical investigations, they were forced to recognize that the norms of faith and the creeds upon which the various groups within the Christian movement relied were the result of an encounter of the Christian faith with the minds of historical cultures.

The theologians were the first to realize that many of these fruits of Christian history must be returned to history because they could be of no direct use to Christians of a rapidly changing, totally new cultural outlook. The official bodies and the lay-people in the churches refused to recognize this necessity and many still persist in the refusal. But facts speak for themselves: The results of the research in the history of Christianity from the time of its beginning until the present time cannot be undone. The process by which the institutions of the church have become what they are cannot be ignored by a refusal to accept well attested historical facts. Moreover, the inability of an ever-increasing number of Christians to understand the traditional forms of their faith and the incapacity even of trained clergymen to comprehend the historical dogmas of the church clearly indicate that the modern cultural consciousness in which the present Christian faith must express itself is separated by a deep chasm from the cultural moods of the past that have endowed the traditions of the church. To cite some examples: The doctrines of the Virgin Birth, of the trinity of the Godhead, of the two natures of Christ, of the atonement by the blood of Jesus Christ, of justification, of the literal inspiration of the Bible, are fully comprehensible only to experts in the history of doctrine. To others they are either sacred parts of a tradition that must be accepted with uncomprehending submissiveness or meaningless remains of the historical past.

Modern theology deserves to be praised for its attempts to restate the Christian faith in terms of the modern world-consciousness and for its efforts to recast the meaning of theological tradition, obtained by critical historical understanding, in forms adequate to modern philosophical, scientific, sociological, psychological knowledge. However, it is its tragedy that it has never succeeded in stating the faith for modern times in a widely accepted authoritative manner and that it has failed to impose upon the churches the necessity of stating their faith for the present day in ways which would accomplish for today what their founders by creeds, confessions, catechisms, church-orders, discipines, platforms, and iturgies had achieved for themselves and their children. Because of this failure, present-day Protestantism interprets itself in a multiplicity of theological forms, old and new, unable with a clear voice to answer the question of the uncertain, disillusioned modern mass-man and of the bewildered Christian preacher or layman: What is the faith? The task of defining the Christian gospel for today is therefore beset by the tremendous difficulty that no traditions of the past can be taken for granted and that the modern interpretations of Christianity are of a confusing variety.

The task of clarifying the Christian faith is therefore beset by grave inner difficulties which have resulted from the inner development of the Christian religion within modern civilization. The person who, bewildered by the events in the present world, looks to religion as the source from which he hopes to derive a clear call to a meaningful existence cannot ultimately avoid the insight that religion itself is entangled in the complexities of life through which to steer his mind he seeks guidance. A realistic self-examination of the faith must take account of this condition. This is why the present turn of Protestant thought to theological questions is so radically different from any other, earlier attempts to render the voice of religion clear and pure by a fundamental examination of its message.

II

It is possible to indicate more closely the nature of the theological questions that burden the mind of Protestantism. The central issue of the contemporary theological problem has been brought to the attention of thoughtful observers of the present scene by the inner and outer disturbances inflicted upon the Christian churches by the Nazi movement. The events that have been happening in Germany during these last decades deserve close searching from all responsible contemporaries of our era.

Many and perhaps the most characteristic features of National Socialism were due to the revolutionary visions and stratagems of its leaders. Others cannot be understood except in the perspective of German history. But many of the problems which confront the Germans of today belong not to them alone, but to the whole civilization of which the Germans too are a part. These problems are common to a large part of the world because they reflect the difficulties of the world order in so far as it is basically determined by the development of the capitalistic system in conjunction with the nationalistic, imperialistic politics of the big powers. Everywhere, this development is characterized by the extension of technology and mechanization into all spheres of life, by the growth of the social processes of urbanization and internationalization, by the subjection of individual destinies to the demands and changes of the economic order, by the rise of the totalitarian power of the state and the threat of international and civil wars which it implies. The life of men has been dragged down to the existence of mass-men.

The man of our era is thus compelled to give up the privilege to make personal decisions concerning his life and to become dependent on those who happen to be charged with the leadership in politics and economics. This surrender is all the more tragic because even the leaders must often subject their initiative to the requirements of the economic and political systems in which they move. Civilization has thus become deeply beset by the danger of dehumanization: man, the builder of civilization, is threatened with the loss of freedom. He stands to lose that endowment which, in so far as it enables him to make decisions concerning his fate and his environment, distinguishes him from all other creatures and is thus the agent of his humanity.

The trend here described has manifested itself most dangerously in Germany. By the war it has been openly extended to other lands. But it has been latent in the life of the entire world for a long time.

Its further implications for human history can be understood by the following considerations: Throughout history the right use of freedom has been man's most important concern. The growth of freedom has therefore justly been regarded as the primary achievement of human culture. Because the right use of freedom is essentially determined by the standards or the sets of values which must guide man in his decisions, this most characteristically human of human concerns has always been religious in nature. For, in the last resort, it is religion which provides man with that sense of the meaning of life from which he derives the norms in accord with which he can exercise his freedom.

Whosoever recognizes the trend toward dehumanization as the main danger of modern civilization must, therefore, hold that the crisis of our life is essentially religious. He will not be surprised to find that the fascist and communist movements of our day have tried to establish new religious sanctions for the institutions and measures which they have initiated. He is thus confronted with an astonishing paradoxial phenomenon: these movements which dramatically represent the trend toward the destruction of human freedom and therefore of the religious norms without which this freedom cannot be, have set up religious standards of reference by which they try to justify themselves before their followers. These new religious ideologies are either artificial or borrowed from old traditions. Their very character is such that the appeal they make will hardly be a lasting one. That they have arisen at all is an indication of the fact that man cannot live without an orientation to religious values. Hence even movements which destroy human freedom and thereby ultimately undo the possibility of human living in the true sense produce religious sanctions of a sort, in order thus to justify themselves before the court

of the conscience of humanity or at least before the tribunal
of the human self-consciousness of its own members.

The position of the Christian religion in these developments is of high importance. Because Christianity has hitherto
furnished the religious motives to Western civilization, the future of Western civilization will be determined by the ability
of the Christian religion to inject its motivating power into
the present situation, and the future of Christianity will strongly depend upon the train of events within Western civilization.
The destiny of Christianity in Germany has therefore a grave
import for the future of the Western world as a whole and not
only for the future of Germany. That the development of the
German churches during recent years has been so closely
watched and that it has received attention even from people
apparently not primarily interested in organized religion is an
indication of the fact that the seriousness of these implications
is generally recognized. It must be said also in this connection
that the events in Germany are largely determined by pecu-
liarly German circumstances. Nevertheless, universally valid
conclusions can be drawn from the reaction of German Christianity to National Socialism.

We shall, therefore, analyze briefly the situation of Protestantism in Germany under the Nazis in order to raise the question whether it may not contain a significant clue to the
understanding of Protestantism in the present world situation.

One can distinguish three groups within recent German
Protestantism. The first one consisted of those who felt that
the church should continue its work by confining itself as
much as possible to its own specific task of providing spiritual
guidance to all who sought it and could be reached. It was
believed that the church could not avoid taking cognizance of
the tremendous changes which had taken place within the
common life and that it could not expect to remain unaffected
by them. But the primary concern of the church, so it was
felt, should be for the maintenance of its own specific task.
It should not be directed to a change in the world situation by
the impact of the Christian gospel. The members of this group
came from various traditions and they desired to stay within
them, loyally rendering them effective in their personal lives.

One must not underestimate the significance of the attitude

of this group, much as one may deplore it for political or cultural or religious reasons. It is an attitude which has been taken by innumerable Christians, clergymen and laymen alike, during the crises that the church has had to endure in the past. It has preserved Christianity until our day and it will assure the continuity of the Christian religion also in times to come. Furthermore, in many respects, it represents the only practical course which can be taken in most actual situations. However, if all Christians had chosen this course in earlier historical days of conflict, Christianity would hardly have become that historically transforming spiritual power it has proved to be.

And indeed, there was a second group of Protestants in Germany which chose to put the church in relation to the political and social order of National Socialism. One should not doubt that many of the much maligned "German Christians" were not merely fanatical Nazis but earnest and sincere men and women who felt that it was the church's duty to come to terms with the cultural environment in which it happened to live so that it could serve the people in a realistic way. They acted from the conviction that Christianity would not have survived the many stages of civilization through which it has passed if it had not found ways of adjusting itself to the social, political, and cultural conditions of its environment.

The price demanded of the so-called "German Christians" for their co-ordination of Protestantism to National Socialism was high. They had to accept not only the hypertrophied nationalism and militarism of the Nazi government, but also the ruthless dictatorial rule of the party which dominated all actions of this government. They had to come to terms with the insane "racial myth" and its terrible consequence—Antisemitism. They had to consent to a radical change (if not surrender) of the Christian principle of universalism. They had to submit to the domination of the inner and outer life of the church by emphatically secular authorities and give up that Christian principle of organization which since New Testament times has been recognized in some measure by every type of Christian church—namely the right of the individual local congregation to have some voice in the regulation of its affairs. They even agreed to eliminate from Christian worship some symbols which, throughout the ages and throughout all lands, have expressed the unique character of the Christian religion. They attempted to interpret the Christian gospel not only in terms of the Bible and its historic interpretations but also and especially in the light of the emergence of the National Socialist party which they regarded as a decisive revelatory act of the God of Jesus Christ in history. To many inside and outside of Germany this policy and outlook of the "German Christians" appeared as a betrayal of the Christian religion. To render Christianity contemporary with such a movement as National Socialism seemed to be equivalent to the rejection of the very essence of the Christian faith. The degradation of the Christian religion to a means of religious ornamentation of an anti-Christian political-cultural party was regarded as a symptom of the mortal illness of Protestantism.

A third group chose a course opposite to that of the "German Christians." The "confessional synods" and brotherhoods heroically defended the spiritual independence of the Christian church. It is wrong to consider them as organizations which, in the name of religion, protested against the general policies of the Nazi regime. A great majority of their members probably had no quarrel with the political principles of Hitler and his party. Their major concern was the freedom of the Protestant church. In order to maintain the purity of the Christian gospel, they barricaded themselves in the fortress of the Bible and the writings and creeds of the Reformation. In the course of their fight, which brought many close to martyrdom, they developed a religion that was a revival of sixteenth century Protestantism. To many of them Luther and Calvin and the orthodox interpreters of the classical Protestant creeds spoke as if they were their own contemporaries. In their struggle for an undefiled Christianity, they were not able to forge spiritual and theological weapons fully adequate for the twentieth century and its atheistic, anti-Christian mass-movements. While they have gloriously upheld the super-temporal freedom and the super-historical majesty of the Christian gospel, they have not been able to relate it to the present day. They have not, perhaps I must go so far as to say: they *could* not make it truly contemporaneous.

Here, then, is the dilemma of German Protestantism: all major groups were confronted by the same pressing question:

What is the Christian gospel for today? In the last resort, each one of them was unable to answer it satisfactorily and effectively. One group tried to ignore the question as much as possible by pressing the perpetual tasks of the Christian church. Another group so ardently identified itself with Germany's "today" that it lost the possibility of preserving the Christian part of the Christian gospel. A third group defended the specific character of the Christian gospel in its Protestant understanding by resuscitating the historical forms of Protestantism belonging to the sixteenth century but found itself unable really to proclaim the gospel to the men of today.

Have we who live in a land which has not known the contortions of political, economic, and cultural life represented by National Socialism, an answer to the question: What is the Christian faith for today? I think that it will be generally admitted that we have not. The problem of relating Christianity to a cultural life largely secular and barren of the dimension of depth is also *our* unsolved problem. The difficulty to actualize the Christian ethos in the technological, mechanical civilization of the modern mass-men is also *our* difficulty. The search for those theological and liturgical forms of the Christian faith which would communicate the truth of the Christian gospel to our contemporaries is also *our* search. In view of this community of seeking, it is highly significant that we should regard the struggles of German Protestantism as a conflict in which we, too, are involved—in another way.

For the question: What is the Christian gospel for today? is the central problem of present Protestant thought. Wherever Protestants are engaged in a re-thinking of their faith they inquire for the form of Christianity which will render its gospel contemporaneous. It is the coming test of Protestant faith whether this inquiry will lead to a positive, constructive end. A way must be found to convey the Christian faith—no other faith and no deformed Christian gospel—to the man of today, who lives in a world that threatens to make him a mass-man.

Must we wait for a new Reformation? It may well be that we are members of a pre-reformation age. Perhaps only those who come after us will be able to reform the church so that the Christian powers of salvation are related to the realities of modern civilization. But as members of a generation belonging to a pre-reformation age, it behooves us to be clear-sighted about the problems that are to be solved. Even if we are merely engaged in the task of diagnosing our troubles (which often seems a vain undertaking because we may not be able to prescribe a cure), we are fulfilling a true historical responsibility.

CHAPTER 16

The Outlook for Religion

W E HAVE become so accustomed to refer generally to "religion" that we are apt to forget that religion is believed in and lived by men who find themselves in concrete cultural situations. Religion is always historical. This observation leads directly to the discovery of the first factor by which the outlook for religion must be determined. It depends upon the cultural conditions in which we find ourselves. The future of Protestant Christianity is closely linked to the fate and destiny of that phase of western civilization of which it is an inherent part.

The recognition of this interrelation at once brings to mind what lately has been the subject of a good deal of public discussion, namely, the outlook for capitalist or bourgeois, middle-class civilization. No one will deny that Protestantism is closely connected with this civilization and that its own future will be shaped by what is to happen to bourgeois culture. If we were to characterize the spirit of this culture by a single word, we should not go wrong in choosing the word "autonomy". The modern world is what it is because it has cultivated and practised the doctrine of the self-determination of man. It is the autonomous mind which has called "modern" philosophy into being, has produced "modern" science, has given the drive to "modern" economics and constantly nourished the spirit of capitalism, has caused the "modern" inventions to be made, and has created and sustained the political democracies. The "Age of Reason" and the "Age of the Machine" are closely connected with each other. The discussion of the problem whether this modern civilization is the outgrowth of the Protestant Reformation has not yet come to an end, but one fact is certain, that Protestantism as an ecclesiastical movement is to-day closely allied to this modern culture. And it is equally certain that, if modern Protestantism has entered into alliance with the "modern spirit," the Reformation belongs to a totally different world from ours. To be sure, attempts have been made to find the source of modern individualism in the teachings of the Reformers, but such attempts have been insufficient to explain the origin of the spirit of autonomy. There is nothing of this spirit discoverable in the Reformation. For the spirit of the modern world is surely not qualified by that disturbing God-consciousness which inspired the Protestant Revolution. As a matter of fact, capitalist or bourgeois or middle-class society represents a growing lack of religious consciousness, if by this we mean a consciousness of the eternal, or an awareness, as Kierkegaard called it, of the qualitative difference between time and eternity. The spirit of modern society is the spirit of temporal self-sufficiency. It rests in itself. It has no faith in a transcendental meaning for existence. It does not hope for the eternal life. Its eschatology is wrapped up in the values of freedom, happiness, immortality, perfectibility, progress.

To-day, this civilization finds itself in a crisis—a crisis which has been advancing since the end of the last century, which came to full expression in the wake of the First World War, and which is now engulfing all parts of the earth touched by the western mind. The fundamental character of our civilization is evident in the bewildering absence of unifying purpose; and its tragedy is revealed by the apparent futility of all efforts, through organization, to achieve the desired unity. The methods of re-organization which we see applied in almost all realms of human endeavour are doomed to failure as long as they spring not from the root of new, healthy thought, but only from the pressing awareness of a great need. The process of reconstruction must therefore be very slow, for we are only beginning to see new and truly productive tendencies emerging in the various fields of human enterprise.

These tendencies are evident, none the less, to those who will look for them. Philosophy, which for so long a time has permitted itself to be reduced to the positivistic discipline of the classification of knowledge or has consumed its best powers in the endless and often futile discussion of the theory of knowledge, is rediscovering the challenge of metaphysics and devoting itself again to the principles which must underlie the totality of existences in this universe. The natural sciences have also outgrown their period of positivistic research. Finality has departed from their findings; and their further progress is assured by their concern for the metaphysical problems which developments in their own midst have forced upon them. The sciences of history and literature are gradually rising above the level of the recording and analysing of facts to the stage of interpreting and understanding them from a universal viewpoint. Psychology and sociology are following the same trend. They are outgrowing their mechanistic methods, fashioned from the natural sciences, are realizing their duty in respect of philosophical interpretation, and are developing special methods for the analysis and understanding of the respective functions of the human mind and of society.

In the realm of art, significant beginnings of a new era are indicated by the fact that Naturalism, Impressionism, and Expressionism are giving place to a new Realism in which artistic form is again being made the means by which life is interpreted by the artist to the observer. This change is most apparent in the realm of painting. In literature the emergence of the philosophical novel or drama is significant.

The politically-minded person is becoming concerned over the problem of the State, and is discovering that its functions should be more than the mere maintenance of order and adjustment within an autonomous society whose members freely pursue the end of acquisitiveness and private happiness. The moral obligation of the State to maintain values higher than organization, co-ordination, and representation is now being discussed, the while the merits of the typically modern constitutional form of democracy are being weighed.

In connection with the present political debates social questions are being approached from fresh points of view. A great moral passion is gradually accumulating against the evils of an acquisitive, individualistic, automistic, brutally imperialistic society, whose formerly glorified virtue of tolerance now appears as a sham for indifference toward the moral obligations of social unity and social justice.

Western mankind is slowly becoming aware of the forces of disintegration which beset a society which has submitted too radically to the attractive lures of the spirit of liberation, inherent in the law of the autonomy of man. And we are now coming to recognize that we must bear the burdens of our times as true and honest contemporaries of our own era. It is not therefore in a spirit of defeat and pessimism that we observe our civilization in the state of crisis and dissolution but in a spirit of courage and even with a will to hasten the process; for out of the old we see a new order rising. We recognize the signs of our time, and we deeply know that if we are to work the works of God in our time, our concern for the progress of man must be deepened, purified, and sanctified by a new obedience to the laws of an eternal world which transcends time.

With this conclusion we are led to the insight that the crisis of modern civilization is religious in nature. To be sure, many do not admit such a diagnosis. Joseph Wood Krutch, and before him Bertrand Russell, profoundly impressed as they were by the power of the modern spirit and its break with old traditions, and yet deeply disturbed by its emptiness, could only express their reactions in agnosticism and stoic pessimism. Their analyses, I believe, are only too true, and if they are met on their own ground almost irrefutable. But their attitude toward the facts which they so keenly analyse does not rise to the highest level. They shrink from entering the temple of religious devotion; they remain spectators who review the scenes of the life about them without actively engaging themselves in it. Their arguments can be met only on the basis of a religious devotion which is perpetually concerned with the search for the meaningful life and which solves the perennial problem, "How Live?", with its practical and positive answer to the deepest of all questions, "Why live?" We may say that our cultural crisis is religious in nature because, as we have seen, in all realms of human endeavour where the crisis is felt, the question "Why?" is being asked. Usually it is answered in a metaphysical manner, but the way from metaphysical probability to religious certitude and affirmation is not long. The principles of being and meaning which the metaphysician asserts are easily transformed into affirmations of faith that give content to religious worship. For it is characteristic of the religious spirit that it daringly assumes the truth of the highest values which constitute the meaning of existence, and inspires man to live adven-

turously in supreme devotion to them. It bids man halt before
the mystery of existence, fills his whole being with a sense of
the awe of it, makes him embrace it with fascinated and daring
love, and thus gives his life indescribable richness and strength.
It is this spirit which sceptics like Krutch lack. For this reason
men of his type are not fully representative of our age, which,
like so many other critical periods in the history of mankind,
when the end of the road of development seemingly had been
reached and the future appeared uncertain, is an age of religious yearning.

Now once more the time is fulfilled and the Church is challenged to live up to its destiny. Is it capable of fulfilling its
task? The answer of this question will definitely determine
the outlook for religion.

First of all, and gladly, we can state that wide sections of
the Protestant Church have become truly contemporary. The
great theological movements of Liberalism and Modernism
have compelled it to recognize new fields of duties toward the
modern age. The tremendous work of the historical criticism
of Christian tradition has returned to history what belongs to
history. Thereby the liberal school has given us understanding
and perspective. In that sense, the church of the future must
and will be liberal. The group of Christians whom we call
modernists have taught us to accept the challenge of the modern
day and, free from the authority of tradition, have begun to
interpret Christianity in terms of the requirements of modern
life and knowledge. In so far as modernism leads us to the
concrete duty of taking our own historical situation seriously,
the church of the future must be Modernist. With the help of
the critical methods of theological liberalism and of the constructive attempts of Christian Modernism, we are charged to
build a Protestant Christianity which cultivates *Wirklichkeits-
religion*.

The recognition of this task forces us to reject the programs which are associated with the reactionary groups of
Orthodoxy and Fundamentalism. It impels us also to avoid the
course of those schools which recommend the revival of powerful, positive movements of the past. We must not and cannot
become Neo-Thomists, and we must beware of a mere Luther-
Renaissance. Nor are we permitted to follow the leadership of

Karl Barth and his friends when they call upon us to submit to a theological authority which is composed of the elements of ecclesiastical tradition. We discern in all these movements the frantic and sometimes desperate effort to avoid the terrific responsibilities of true contemporaneousness. They try to substitute programs and formulas which were once adequate, for the new creations for which a new age calls.

And yet few of us will be insensitive to the appeal of these reactionary tendencies. They are not blind tendencies. The reason they react so violently to the mind of liberal and modernist Protestantism is because they sense in it a weakness of religious conviction which they would never tolerate or exchange for the positive certainties they themselves enjoy. And it must be admitted that modern Protestantism has liberated itself from the chains of a dead past with the sacrifice of religious conviction. It is not fair to declare that modern Protestantism since Schleiermacher has betrayed the Christian cause, but it would be fair and honest to say that it has undertaken an adjustment to the spirit of the modern age which, in these days of the crisis of that age, finds it without a positive message. It could not be otherwise. The methods by which the emancipation from antiquated authority and tradition was effected were furnished by the same spirit which brought about the sickness and tragedy of modern culture. Religion, too, became subject to the law of autonomy. The word of God was replaced by the experience of man, submission to the revelation of a supernatural, miraculous Sacred History by the adventure of experimentation with human ideals. Opposition to the heteronomy of ecclesiastical authority and of absolutized dogmas and doctrines of historical origin and temporal validity often carries in itself the refusal to accept the theonomous character of true religion.

The religious man can never be autonomous. The spirit of devotion which lives in his soul implies the worship of one greater than himself. It thrives on submission to the revelation of the divine; it recognizes gladly that there are factors and aspects of life which transcend the control of man. God is the unconditioned ground of all conditioned existence. He transcends all we are and have, and lives therefore in a light no man can approach unto. And yet He is nearer to us than breath-

ing because without Him we would not and could not live.
Faith in Him is therefore directly opposed to the spirit of
autonomy. It precludes the possibility of man's self-determination. From this aspect, all true, vital religion is theonomous
and theocentric. It expresses itself in obedience, for God is
the primary fact, with the recognition of which all religious
thought and action must begin. The authoritarian theological
systems of historical Christianity have preserved more of the
proper religious attitude than has modernist theological thought
but they have objectified God. They have imprisoned Him in
a miracle or an institution or a book. When modernism began
to tear down the walls of authoritarianism, it opened a new
direct way to God. But it presently proceeded to subjectify
Him by making His reality dependent upon religious experience, so that finally the question could be asked whether all
theology was not merely anthropology and whether that reality
which was meant by the word of God was not merely a supposed
reality and actually only a dream of man, an image of himself.
It is the appropriateness of this question which gives authority
to the so-called orthodox and reactionary groups within the
Church. But the truth lies neither with those who stress the
objective nor with those who emphasize the subjective character
of God. This we are beginning now to discover. There is no
revelation without faith and there is no faith without revelation. *Gott und Glaube gehören zuhaufe,* taught Luther. In
other words, neither the immanence nor the transcendence of
God can be made absolute or exclusive, for He is both immanent and transcendent.

Modernism has over-emphasized the immanence of the
divine in man and in the world. Thereby it has narrowed the
truly religious spirit, and the Barthian criticism, which has
fallen upon it with a vengeance, is largely justified. To be sure,
Barthianism is of value primarily as a corrective and not as a
constructive theological movement. For in contrast to modernism it has isolated the doctrine of the divine transcendence and
has finally even been led to an over-appreciation of theological
tradition as given in the teachings of the Reformers and even
in the church fathers and scholastics. It does not actively
participate in the responsibilities laid upon us by the present
day. It is not truly contemporary.

All this may seem extremely abstract. It is so in thought and on paper. But it concerns the fundamental problems of living. Its truth or untruth can only be discovered in actual life itself. For the validity and power of man's religious devotion expresses itself in his conduct in the affairs of the world. It gives life a new quality which may be characterized by the words "freedom" and "obligation", or better yet by the good Christian words "faith" and "love". Faith in God creates in us a new spirit of liberty from the dangers of self-sufficiency. It is now often called "disinterestedness". It makes us see life *sub specie aeternitatis,* enabling us to be realists in the sense that by inner necessity we accept things as they actually are. It gives us new knowledge in the form of an understanding of things which is not baffled by utilitarian necessities nor limited by mere idealisms. It invests us with new insight as to the forces which hinder the full unfolding of life. Nothing ultimately prevents growth more drastically than self-sufficiency—which may disclose itself not only in sheer selfishness but also in a conservatism that glorifies the *status quo,* and even in a radicalism which, for the sake of satisfying reformatory ambitions, attempts the break-up of what is.

This "faith in God", when it is real, is always coupled with love, *i.e.,* with action in the world performed in the spirit of freedom. It flows into the making of a community which differs from all other types of community in that in it neighbors are bound to neighbors not by mutually attractive qualities and special endowments, but simply by the fact that they are neighbors. As believers in God we love our neighbors as neighbors. And we love the world for no other reason than that it is our world—and God's. It is God who lets the neighbor cross our path and who places us in the world. Life is meaningful only when it is recognized as God's life, i.e., when its being and value are recognized as inherent in it, when its existence and meaning are understood as transcending our making. We are then co-operators with God in eliciting from life what it is by God's grace and in bringing it to full expression.

The Christian world is rich in thoughts and deeds which illustrate this conception. What we have described is already implied in the word-symbols of traditional Christianity—"Holy Spirit", "eternal life", *etc.* It is what the great theological thought-complexes of creation and salvation, sin and grace, justification and sanctification, repentance and forgiveness, law and gospel, light and darkness imply. We have indicated the source of that peculiar vitality which gives a person a Christian character. A study of church history discloses the secret of the life hid with Christ in God in many a biography and in many a special act. There are to be found concrete examples of the God-life in the stream of history. Only one thing is required of us: that we ourselves understand the mystery of divine revelation before we embark upon the study of its work in our own contemporary and in the historical world. The *testimonium spiritus sancti internum* is still the pre-requisite of religious understanding. Whenever we depend on it, we are given power to see clearly. We can then distinguish between the chaff and the wheat, realizing that the absolutization of self-sufficiency, the uncritical defense of the *status quo*, the resting in what is deemed perfection—that these are the means by which the full life is limited and often destroyed.

The authority for the truth of our religious faith rests, therefore, nowhere but in living itself. Our own living is to be constantly nourished by the rich lives in which God is and has been a reality. This means practically that we are charged with the duty of translating eternal life into practical life. Hence the future of the Church as the communion of believers in God depends upon the willingness of its members to develop a theology of translation, an ethics of translation, lives of translation. Saintly men and women have lived in every human generation. The theology and ethics of translation are still rarities, but they are in the making.

Two things then, determine the outlook for religion: the question is whether we will take our own historical situation seriously, and whether we will take God seriously in His divinity. If we take seriously both God and our own situation we shall be led to a life derived from God which is truly contemporary. From such a viewpoint, the break-up of the self-sufficient, autonomous, bourgeois civilization is a most hopeful occurrence. The trends of renewal which we have observed are, we may now conclude, hints of a revival of a religious consciousness, at once free from earthly boundaries and rich in love.

CHAPTER 17

An Exposition and Criticism
of Liberalism

A PROMINENT feature of the present discussion of public events is the debate on the merits or demerits of economic liberalism which has dominated modern economic life. The "laissez-faire" economy, also disparagingly called the profit system of "rugged individualism," is said to be responsible for the disaster which has befallen modern civilization. The principle of the free play of economic forces is declared to have exhausted its possibilities of application.

I

In the classical works of its first scientific interpreters, Adam Smith and David Ricardo, this economic system was expounded on the basis of a world-view which rests on the belief in the reasonableness and harmony of the world-order. They assumed the knowledge of this nature of the universe to be within the reach of human reason, and they considered man's free application of his natural reason to all facts of life, but particularly of the economic realm, as the guarantee of a progressive unfolding of the harmonious character of the world. All men appear as co-operators in the realization of the cosmic world-plan. In the economic field, every single individual contributes to the production of economic goods and, according to the value of his contribution to the life of society, he receives the claim and the right of the consumption of goods. The stability of the economic system is considered safeguarded by the economic law of supply and demand and its creative elasticity guaranteed by the freedom of private property and by the individual responsibility of the participants in the economic process.

This system was conceived in order to liberate economic life from the subjection to the power of the political state and to enable it to unfold its own full character. The free play of economic forces was demanded in reaction against an irrational, extra-economic power in order to bring to light the rationality of the economic forces. The actual consequence of the application of these principles was not only an economic productivity (which could more and more effectively supply the economic needs of men), and a most remarkable raising of the standard of living, but also the development of new irrational power in the economic order itself. It was caused by the ever rising inequality in the possession of the means of production; it was tremendously increased by the rise of machine-industrialism; and it was finally dramatically demonstrated in the fate of the disinherited proletariat of the workers. The formula of the free play of economic forces gradually became the means for the maintenance of economic power and control on the part of the privileged owners of economically productive property. The vision of the first interpreters of economic liberalism was replaced by a picture of economic chaos. Instead of a reasonable harmony of individual economic forces a struggle of all against all and a conflict of economic classes has come into being. All efforts of demonstrating the reasonableness of the universe by a laissez-faire economy are refuted by the hopeless disillusionment of modern man and by his fear of the irrationality and meaninglessness of the world-order as a whole.

It has become plain that the debacle of the philosophy of economic liberalism is no isolated feature in modern cultural life. In so far as liberalism is recognized as the philosophy of life which has characterized modern civilization it is now challenged and questioned in its totality. The ideals of the freedom of property, of government, of the press, of speech, even of faith have fallen in disrepute or they are the center of discussions which test their validity. The life of whole nations is being transformed under the influence of powers which have pronounced anathemas upon these ideals. In some parts of the world anti-liberal revolutions have taken place and are in full progress; in others they are being feared. We have little right to interpret these events and attitudes as temporary disillusionments, representing after-effects of the catastrophes of the World

Wars. We must rather recognize that we live in a period of transition and that the history of these years represents the end of an era.

This era may be generally described as that of the middle-class, bourgeois civilization which replaced the so-called medieval system of feudalism. It came to life in the medieval towns and cities, partly nurtured by cultural forces of ancient Graeco-Roman times which had been quietly preserved in the feudalist-hierarchial order of the Middle Ages; it first blossomed forth in the period of the Renaissance; and, after having been both retarded and transformed by the Protestant Reformation, it developed its full strength in the period of the Enlightenment which is also known as the Age of Reason. Its character lies in the increasing assertion of the autonomy of human reason, which ultimately led to an emancipation of man from the heteronomous traditions of the past as they prevailed in all realms of human endeavor. Natural reason, the principle according to which the universe was believed to be organized in a pre-established harmony, now became the norm by which all values of life were measured. The ideals of progress and the perfectibility of the human race coupled to the proclamation of human liberty acted as the impulses by which modern man released himself from the supernatural authorities of church, state, and society which had held his development in check. The modern world is what it is because it has cultivated and practiced this doctrine of the self-determination of man. It is the autonomous mind which has called "modern" philosophy into being, has produced "modern" natural and historical science, has given the drive to "modern" economics and constantly nourished the spirit of capitalism, has caused the "modern" inventions to be made, and has created and sustained the political democracies.

To be sure the achievements of this bourgeois civilization present themselves in such a complexity that the picture here given may appear as an undue simplification of its character. But even if all the positive attainments of this civilization are taken into account, namely, the expansion of natural, historical, sociological, psychological, economic, technical knowledge, the control of nature and life by the application of ever more refined processes of reason, the conquest of time and space, the defeat of superstition and disease—the fundamental nature of this culture has remained what it was in its beginnings. It is the expression of the autonomy of man as a reasonable being who by his rationality conforms to the universe which as a unity proceeds according to the norms of reasonableness that can be described in the terms of so-called natural laws. The unity of this world-view expresses itself in the midst of all the various ramifications which its own application to life produces. But it must also not be denied that it is constantly overshadowed by the traditions of other ages and civilizations of a different nature which live on and cannot be absorbed, and that it is continuously disturbed by those elements in the nature of man and the world which do not permit themselves to be drawn into the unity of rationality. Whenever these elements were in the ascendance, "modern" civilization has found itself in a state of crisis. This crisis was never as extensive as it is now.

II

We now turn to theological liberalism which is the central subject of our consideration. It is evident that it is part of the cultural process of the bourgeois era. Its opposition against the ecclesiastical authority of tradition and against the supernaturalist system of orthodoxy is one of the phases of the assertion of autonomous human reason. When it developed the methods of historical criticism and applied them to the history of religion in general and to the history of Christianity in particular it shared in the expression of the free human spirit. The introduction of scientific method into the field of religion is merely another step in the evolution of the spirit of modern civilization. No truly modern contemporary could and can escape from the necessity of accepting it. For the methods of scientific research and understanding as they have been cultivated by the modern scholars can no less be refused than the machines that have been built with their help. Theological and ecclesiastical orthodoxy resisted the application of the modern methods of the study of life and its becoming much more stubbornly than other historical institutions dared to do. Even today it is represented by a large number of Christian theologians and laymen, but it is nevertheless a fact that actually it has become profoundly affected by the results of scientific research inside and outside of the church. In so far as it still clings to its own heteronomous traditionalism it is anachronistic.

One of the chief results of the study and analysis of the Christian religion on the basis of "modern" methods of research was the discovery that Christianity as a religious movement survived the various civilizations in which it lived because it adjusted itself to its social, economic, political, cultural environment under maintenance of its own characteristic identity, consisting in the belief of the revelation of God in Jesus Christ. The modern church proceeded, therefore, to adjust itself to the civilization of its own age. Developing a modernist theology, it interpreted itself to modern civilization and modern civilization to itself, thus claiming to repeat with reference to the modern world what in other ages the church had undertaken in relation to its environment. Modernism was thus understood as a method by which the church must proclaim its message to the changing generations of men. The so-called orthodox systems of theology and church life appeared as modernist forms of the past. They seemed to exert an influence upon present-day life only because of the refusal of their adherents to become contemporaries of the present era. Modern "liberal" theology could then be interpreted as a theology which "uses the methods of modern science to find, state, and use the permanent and central values of inherited orthodoxy in meeting the needs of a modern world. The needs themselves point the way to the formulas."[1]

Thus it happened that a constructive liberal Christian theology came into being. Abandoning the fixed creeds of tradition and dedicated to the modern mood of the freedom of thought and faith it interpreted and restated the Christian religion in terms of modern civilization. Following the trends of the modern mind in science, history, philosophy, and all other fields of cultural life, it bestowed upon itself a vitality and a willingness to change which heretofore had been unknown in Christian history. With each turn of modern culture, new theological schools came to the fore. The rationalism and moralism of the Enlightenment were replaced by the psychologism of Schleiermacher and the speculative idealism of Hegel and their schools. The historicism of the Ritschlian school was followed by the religio-historical and the socio-historical types of theological thought. All these generations of liberal Christians acknowledged their loyalty to the principles of the individualism of Christian experience and of the relativism of its historical nature.

In spite of the variety of theological systems, the Christian liberals agree in the fundamental tenets of their faith. In harmony with the spirit of bourgeois civilization they assert the continuity between God and man. The world is essentially one. Its character and meaning is disclosed in the values of rational truth, artistic beauty, and moral goodness which are accessible to human reason and express themselves in its functions. The task of man consists in the achievement of perfection by the realization of these values, in the attainment of an integration of his own personality by obedience to the demands of the value-character of the universe. God is the unified and unifying background of all processes of integration.[2] Wherever perfection is achieved there God is revealed. He lives in the soul of every striving man. History discloses the gradual manifestation of the divine in human life. The highest point in the historical development of perfection has been reached in Jesus of Nazareth, in whose prophetic personality the divine has found clearest and most challenging exhibition. He is therefore both the revelation of God and the goal of man's longing for salvation. The church is the movement of those who have dedicated themselves to the principles and ideals involved in the religion of Jesus. As a brotherhood of his disciples, devoted to the ideal of following his example of an unselfish life of love, they are engaged in the building of the Kingdom of God on earth. Considering their own religion as the highest form of the devotion to the good life and their own master and leader as the profoundest and purest of the great religious personalities of mankind, they are nevertheless ready to approach other non-Christian religious groups in a spirit of friendly sharing and interchange of experience. Ever ready to accept new truth, because all truth is the expression of the inward divine nature of the universe, the modern Christian is a seeker of the best ways in which he can contribute to the realization of the divine purposes which are immanent in the process of life.

This is, I believe, the interpretation of Christianity which is offered by the liberal theologians. In their learned works it seldom appears as simple as it is here outlined, for they present it in constant interchange with contemporary philosophy and science and with continuous reference to the history of the church. The "essence of Christianity" has taken the place of the authoritative creed or the inspired Bible or the supranatural church institution. It consists of those abiding values of the Christian faith which each age must recover for itself in a decision which involves a relation of the inherited faith to the needs of a new day. An "absolute" definition of the essence of Christianity is, of course, impossible, for whatever a member of a new age declares it to be will depend upon the relativity of his understanding of the needs of his age. The individualistic, subjective nature of their definition of Christianity is indeed readily admitted by the liberal theologians. They point out, however, that the arbitrary element in this subjectivism is checked by the reference to the historical character of the Christian religion, represented not only by the historicity of its founder but also by the historical continuity of the Christian fellowship.

The practical effect of this interpretation of Christianity expresses itself in all sorts of individualistic ways of behavior. The ideal of tolerance regulates the relationship of Christian groups with one another and with non-ecclesiastical orders of society as well as the attitudes of individual Christian persons toward each other. The church is understood as a fellowship of those who because of the same or a similar religious experience have decided to worship together, thus expressing the social nature of religion. The sermon is a more or less subjective exposition of the Christian faith on the part of one who by personal inclination and training has chosen for himself the profession of a minister.

III

Opposition against this theological liberalism has come from various quarters. Orthodoxy condemns it in self-defense against a foe who has persistently undermined the foundations upon which it stands. But it also claims to have preserved the Christian gospel in its true nature, while the liberals are said to have betrayed it. The first criticism is invalid, because the destruction of the authority of a supernaturalist world-view and the break-down of absolutized church forms or theologies of the past have proceeded with inescapable necessity on the basis of irrefutable, factual, historical, and scientific knowledge. The second criticism has considerable validity, for it cannot be denied that the liberal principle of the immanence of God in a unified world and the resultant liberal attitude of "at-home-ness" in the world contradicts the insistence of all pre-liberal Christianity upon the dualism of creation and salvation. The liberal doctrine of the continuity between the world and God, and between man and God, stands in sharp contrast to the teachings of historic Christianity ,which center around the doctrine of the discontinuity between God and the world.

The *concept* of revelation which is defended by orthodoxy must be rejected, because it is based upon supernaturalist metaphysics which justify miracle and magic, but the *idea* of revelation which is implied in this inadequate concept must be taken much more seriously than liberalism has done. The meaning of the idea of revelation in religion points to those factors and aspects of life which transcend the "given-ness" of existence and are therefore not accessible to human control. The protest of the Barthian theologians against the immanentism of modern Christian thinking is here in accord with the orthodox objection against liberalism. It is Barth who has dramatically called attention to the fact that historic Christianity has lived of the gospel that the transcendent, eternal God has disclosed himself in Jesus Christ. The "word of God" which the church preaches is a "word" addressed to man from without himself and not a "word" which he speaks to himself, as if it were coming out of the depth of his own psychological or historical consciousness.[3] Orienting himself again to the dogmas of the ancient church and to the teachings of the reformers, Barth bitterly attacks liberal theology, because, in his opinion, it has forsaken the truth of the gospel as it is proclaimed in the Bible and expounded in the dogma of the church. Radically opposing modernism he attempts to reconstruct the theology of the church on the basis of an absolute affirmation of the transcendence of God, declaring that God can be known only as he has disclosed himself in the death and resurrection of Jesus Christ, of which the Bible, and through it the church, give witness. He does not reject the critical examination of Christianity as undertaken by the liberal theology in so far as it describes the process of Christian history. However, he denies with conviction that the modernist theological interpretation and evaluation of this history does justice to its meaning. In his eagerness to assert the sovereignty of God and to recognize the chasm which separates unredeemed mankind from salvation by the act of God alone, he even refuses to admit that there is a point of contact between God and man, that there exists a human possibility to come to the knowledge of God. He opposes the principle of the autonomy of man with such a radicalness that his attitude toward the life of man in the world must be qualified by a perennial "No." But this negation of human possibilities in the name of the "totally other" God can actually be of little practical significance for the church and its work in the world. It leads merely to an emotional or intellectual restoration of the fundamental theological tenets of historical Christianity and offers no real guidance to man in the problems of living.

This criticism of Barth's theology must not prevent us from a serious consideration of the protest which has called it into being. For Barth's whole thought is a violent outburst against modern civilization and its dependence upon the principle of the freedom and the self-determination of man. His antagonism against liberal theology is so sharp because he feels that it has given religious sanction to the efforts of modern man to control life by his autonomous reason and to "improve" it by a confident reliance upon his goodness and his natural power to be good. He accuses modern Christians of having closed their eyes to the power of sin and evil which again and again destroys the unity not only of individual persons and of social groups, but also of the world. I think that Barth is justified in making this accusation.

IV

To be sure, also liberalism knows of sin and evil, but too often it interprets them in terms of imperfection, ignorance, maladjustment, immaturity. It praises persuasion and education as weapons against them. Thus it shows its trust in the fundamental goodness of nature and in the possibility of man to grow and develop in adjustment to this immanent character of the universe. Salvation is the removal of those hindrances which prevent the unfolding of the inner nature of things. It is the liberation of that perfection which is thought to be directly available to him who knows the right methods of releasing it.

But this view of life cannot be defended in the light of the actual reality of existence. Sin and evil are positive, concrete powers of destruction. They are the real opposites of holiness and goodness. Life must not be understood as a progress toward perfection, but as a conflict between good and evil, between holiness and sin, between belief and unbelief. The solution of this conflict does not lie in a goal toward which one can directly move, but in a "yonder" of good and evil which can only be believed.

A dualism can certainly not be affirmed by the Christian. For he puts his faith in one God, the creator of heaven and earth and the savior. He trusts in the meaningfulness of life and the universe; he is persuaded that what ought to be can and will become actuality, that the Kingdom of God will come.

There can be no quarrel with liberalism because of this vision of the end. But liberalism is wrong when it expects this end to come in the course of a continuous, directly ascending progress. Historic Christianity has held a profounder view. Its symbol of heavenly bliss (perfection) is the resurrection and not immortality. Belief in immortality implies that there is a direct continuity between the life "on earth" and the life "in heaven." But belief in the resurrection implies that the life "in heaven" will come as a new creation. The continuity between the unredeemed life and the redeemed life is not a direct but a broken one.

All this means that the conflicts of life must neither be interpreted in terms of monism nor in terms of dualism. Good and evil are neither reconcilable in the unity of the good, as if evil were a *minimum* of good, nor are they irreconcilable because of their absolute disunity; but there is a yonder of good and evil, a transcendent aspect of reality, a depth beyond all conflicts, which man calls "God." "He" is holy.

Who partakes of this divine holiness is saved. He has risen not only "above" the conflict between good and evil, but also "above" any conflict which may have beset his life. He *is* what he *ought to be*. There is no longer a tension between the actual and ideal. For he is related to that togetherness of the actual and ideal (God), which is the transcendent–immanent underground of all existence.

The old Christian myth of the new Paradise beautifully expresses this belief in salvation. There everybody and everything are again what they were meant to be, where every single part of the universe fulfils the meaning which it was intended to realize; God is all in all. The participation in this fulfillment of life takes place only in anticipation. But as such it qualifies the whole character of living. Who believes in this future Kingdom of God considers the conflicts of existence in their true relativity. He views them *sub specie aeternitatis*. Hence he can deal with them in a realistic manner.

This view is set both against the liberal teaching of the divine immanence and against the Barthian teaching of divine transcendence, but it includes the right emphasis of both these doctrines. God and the world are not one, nor is there an *"infinite* (absolute) qualitative difference" between them. God and the world stand in that relation to one another which is suggested in the historic Christian teaching that God who has *created* the world also saves it. The unity between God and the world, between God and man, is dialectical, as the dialectical nature of all Christian doctrines suggests. In them creation and salvation, sin and grace, repentance and forgiveness, law and gospel, light and darkness, time and eternity, divinity and humanity, death and resurrection are correlated to one another in a unity which is not direct but dialectical.

We have more than once suggested that what is meant by these teachings of historic Christianity is a more realistic, *i.e.,* truer understanding of the nature of life than what is suggested by the underlying philosophy of liberalism. Our concern with these doctrines is dictated by the conviction that they offer a better understanding of the character of existence. We do not consider them more valuable because they are traditional, and we certainly dissociate ourselves from those who declare them true because they were taught by prophets and apostles, church fathers, and reformers. We also admit that the manner of their formulation reflects definite historical backgrounds and particular kinds of historical philosophies. Hence, they cannot become directly significant for us but only indirectly, namely, in so far as we are able to comprehend the meaning which is expressed in them. We do not separate ourselves from the movement of liberalism. We clearly accept the liberation from arbitrary historical or traditional authority which it has achieved. We do our thinking on the basis of the liberal protest against heteronomous authority. We refuse to submit to the decrees of councils and popes, creed-makers, and self-appointed guardians of orthodoxy as we should refuse to consider the validity of the claim of one who should today arise and declare that by the grace of God he had obtained the right to rule over us.

But we also deny that the freedom which the liberal protest has achieved is true freedom, *i.e.,* freedom which corresponds to the real nature of life. We maintain that the interpretation which liberalism has attached to its principle of the autonomy of man as a rational being is wrong.

We too say that man is created free. He alone among the creatures is endowed with the possibility of controlling his being. He alone among all creatures can make decisions for his life. He can even carry this possibility to the negative extreme of committing suicide by his own free decision. Now it is a fact that as soon as man awakens to the realization that he is free, that he *can* decide about the norms, the laws which shall determine his life, he discovers that he is unfree. He is part of a physical and spiritual universe. He can therefore exercise his autonomy only in so far as he decides to obey the physical and spiritual laws which govern the life of the universe. He cannot choose to live on the moon, he is bound to the earth; he cannot choose what shall constitute the nature of truth or beauty or goodness, he must submit to their objective normativeness. He therefore recognizes that in order to fulfill his destiny he must use his freedom for the purpose of becoming what he ought to be. He can become what he ought to be only by establishing his being in such a way that the ideal values are actualized in the reality in which he is placed. He can be what he ought to be if the actual and ideal are together in his existence. This togetherness he recognizes as the meaning not only of his but of all life.

But does the knowledge of this meaning enable him to realize it in his life? Does his insight in the physical and spiritual nature of the universe, of which he is a part, enable him to actualize this nature? Does the qualification of his autonomy by this knowledge render it possible for him to reach perfection? The liberal philosophers and theologians answer these questions in the affirmative when they declare the reasonableness of the universe and of man and the continuity between God and man. But they overlook the concrete nature of *autonomy*, self-determination. For the self which is the determinant is an active self. It is of such a nature that it asserts itself in selfishness. The autonomous man is always inclined toward self-sufficiency, individualism. He acts not according to the dictates of his insight but according to the dictates of his *power*, and he uses his insight for the sake of expressing and increasing his power. It is this power of free men which constantly destroys the harmony of humanity. And it is the recognition of this element of power in all freedom which invalidates the liberalist interpretation of life. Rationality, harmony, unity, continuity, cannot be the keywords of a philosophy which claims to interpret life truly, for as long as life is dominated by the element of power there is irrationality, disharmony, disunity discontinuity in life.

*   *   *   *

We may now return to the beginning of our discussion by asking: Why is economic liberalism today in discredit? In the light of our analysis of the philosophy of liberalism, we can answer: Because the economic freedom which it bestowed theoretically and practically has been abused by those who could exert the greatest power to limit and destroy the freedom of their fellow-men. Because similar phenomena can be observed in all other realms of "modern" civilization, it is in a state of crisis.

We must not fail to observe that the civilization of liberalism achieved the emancipation of Western mankind from the arbitrary power of kings and castes and hierarchies, that it actually has been a civilization of liberation. The glories of modern culture testify to this fact. But the age of feudalist power was succeeded by the age of individualist power.

Is it to be the destiny of mankind that the age of individualist power will be superseded by an era of the power of race or nation or class? Are the achievements of autonomous lib-

CHAPTER 18

A Defense of Liberalism

IN A paper entitled "Calvinism in American Theology Today," Dr. Clarence Bouma, professor of systematic theology
at Calvin Seminary, Grand Rapids, Michigan, undertakes an
analysis of the present theological situation in America. He
writes from the point of view of Reformed orthodoxy and as
a defender of "historic Calvinism". His evaluation of theological liberalism is determined by the belief that Protestant
orthodoxy will come again into prominence. I am convinced
that this expectation is not well founded. The present prospects of orthodoxy are not as good as Dr. Bouma thinks they
are. I shall try to prove this judgment by an analysis of his
thesis.

I

Dr. Bouma's thesis may be briefly stated as follows: Calvinism, which once upon a time dominated the American theological scene, has today been so reduced in its influence, even
upon the life of the Calvinistic churches, that only a mere
trickle of it remains. The original strength of its God-centered
faith has been eaten away by the man-centered religiousness
of liberalism. But liberalism today is in a state of disillusionment. Its own spokesmen appear to turn away from it. They
are longing for the recovery of the faith in the living God of
the Bible and are rediscovering the truth of the Christian
doctrine of sin. This reorientation of liberal theological thinking seems to hold the promise that Calvinism will once more
come into its own.

If this is a fair general summary of Dr. Bouma's article, I
find myself in the strange situation that I can subscribe to his
thesis in so far as it states the present condition and trend of

American theological thinking but that I must radically disagree with him concerning its significance.

In agreement with Dr. Bouma, I do not hesitate to acknowledge the fact that, under the impact of modernism, the old
Calvinism has largely disappeared from the American theological scene. But I disagree with him when he regrets this fact,
for I hail it as an inevitable and good historical achievement.

In agreement with Dr. Bouma, I grant that orthodox Calvinism is adequately embodied in the life and teaching of the
Christian Reformed Church and of the Orthodox Presbyterian
Church. But I disagree with him when he finds great satisfaction in the thought that in the former of these denominations
(to which he belongs) "the most vigorous and intellectually
respectable championship of the historic Reformed faith is carried on," for I think that he has no good reason to be so
gratified, because I hold that the position which he and his
church take cannot be defended with good theological arguments and that his descendants will in all probability be compelled to give it up.

In agreement with Dr. Bouma, I recognize that Protestant
theological liberalism is today in a state of crisis. But I disagree with him when he tends to think that this liberalism is
about to die, for I am of the conviction that the historical point
of view which liberalism has introduced into Christian thought
is a permanent achievement and that its present tendency to
criticize and to rethink its own theology is a sign of its true
vitality.

In agreement with Dr. Bouma, I acknowledge that the
thought of the Reformers and especially of John Calvin should
again be sympathetically studied by Protestant theologians. But
I disagree with him when he interprets the turning of modern
theological thinkers to the Reformation as the beginning of a
possible reinstatement of Calvinist orthodoxy, for I am persuaded that those who newly concern themselves with the teachings of the Reformation do not seek to restore the "historic
faith" of the Reformers but are so inspired by the Reformers'
prophetic apprehension of the Christian gospel that they hope
to find a prophetic form of Christianity of their own that will
confront the people of today as decisively with the Christian

gospel as the theology of the Reformers did in the sixteenth century.

II

In order to justify these statements, I now proceed to review Dr. Bouma's analysis under four headings: (1) the breakdown of orthodoxy in Protestant history; (2) the present-day prospects of theological orthodoxy; (3) the vitality of Protestant liberalism; and (4) the significance of the contemporary rediscovery of the Reformation.

1. In his description of Calvinism as a "historic faith," Dr. Bouma seems to assume that it can be taken as a theological entity of a specific character. But a study of Calvinism proves that it underwent considerable changes in the course of the centuries. To be sure, it cannot be denied that Calvinism represents a type of Protestant Christianity which, since its beginnings in the thought and work of John Calvin, has maintained a character of its own. In this respect, it is analogous to Lutheranism and Anglicanism, which also have succeeded in preserving definite special traditions.

In describing the nature of Calvinism, one may place special emphasis on its "God-centered faith," as Professor Bouma does, for the doctrines of the sovereignty of God and of divine predestination and providence have always been of special concern to all Calvinists. But one should also not fail to stress the "Reformed" insistence on the understanding of religion as obedience to the divine law. For from this special conceptions of the nature of Christian ethics and particularly of church order and polity have been derived. Indeed, the organization of the church which Calvin prescribed in terms of his reading of the biblical law represents to this day the one feature which all Calvinist bodies have in common and by virtue of which they constitute a special church family. In the light of this fact, it cannot be denied that the American Presbyterian and Reformed denominations which Dr. Bouma says have largely become indifferent to historic Calvinist teachings still stand in the genuine Calvinist tradition.

When one is made aware of the importance which churchmanship has always had in Calvinism, one is led to the observation that theology never occupied the central place in its life. Here lies a major difference between Calvinism and Lutheranism. The latter is primarily anchored in a theological tradition. As a church whose nature its adherents have been accustomed to define by the criterion of the right preaching and hearing of the word, Calvinism could, of course, never neglect theology. It has therefore made much of the several historic creeds and catechisms to which Dr. Bouma refers. But, nevertheless, conformity with creedal and theological orthodoxy can hardly be regarded as the most important feature of Calvinism. Had it ever been so considered, the Calvinistic religiousness and the Calvinistic theological emphasis (I am using this vague phrase intentionally) would never have been adopted by so many Protestant denominations which, strictly speaking, do not belong to the Calvinistic fold, e.g., Anglicans, Congregationalists, Baptists, etc.

Indeed, there are many Calvinist theological traditions. The Reformed theologies of the Swiss, the German, the French, the Dutch, the Scotch, etc., are not so uniform as the theologies of the various Lutheran bodies are. The Arminians belong as definitely to the Calvinistic tradition as the defenders of the decisions of the Synod of Dort. Jonathan Edwards was a representative Calvinistic theologian just as clearly as Abraham Kuyper was—and yet they differ from each other not only because they were of different times and places. There is no good reason to suspect, as Dr. Bouma does, that Karl Barth and Emil Brunner do not stand firmly in the Calvinistic theological tradition. Yet they have much to criticize in the thought of J. Gresham Machen, whom Dr. Bouma regards as a champion of Calvinist orthodoxy and as such as a true heir of the historic "gospel of John Calvin."

Dr. Bouma seems to identify true Calvinism with a certain kind of orthodoxy which is based on conformity with creeds and confessions and on the belief in the literally inspired Bible. This judgment is arbitrary, because it implies an indefensible disregard of the historical interpretation of Christianity. The Reformers and the orthodox Christians of the sixteenth and seventeenth centuries had understandable reasons for defending the truth of Christianity by means of the authority of Scripture and creeds. Moreover, the work of the orthodox builders of systems of "pure doctrine" is worthy of highest respect. But today Christian theological thinking can no longer be cast in this mold, simply because the modern philosophical, natural, and social sciences forbid it. It is nothing but obscurantism to base the defense of the truth of the Christian faith upon norms containing philosophical and social implications which are irreconcilable with the evidences of the modern knowledge of the world. This denial of the adequacy of orthodoxy does not mean that the antisupernaturalistic scientific world-view and the historical conception of life stand in an irreconcilable conflict with the Christian religion, as the spokesmen of orthodox churches are wont to claim. They merely render impossible the preservation of theological ways of thinking which were practiced before the rise of modern science and history.

It is true, Calvin had a God-centered faith. It is also true that the religion of modern men has often tended to assume man-centered forms. It is further true that, whenever man tries to deify himself, he is, sooner or later, brought to a fall and is threatened with destruction. Religion should therefore be theocentric and not anthropocentric. But from this it does not follow that the forms of theocentric religion must be of a certain historical kind.

Least of all can one claim the support of the Reformers for such an undertaking. It was their one and foremost concern to make room in the world for the free and unbound gospel of salvation by the grace of God in Jesus Christ. Age-old traditions and dogmas in which the Christian faith had been held fell before the blows of their prophetism. They linked the gospel of Christ closely to biblical authority, but it was always their intention to interpret the Bible by the gospel and not the gospel by the Bible. Their exegetical works are proof of this. They were wrongly persuaded that the Bible was its own interpreter; and Calvin in particular came closer to the later Protestant teaching of the verbal inspiration of the biblical writings. But in all this, they were children of their times and heirs of a long tradition. Could they have known what we now know of the origin of the books of the Bible and of the world in which they were written, they would not have hesitated, I am sure, to free the gospel from biblical literalism. At any rate, it is in the spirit of the God-centered faith of the Reformers to free the Christian religion from the encumbrances of a doctrine which goes counter to well-substantiated, irrefutable evidence.

If it was good and right and honest to say that papal authority is not of the essence of Christianity, it is also right and honest to admit that biblical literalism is not of the essence of the Christian gospel.

Just as Roman Catholicism deforms the Christian faith by demanding that anyone who desires to be a Christian acknowledge the authoritarianism of the hierarchy, Protestant orthodoxy impedes and confuses the free expression of the Christian faith by insisting that anyone who wishes to be a Christian submit to the authoritarianism of antiquated knowledge now proved untrue.

Roman Catholic authoritarianism was broken by the impact of the Reformers' prophetic attack upon it. Protestant authoritarianism should have been made impossible by the spirit of the prophetic religion in defense of which the Reformation was undertaken. But it was actually undone by the spokesmen of human freedom and the defenders of the right of reason. In the name of the autonomy of reason they shook off the heteronomy of arbitrary and untenable dogmas, and it was right that they did so. For, in spite of the fact that most of them failed to be aware of the possibility and even denied it, the autonomy of reason can be in league with the theonomous spirit of God-centered religion; heteronomous authoritarianism is their common enemy. Theological dogmatism finds itself opposed by prophetic religion as well as by enlightened reason.

It is a regrettable fact that, because Protestant orthodoxy actually killed prophetic religion by substituting doctrinal knowledge for it, modern men found themselves unable to break their servitude to dogmatism in the name of a God-centered faith. They had to rely on enlightened reason. In the course of time, most of them came to feel that the reason they tried to live by was irreconcilable with any religion. Such is the belief and conviction of the majority of our contemporaries who have come under the influence of modern education.

2. In view of this situation, theological orthodoxy appears to be in a hopeless condition. It can maintain itself only by secluding itself from the modern world or by permitting a double standard of truth. Both methods are actually widely employed, the former primarily by Protestant fundamentalist groups, and the latter chiefly by the Roman Catholic church.

Neither of these methods can be expected to be successful in the long run. As the technological means of communication make all sorts of isolation and isolationism increasingly impossible, the teachings of all human groups will be brought under the scrutiny of public discussion. In due season, all orthodoxies which try to arrest the march of truth will be dissolved. For a time, they may attempt to preserve themselves as relics of the past, but they can have no future. They are doomed, whether they are Protestant or Roman Catholic. When nationalisms and national sovereignties will have ceased to confound the political life of the world—and, one day, they will be done away with—orthodox dogmatisms will also no longer be.

To be sure, at the present moment, historic dogmatisms appear temporarily attractive to many, especially in the field of religion. The political and economic upheavals of the past decades have led many to the realization that the disregard of religious culture or the cultivation of a humanistic religiousness have deprived civilization of ultimate sanctions. They have come to see that freedom and justice cannot be maintained unless they are related to eternal structures of being, i.e., derived from God and nurtured by a God-centered devotion. Never having had such a faith or having lost it, they find the historic religious-theological dogmatisms attractive, because these seem to be the most reliable guardians of religious culture. So it happens that, in this period of transition, Roman Catholicism can acquire new prestige, especially here in the United States. Also Protestant orthodoxy is gaining new power, particularly in continental Europe. But these gains can hardly be lasting. They will be swept away by a new wave of rational skepticism, or they will be undone by the rise of new forms of prophetic religiousness.

3. There is promise that such forms may develop within the ranks of religious and theological liberalism. I dare say that this modern Protestant movement is about to enter the truly positive stage of its development. Its critical work is practically completed. It has subjected all parts and aspects of the tradition of Christianity to historical investigation. The major Christian writings, including the Bible and the works of the great theologians, have been analyzed or edited by means of reliable critical methods. They can now be understood more

adequately than was possible in any previous period of Christian history. Indeed, this critical historical interpretation of the Christian tradition constitutes the permanent achievement of liberalism. Failure to recognize this is nothing but arbitrary wilfulness.

Historical research has persuasively shown that throughout the generations the Christian faith has succeeded in maintaining its distinctive identity while entering into the cultural environment of its adherents.

No Protestant theologian who has ever been under the influence of liberal theology will deny the validity of this historical interpretation. The criticism which liberals themselves now apply to theological liberalism is not directed against this historical work. In explanation of the reasons for this self-criticism, it may, generally speaking, be said that when the liberal theologians of the nineteenth and early twentieth centuries undertook to interpret the Christian religion to the modern man, they tended to overemphasize the importance of one part of their historical undertaking, neglecting the other one: They stressed the task of relating the life and faith of Christianity to the cultural life of modern man and they simplified the concern for the purity and indigenous distinctiveness of the Christian faith. All that which was subsumed under the phrase "the essence of Christianity" was therefore often too easily determined by a premature and shallow assessment of the results of historical criticism or by a too hasty eagerness to cast the Christian faith into contemporaneous forms. Many of the liberals, even the great ones among them, did not fully understand the secret of the relation between "substance" and "form." In particular, they did not realize that the historical forms of religion (creeds, liturgies, church orders, moral standards, etc.) are cast by communities of believers and that they must be recast by communities. They were too individualistic. Moreover, they underestimated the capacity of most men to develop a proper attitude toward history. Hence they did not sufficiently counteract the tendency of many to relegate to the past what was historically understood in terms of the past, as if it were worthy only to be forgotten. Thus they allowed modernizations of the Christian faith which were unwarranted by their own critical-historical work. It was also inevitable that, because their historical and theological methods were bluntly rejected by the orthodox and fundamentalist reactionaries, they and their followers often felt more kinship with those moderns who had left the churches than with the defenders of the "historic faith."

In recent years, liberals themselves have learned properly to estimate these shortcomings of their teachers and predecessors. They themselves have pointed "beyond modernism." They have studied and interpreted the historic dogmas and doctrines of Christianity with new appreciation. But there is no evidence that they wish to return to the dogmatism of any of the orthodoxies, be they Calvinist or Lutheran or Roman Catholic or whatever. Some of the reformed liberals are called neo-orthodox by the unrepentant and unregenerate modernists. But this propagandistic name should give no comfort to the orthodox party men. As a matter of fact, it does not, for as Professor Bouma's attitude and Professor Van Til's book *The New Modernism* show, they are quick to dissociate themselves even from such extreme neo-orthodox theologians as Barth and Brunner. If they were only fully consistent! Then they would refuse to think that the liberals' rediscovery of biblical religion and of the doctrines of grace, sin, and eschatology marks the beginning of a turning-back to the "historic faith"! This rediscovery is not a "turning-back" but a sign of the religious vitality of Protestant liberalism. It proves that it is capable of criticizing itself! But a self-critical orthodoxy is a *rara avis!*

4. One of the most important phases of the rethinking of Christian theology as it is undertaken by liberalism is the concern with the teachings of the Protestant Reformers. It should be recognized that the "Luther Renaissance" and the "Calvin Renaissance" are the direct results of the preoccupation of historically minded liberal theologians with the Reformation. It was they who produced reliable critical editions of the works of the Reformers. They proceeded to investigate the development of the thought of the Reformers and to study it in relation to their antecedents and in terms of the changes which their successors wrought in it. Then they reversed the long-established order and interpreted the creeds and confessions of the Reformation in the light of the teaching of the Reformers instead of adapting the dynamic faith of the Reformation to the

doctrines of the creeds. Thus they liberated Reformation research from the denominational bias which had beset it for
centuries. They let the Reformers speak for themselves.

Thus it has come about that their voices speak to us from
the sixteenth century with a directness which no creedalism
has ever achieved. They are calling us to pay attention to the
timelessness of the Christian gospel as it is expressed through
ever changing time-bound forms. They speak to us as voices of
an ecumenical Christian faith and not of a denominational par-
tisanship.

We respond to them with an understanding that their own
contemporaries could not give them, for we find it no longer
necessary to insist on religious and creedal uniformity. The
freedom of religion which was established by the democratic
state has made it possible for us to search for the ecumenical
gospel in the particular historical traditions of the various
denominations, transcending historical limitations without arbitrarily absolutizing or denying them. To this ecumenical
Christianity which would not be what it is without the freedom
which modern liberalism in all its forms has accomplished, the
historical voices of the Reformers are speaking.

The Protestant churches are beginning to understand themselves as participants of a world-wide movement. They are done
with denominationalism and its tendency to absolutize particular traditions as if they were the only true expressions and
embodiments of the Christian faith. As the various denominations and churches are brought into close touch with one another, they are forced to recognize that they hold the eternal
gospel in temporary historical forms. They are thus compelled
to seek a confrontation with the gospel itself, so that they
may develop a loyalty to the divinely creative core of Christianity and not to its perishable human conventions. But this
gospel is available only in historical man-made tradition. It
must therefore be sought *in* them and not *apart* from them.
This is why the activities of the ecumenical and interdenominational organizations are so important. They furnish opportuni-
ties to the various churches to compare their own particularities
with those of others, to distinguish the essential from the unes-
sential, and to recognize that one religious faith can be held
in many ways and nurtured by pluralistic practices. Individual

churches or denominations may be led to see that their particular traditions are not worthy to be perpetuated in view of the religious demands of the gospel itself.

All this is actually happening among us. Mere loyalty to traditions has therefore become questionable. It is no longer really important to us whether we are Anglicans, Lutherans, or Calvinists but whether we are Christians. It is not unimportant that we ask ourselves what has happened to particular traditions in the course of history and what the present prospects of Calvinism, for example, are. Yet we ask such questions not in order to hope for the restoration of lost prestige but in order to learn the difference of the permanent from the passing, of the dynamic from the static, of the living from the dead.

Being of such a mind, we turn with fresh attention to the creative periods in Christian history, to the age of the New Testament and to the Reformation. We do not turn back to them, as if we would escape from present responsibilities, but we hope to obtain guidance from them to the divine sources and the human resources of the Christian faith, aware of the fact that we must bring it to a concrete expression in the life of our times by means which our ancestors, including the apostles and reformers, could not possibly know.

CHAPTER 19

The Prospect for Ecumenical
Theology Today

A RENAISSANCE of theology is taking place in contemporary Protestantism. It does not yet affect the churches in such a way that older theological attitudes and views are replaced and that a new Christian outlook upon the world is determining the work of the churches. To be sure, such tendencies do manifest themselves, but they have not yet gained decisive power.

In spite of the changes which occur in the cultural whole, the traditional life maintains itself. Although naïve historians are wont to speak of periods of historical transition in terms of catastrophes, a cataclysmic breakup of the historical process never actually occurs. Also in eras of change historical continuity is preserved. Cultural transformations are of a gradual character. Their radicalness can often be clearly observed only in the perspective of later developments. The revolutionary importance of the Renaissance or the Reformation in the history of Western civilization was not clearly discernible to their contemporaries, for, by supporting or opposing these movements, they believed that they were fulfilling their obligations only to their immediate past and present.

In our day the Christian church continues to exercise its accustomed function, providing its people with religious instruction and practice in ways determined by historical inheritance. We may be sure that, in spite of the present religious and cultural crisis, the church will preserve its traditional character. But, gradually, new attitudes will assert themselves and, in time, dominate the mind of the church. Then orthodoxy and pietism, fundamentalism and liberalism, which now, together with the national, social, and economic forces that have shaped their history, determine the life of the churches, will make room for new attitudes. These will perhaps arise out of the theological movements which today are slowly gaining in strength. These movements have come to the fore in anticipation of the changes which the church will have to undergo.

One can distinguish three main types of a new theological orientation: (1) a radical theological liberalism, (2) a new evangelicalism, and (3) the ecumenical theology.

The features of these theological programs are not sharply cut. It is not possible to regard them as fully developed plans of thought and action. They appear as broad projects, the outlines of which are fairly clear. But the promise they may hold for the future is still hid in the fluctuations of the process of becoming. Nor can any one attribute any of these programs to individual leaders, although each one of them is being shaped by strong individual contributors to theological thought. Leaders who seem to further the same program do not agree in their specific views.[1]

It is also impossible to state that these programs are advocated by whole Protestant church groups, visibly set apart from other groups. However, it is highly important to note that the exponents of these programs come from different denominational traditions. This fact seems to indicate that the old denominational alignments have lost much of their theological significance.

Finally, it is perhaps permissible to say that there are individual theologians who sympathize with all three programs. Attracted to the point of view expressed in each of them and yet unable to decide for one of them, they represent the probably large number of contemporary Protestants who know that the mind of the church is changing but cannot tell the direction of the change.

I

The program which may be labeled "radical theological liberalism" depends primarily upon the methods and attainments of modernism. It is based on the presupposition that many of the historical beliefs of Christianity have outlived their usefulness. Its advocates differ from the older liberals in so far as they adhere to this opinion with a radical earnestness. The modernists of the nineteenth century and the early decades of this century relied upon the distinction between the abiding content and the changing categories of the Christian faith (and there was truth in this distinction!). They considered it possible to create proper contemporary expressions of the super-historical "essence" of Christianity. They took a position inside the existing churches and hoped gradually to transform their thought and worship by means of education. They were successful particularly in so far as they accomplished a loosening of creedal authority and a broad enlightenment of the church people about the temporary and relative character of theological doctrines. But they always preserved the existing ecclesiastical institutions and introduced no revolutionary innovations.

The new liberalism is much more radical. Its representatives are not primarily concerned for the preservation of the existing churches. While they regard themselves as Christian thinkers, they do not take a position within any of the existing churches. Not unaware of the historical effectiveness of the Christian tradition, they define the religious attitude of modern man on the basis of the scientific interpretations of the universe, in dependence upon the new biological, psychological, and sociological knowledge of man, or in terms of the modern philosophy and history of religion. The radicalness of their point of view is to be seen in the fact that they are not primarily interested in serving the churches. Their first concern belongs to those modern men who, emancipated from the Christian tradition, long for religious guidance amid the confusions and pressures of present-day living. Their interpretation of religion is determined by the desire to give recognition to the truth which, they feel, must inhere in all high religions. Some of them look forward to the day when one world-religion will serve and express the religious needs of men everywhere. They trust that the scientific advance will continue and gradually overcome the inward and outward limitations which still separate the people of the world from each other. Therefore, they subject the historical faiths to an examination on the basis of norms which are derived from the sciences or inspired by scientific philosophy, and they hold that only those religious ideas deserve to be cultivated which have stood the test of this scrutiny. They pin their hopes on the philosophy of religion. They expect that, when its furtherers will have developed universal methods for the interpretation of religion that can be as generally recognized as the methods of the sciences now are, it will replace the "discipline" of ecclesiastical theology.

The influence of these radical liberals extends far into the churches, and they have a hold upon many Christian leaders, especially ministers. These may not be fully aware of the implication of the teachings by which they are attracted. But precisely these implications point to the possibility of a radical transformation of Christianity in the future. For it may be that, in times to come, the existing church organizations will be dissolved from within by the power of interpretations of the religious life which are free from a direct dependence upon the Christian tradition and emanate from individual teachers of religion who address themselves not to Christians exclusively but to religious individuals wherever they may be found.

In the light of the history of Christianity, these prospects appear questionable. While it is undeniable that there are tendencies in contemporary cultural life which point to the possibility that there will come a time when the church will no longer be, it is doubtful whether, even in these times of rapid change, the church can be conquered and dissolved by religious-philosophical teachings not primarily inspired by history and tradition. It must be obvious to a critical observer that the "new radical liberalism" is a modern form of the mystical approach to religion. Indeed it may be said that the power of attraction which it exercises upon its representatives is derived from its propagation of a mystical religious devotion rather than from its criticism of ecclesiastical theology in the name of "modern" methods of the philosophy of religion.

The history of religion and of Christianity in particular shows that mysticism has been effective only when it was grafted upon historical religions. It therefore appears not improbable that the modern "radical religious liberalism" also lives by the church. If the church should break up, it too would disappear.

II

Another new theological program has come to the fore in the form of a "new evangelicalism." It is sometimes described

by the name of "neo-orthodoxy." This name does not adequately suggest the character of this movement. For, while it
turns with a fresh appreciation to the teachings of the Christian tradition as they are contained in the Bible and in the
historical dogmas and creeds, it has little in common with that
type of orthodoxy which, largely for reasons of conservatism,
has clung to the old forms of ecclesiastical life and thought and
refused to admit the validity of the historical understanding of
the Christian faith. The new evangelicalism is fully conscious
of the inward and outward involvement of the Christian religion in the situation of modern civilization and its crises. It
therefore not only accepts the critical understanding of the history of Christianity but also relates itself to the special condition of the Christian churches in the present world. As a matter
of fact, its point of view has developed primarily from a consideration of the present world situation. The recognition of
the irreconcilability of the Christian religion with the philosophies and doctrines of the warring political, economic, social,
and cultural groups and parties of today has caused its representatives to advocate a detachment of Christianity from its
entanglements with modern civilization. This detachment has
sometimes, in the case of Karl Barth, for example, been interpreted as a retreat from responsibility for the present, a theoretical retreat in the forgotten—and rightly forgotten—teachings of the past, and a practical retreat from the present enemies
of Christianity, a retreat which in actuality is said to amount
to a surrender to those forces of modern civilization which
threaten to destroy it, because it leaves the field to them. Such
a judgment is unjust, for it fails to comprehend this "retreat"
as the assumption of a position in a fortress for purposes of
defense as well as of attack.

The representatives of the new evangelicalism regard their
rediscovery of a positive understanding of the Christian "tradition" as the beginning of a spiritual battle in the course of
which the truth of the Christian faith is to be defended and
its enemies in modern life attacked. The "old" doctrines are
regarded as a fortress not because they are old and tried in
storms but because they contain an understanding of the Christian gospel in which its full uniqueness is preserved. This
uniqueness is primarily seen in the message of salvation, funda-

mentally different from all other teachings of salvation in so
far as it asserts the full and unqualified need of sinful, finite
man for the mercy of the only holy, infinite God.

The new evangelicalism thus gives fresh attention to the
old Christian teachings of revelation and of grace and sin. Rejecting the reinterpretations of these teachings by "modernist"
theology because they adjust the true content of the Christian
gospel to an essentially un-Christian assertion of man's ability
to achieve the good life and the Kingdom of God by his own
rational and moral and religious efforts, it has anchored itself
in a new biblicism. For it holds that only constant attention
to the message of the Bible and a measuring of Christian teachings and institutions by this message can guarantee a true encounter of man with the Christian gospel. This attitude is
held on the basis of the premise that the content of the message of the Bible, and particularly of the New Testament, can
be clearly ascertained within its historically relative, fragmentary and even dubious forms, and that, in a similar way, the
true intent of the ecclesiastical dogma, outlived as its terminology may be, can be comprehended.

The church appears to the defenders of this point of view
as the fellowship of believers who, responding to the self-disclosure of the eternal God in Jesus of Nazareth, feel themselves
set into the world as witnesses of a way of life which is inspired
alone by the trust in the sovereignty of the God of Jesus Christ
and in no way by reliance upon the sufficiency of powers which,
in the illusion of his mastery of the world, man may proclaim
as instruments for the establishment of the good life on earth.
If the actual church does not reflect this character, they say, it
must be reformed. Indeed, the whole movement of the new
evangelicalism, by whatever protagonist it may be represented,
is a movement for the reformation of the church. It calls Christians back to the distinctive resources of their faith. It does so
by pointing to the doctrines, creeds, and liturgies of the "tradition," not for the sake of a revival of this "tradition" but in
order to bring contemporary Christians again in touch with
the unique content of the Christian faith. The traditionalism
is therefore not an end in itself but merely a means to an end.

The power of this call is particularly impressive because of
the fact that it has awakened in the churches a new realistic

awareness of the nature of evil and sin. The strength of the new evangelicalism lies therefore in the realistic understanding of the powers of evil, now dominating the world.

Whether the reform of Christianity, which the defenders of this point of view envisage, can and will really take place depends largely upon the question of whether the new appreciation of the traditional teachings of the church will remain a means of awakening the church to a consciousness of the special character of its gospel, or whether it will become an end itself. If this movement can succeed in erecting contemporaneous forms of the faith which will truly correspond to the historical dogma, it will inaugurate a true reform. If it does not succeed in this, its importance will merely be that it has shown the need for a new formulation and expression of the Christian message. Only that expression of the Christian message will be adequate, today and in the future, which states the gospel of the Kingdom of the God of love in a form which does justice to the mature status of reason, achieved during the last century, and which expresses the vision of a social order and a world order, in which the strife and destruction of political nationalistic imperialisms and of economic capitalistic competition are seen as utterly incompatible with love and reason alike.

III

The "radical liberalism" regards itself as part of the wide historical development of religion in general and of Christianity in particular and is distinctly undenominational. The "new evangelicalism" takes its position within the churches and denominations, although it does not intend to further any form of denominationalism. A third movement in the present theological revival combines the long historical perspective of "liberalism" with the "traditionalist" emphasis upon the responsibility of the existing churches and is distinctly interdenominational. It is the "ecumenical theology." It has gradually come into being under the impact of the ecumenical Christian conferences of the years after the first World War. Particularly from the recent conferences of Oxford, Edinburgh, Madras, and Amsterdam, it has received a significant impetus. The chief concern of the ecumenical movement is the conquest of the present diversities of Christendom, particularly Protestantism, by the spirit of unity and co-operation. Recognizing the interdependence of all parts of the world as the basis of the productive development of civilization, it endeavors to accomplish a Christian ecumenism. Thereby it hopes to extricate the Christian churches from their entanglement in the competing nationalist economic-political orders and to unite them in a common front against the destructive secularist and pagan absolutisms of the present day. The unity of Christendom, which it tries to establish, is to express itself primarily in a worldwide proclamation by all churches of the irreconcilability of the Christian ethos with the egotism of national, political, and economic groups and movements.

It is now fully aware of the fact that such a unity in the Christian ideals of life and work cannot be established without a common concern for the standards of faith which underlie these ideals. Particularly the Oxford Conference has done its work on the assumption that, without an ecumenical theology, no unity of Christian life and work can be accomplished. It succeeded in enlisting individual theologians from all co-operating church groups for the work of a common examination of the fundamental theological premises of a Christian world order. This theological collaboration of thinkers, who came from various traditions and who exercised different concrete responsibilities in Christendom, was an entirely new phase in the history of Protestantism. In spite of the interruptions which it has encountered during the last war, it has been continued. In the course of time, it may produce a theological attitude in which the "radical-liberal" emphasis upon contemporaneity will be combined with the "new evangelical" insistence upon the uniqueness of the Christian gospel. This theological attitude may prove all the more influential because it originates from a world-wide confrontation of the Christian religion with the critical conditions of present civilization.

We may not expect that this ecumenical theology will be specially produced by the ecumenical movement, as if it were possible for the World Council of Churches to set forth its own ecumenical theological teachings. To be sure, the activities of the ecumenical organizations will stimulate ecumenical theological work in the future as they have done in the past — through international theological study groups and through their general impact upon the life of the churches, especially in the mission fields. The ecumenical theological spirit which will thus be aroused will effect a change in the outlook of those churches which are active particpants in the life of the World Council of Churches.

The time has passed when the ideal of the *Una Sancta* was so conceived that one Christian World Church or even one Protestant or non-Roman Catholic World Church could be envisioned. It is now clear that the goal of the ecumenical movement cannot be the accomplishment of unity through uniformity but that it must be the achievement of unity in multiformity. While it is to be hoped that the division of Christendom will be increasingly undone by the gradual development of interdenominationalism in and by means of the union of such denominational churches as are able to merge, it cannot be expected that the historic churches which represent particular expressions of the Christian spirit within the stream of human history will or should be replaced by new, more inclusive ecclesiastical bodies. At any rate, it is inconceivable that the major types of Protestant Christianity, namely, Lutheranism, Calvinism, Anglicanism, and that noncreedal, nonauthoritarian Protestantism which originated in the so-called sectarian movements of the Reformation and has blossomed in various forms particularly in English and American Christianity will cease to be special independent entities in the life of Christendom. Within the ecumenical movement the Christian ways represented by them will continue to assert themselves — yet without the spirit of absolutism and without particularism. Thus they will become ecumenical churches. Indeed, the denominations, so we may expect, will be related to the ecumenical church of the future in the same way in which local churches and church associations are now related to the national or international bodies to which they belong. For, in spite of the considerable differences in the polity of the various denominations, the togetherness of localism and universalism, of congregationalism and catholicity, which was characteristic of Christian church life even in New Testament times, is characteristic of the ecclesiastical spirit of them all.

The ecumenical theology of the future will then be the product of the churches that participate in the work of the ecumenical movement. It will not be super-imposed upon them, but it will grow within them. It will be primarily an expression of an ecumenical spirit within the particular tradition prevailing in a given historic church. This spirit will manifest itself in the abrogation of all theological or creedal absolutisms. It will lead to a catholicity of outlook which, on the one hand, will be radically distinguished from that intolerant exclusiveness which now characterizes the catholicity of the Roman Catholic church and, on the other hand, will be marked by a definiteness of position unhampered by either electicism or syncretism but oriented to the gospel of Christ.

The display of such an ecumenical theological spirit will be nothing new in Protestantism. Ever since the days of the Reformation, efforts have been made by farsighted men to cast the theological expression and defense of the Christian gospel in an ecumenical form. Melanchthon, Butzer, and particularly Calvin endeavored to be theological spokesmen of a "unitive Protestantism," and, under new circumstances, their example has been followed by many theologians down to the days of Schleiermacher and the liberal theologians of our day.

Despite the different theological methods they employed, they spoke and wrote about the true Christian gospel as they conceived it to be relevant for their own times. They regarded themselves as representatives of the church to which they belonged, and, as such, they interpreted the Christian gospel. They did not desire to absolutize their theological interpretations in so far as they were characteristic of their church, but they also did not wish to invalidate the determinedness of what they had to say about Christian truth by their particular place in Christendom and in the life of historical civilization.

In our day it is much easier for theologians to work in the spirit of ecumenical theology than it has ever been before. The historical understanding of the Christian religion has liberated them from that orthodoxy which was bound to the literally inspired Bible, to authoritarian creeds, and to other unchangeable norms. It has enabled them to see that the Christian gospel can be comprehended only in and through pluralistic historical forms and that the Christian faith cannot be anything else but that dynamic response to the divine call in Jesus Christ which comes to individual men and groups of believers only through the media of many historical forms of Christian faith and order, life and work. The theological interpreters of Christianity cannot do their work except on the basis of historical and comparative theology. They are thus required to practice an open-mindedness that makes them willing to listen to all serious interpretations of the Christian religion. They must possess a readiness for rethinking which will permit them to recast their own views in the light of discussions with those who disagree with them.

The possibility of an ecumenical theology is thus given wherever Christian thinkers find themselves ready freely to learn from one another as they share with one another what they believe the Christian gospel to be in the light of their loyalty to the Christian tradition in which they stand and in terms of their responsibility to the times in which they must serve. Such a theology will combine within itself that concern for the specific elements of the Christian religion which the new evangelicalism of our day stresses and that passion for contemporaneity which the radical liberalism emphasizes. It can avoid the one-sided preference for the traditional teachings which is characteristic of some of the so-called neo-orthodox theologians and also that exaggerated devotion to contemporaneous issues and that neglect of history which mark the radical liberals and especially the philosophers of religion among them. This ecumenical theology can be both churchly and free. It must ever be in motion and can never be static.

I believe that it finds its foremost expression today not primarily in the enterprises of the ecumenical movement itself but in the work of the modern American interdenominational (or interdenominationally minded) seminaries and divinity schools. It is reflected also in the spirit which determines the American theological societies. What is going on and is being accomplished in these institutions and groups deserves to be brought to much wider attention in Christendom. The actuality of the ecumenical theology which has been accomplished by them should be heartily celebrated and fully realized. And those who have the privilege of sharing in this actuality should recognize more fully than they now do its importance for the theological work of the church. If they would, they would be led to stress their churchmanship in the denominations in which they now stand in such a way that their own churches would benefit from their work in a much more concrete way than is now the case.

It should perhaps be particularly noted that the interdenominational theological work being done in American seminaries is unique in Christendom. It is, of course, made possible by the freedom of religion which Americans enjoy by virtue of the Constitution of the United States. It is thus a very positive product of the same opportunity which has called into being that diversity of Christendom which is represented by American denominationalism. Thus it has come about that many American theologians pursue their work with a constant concern for the life and thought of all denominations and not merely for that of their own, because they have an immediate opportunity of doing so, and that they are open to the thought of the Christian thinkers of all lands to an extent characteristic of the theologians of no other country. It is time that American theologians should fully appreciate this great privilege and that they should consciously assume the leadership in the further development of the ecumenical theology.[2] Their own church situation has given them the methods of ecumenical theological thinking—the situation of world Christianity demands of them that they be fully applied.

This review of the features of the three main types of the "theological renaissance" will have shown that the field of theological work that has been opened for the Christian churches under the impact of the crisis of Western civilization is wide and rough. The clarification of the Christian faith for the present time and the re-examination of its standards for the purpose of preparing for the future of mankind is no simple task. But it can be said that he who enters into a debate with those who pursue one of these theological programs is brought directly face to face with the urgency of the need of finding a theological form of the Christian faith by which its saving power can be fully communicated to the desperate spiritual hunger of the men of today.

Acknowledgments

The following list explains the origin of the individual chapters of this book. Grateful acknowledgment is herewith made to the editors of the several journals for their permission to reprint the materials. It should be emphasized that all of the articles have been revised for publication in this volume.

1. First published in *Theology Today*, vol. III (1946), p. 314-327.
2. First published in *Religion in Life*, vol. XVI (1946-47), p. 3-11, written in commemoration of Luther's death on February 18, 1546.
3. Hitherto unpublished.
4. First published in *Church History*, vol. XV (1946), p. 17-27.
5. First published in *The Journal of Religion*, vol. IX (1929), p. 85-98.
6. First published in *The Journal of Religion*, vol. IX (1929), p. 237-256.
7. Hitherto unpublished. The substance of this chapter was delivered as a lecture at the Joint Meeting of the *American Historical Association* and the *Catholic Historical Association* in Cleveland, Ohio, December 28, 1947.
8. This is a much revised version of an article first published in *Church History*, vol. VI (1937), p. 3-23.
9. The substance of this article constituted the *Dudleian Lecture* for the Academic Year 1938-1939 in *Harvard University*, delivered in Andover Chapel, April 18, 1939.
10. First published in *Christendom*, vol. XI (1946), p. 373-381.
11./12. Parts of these chapters have been published in *Theology Today*, vol. V (1948).
13. First published in *Church History*, vol. XV (1946), p. 220-234.
14. This chapter and the preceding one represent *University of Oregon Lectures in Religion*, delivered in January 1945.
15. Hitherto unpublished.

16. First published in *Congregational Quarterly* (England), vol. XII (1934), p. 156-163.
17. First published in *The Journal of Religion*, vol. XV (1935), p. 146-160, here considerably revised.
18. First published in *The Journal of Religion*, vol. XXVII (1947), p. 48-54, in reply to an article by Clarence Bouma entitled *Calvinism in American Theology Today* (ibid., p. 34-45).
19. First published in *The Journal of Religion*, vol. XXV (1945), p. 79-87.

Notes

NOTES TO CHAPTER TWO

1 Ernst Wolf, *Martin Luther* (Theologische Existenz heute. Heft 6). Munich, 1934, 7.

2 30, III: 290, 28. (All quotations are translated from the volumes of the *Weimar Edition* of Luther's works. The quotations taken from the Table Talk (*Tischreden*) are indicated by the sign T.R.; those taken from the Letters, by the sign B (*Briefe*).

3 10, II: 105, 17.

4 10, II: 228, 27.

5 8: 683, 13.

6 B. 11: 39.

7 T.R. I: 42, 17.

8 T.R. V: No. 5342 b.

9 6: 157.

10 T.R. (IV): No. 3944.

11 T.R. I: 176, 15.

12 8: 685, 6.

13 30, III: 366, 8.

14 T.R. V: No. 6409.

15 31, I: 174, 26.

16 18: 709, 21.

17 15:574, 14.

18 23: 133f.

19 26: 339f.

20 19: 492, 12.

21 40, III: 154, 9.

22 23: 151.

23 40, III: 56.

24 I: 225, 1.

25 30, I: 28.

26 18: 709.

27 40, I: 546, 25. See the very illuminating discussion of Erich Vogelsang, "Die Unio mystica bei Luther" in *Archiv für Reformationsgeschichte*, Vol. 35 (1938), pp. 73 ff.

28 See Fritz Frey, *Luthers Glaubensbegriff*, Leipzig, 1939, 110.

29 40, I: 228, 15.

30 10, III: 3, 329.

31 40, I: 589, 8.

31a See Roland H. Bainton's interesting analysis "Luther's Struggle for Faith" in *Church History* XVII (1948), p. 193ff.

32 10, I: 2, 335f.

33 T.R. I: 203, 36.

34 T.R. I: 146, 12.

35 19: 226, 12.

36 B. II: 430ff.

37 10, III: 18ff.

NOTES TO CHAPTER THREE

1 Cf. the treatment of Luther's doctrine of the church in the book by Paul Althaus, *Communio Sanctorum*. Gütersloh: Bertelsmann, 1930. The best discussion of the development of Luther's conception of the church is that by

Karl Holl (See his essay entitled *"Die Entstehung von Luthers Kirchenbegriff"* in *Gesammelte Aufsätze,* Vol. I: *Luther* (Second Edition, Tübingen: Mohr, 1923). I regard the essay by Ferdinand Kattenbusch, *Die Doppelschichtigkeit* in *Luther's Kirchenbegriff* (Gotha: Klotz, 1928) as the most suggestive and most competent treatment of Luther's ecclesiology.

[2] W. A. (Weimar Edition (*Ausgabe*) of Luther's works), 12,488: *so wyr denn mit Christo eyn Kuchen sind, so wirckt das selbige soviel, das wyr auch untereinander eyn ding werden; . . . die korner, die tzermalen werden, so sprengen sie sich ynn einander, keyns behelt mel bey yhm, sondern mengens ynn eynander, bis es eyn ding wird . . .keyner ist fur sich selbst, sondern yeglicher wyrfft und breyt sich unter den andern durch die liebe.*

[3] *Ausser der Christlichen kirchen ist keyn wahrheytt, keyn Christus, keyne seligkeyt.* (W. A. 10, I; Pt. 1, 140)

[4] W. A. 7, 721, 9: The whole life and substance of the church is in the word of God.

[5] W. A. 2, 509: *Solum verbum est vehiculum gratia Dei.*

[6] W. A. 39, 1, 332: *Verbum non est opus nostrum, sed est regnum Dei efficax et potens in cordibus nostris.*

[7] W. A .25, 97: *Unica et perpetua et infallibilis ecclesiae nota semper fuit Verbum.*

[8] W. A. 50, 629, 34: *Gottes wort kan nicht on Gottes Volck sin, wiederumb Gottes Volck kan nicht on Gottes wort sein, Wer wolts sonst predigen oder predigen hören.*

[9] W. A. 40, 1, 259, 11 ff.

[10] W. A. 30, I, 1:192.

[11] W. A. 18, 1:689.

[12] W. A. 8; 141, 30: *Was seyn nu Bapsts gesetz den eytel tzusatz.*

[13] W. A. 39, II, 61, 4.

[14] W. A. 1; 639: *est autem fidelium communio duplex: una interna et spiritualis, alia externa et corporalis; spiritualis est una fides, spes, charitas in deum, corporalis participatio sacramentorum,* i.e. *signorum fidei, spei, charitati, quae tamen ulterius extenditur usque ad communionem verum, usus, colloquii, habitationis aliarumque corporalium conversationum.*

[15] W. A. 6; 295, 25: just as the body is a figure or image of the soul so the corporeal community is a likeness of this spiritual Christian community.

[16] *Ibid.,* 296, 36.

[17] W. A. VII; 683, 9: *Da ich Christliche Kirch ein geystlich versammlung genennet hat, spottistu meyn, als wolt ich ein Kirch bawen, wie Plato ein statt, die nyndert were und lest dyr deyn zufall so hertzlich wolgefallen, als habstu es fast wol troffen.*

[18] W. A. VII; 719, 34ff: *quamquam ecclesia in carne vivat, tamen non secundum carnem vivit, Paulus dicit in Gal. 1 et 2., Cor. 10, Ita in loco, rebus, operibus mundi versatus, sed non secundum hos aestimatur . . . sicut enim ecclesia sine esca et potu non est in hac vita et tamen regnum dei non est esca et potus secundum Paulum, ita sine loco et corpore non est ecclesia et tamen corpus et locus non sunt ecclesia neque ad eam pertinent.*

[19] W. A. IV; 169, 30 . . . *ecclesia semper nascitur et semper mutatur in successione fidelium, alia et alia est ecclesia et tamen semper eadem.*

[20] W. A. 7, 97: *ut sit ipsa per sese certissima, facillima, apertissima, sui ipsius interpres.*

[21] See my articles *"Martin Luther's Glaube"* (in Arnold Bergsträsser [ed.], *Deutsche Beiträge zur Geistigen Überliefernug.* Chicago: University of Chicago Press, 1947, p. 58-72) and "Martin Luther's Faith", but particularly the essay by Karl Holl, entitled "Luther's Urtele über sich selbst" in *op. cit.,* p. 381-419.

[22] W. A. 7: 670, 20: *Ich begere nit loss zu seyn von menschen gesetzen und leren. Ich begere nur, das gewissen los zu haben.* (I do not desire to be free from human laws and teachings. I desire only to have a free conscience).

[23] I have adopted these terms from Ferdinand Kattenbusch, *op. cit.*

24 This point is well borne out by the following sentence of the theses prepared by Luther for the Disputation of Leipzig in 1519: *ita iure divino quiquid habet Romana ecclesia, habet qualibit ecclesia quantumlibet parva* (W. A. 2, 208, 17ff). (Any church however small has by divine right whatever the Roman church has.)

25 That what the Papacy had made of Christianity was heresy, he did not doubt. So he regarded also Scholasticism as heretical and particularly the teaching of Thomas Aquinas. (W. A. 7, 710; 15, 184).

26 Wider Hans Worst.

27 Cf. Holl, *op. cit.*, p. 368f. He quotes the following sentences from a disputation of Luther (W. A. 39, 2:167, 20): *in ecclesia papistarum mansit vera scriptura et conservata est ipsa mirabili dei consilio, mansit baptismus, sacramentum altaris, absolutio conservata divino miraculo, item multi in vera fide sunt mortui . . . item vixerunt multi boni monachi ut Bernhardus et Bonaventura, qui sunt salvati, sed non habent illa tam clare ut nos iam habemus, item multi parvuli sunt salvati quos liberavit deus* (cf. also 666, 682) (In the church of the papists the true scripture is remaining, having been preserved by the wonderful counsel of God. There also remained in it baptism, the sacrament of the altar and absolution, which has been conserved by a divine miracle. Moreover, many have died in true faith . . . many good monks like Bernard and Bonaventura have lived, who had salvation. But they (the papists) have all this not clearly as we have it now. Also many ordinary people have been saved (in the Roman Church) and God has freed them (from their sins).

28 W. A. 8, 685, 6ff: *"Was ist Luther? Ist doch die leer nit meyn; Szo byn ich auch fur niemand gecreutzigt. . . . Wie keme denn ich armer stinkender madensack datzu, das man die Kynder Christi solt mit meinem heiloszen namen nennen. . . . Ich byn und wyll keynes meyster seyn. Ich habe mit der gemeyn die eynige, gemeyne lere Christi, der allein unszer meyster ist."*

29 As one example, I quote the following (W. A. 2; 492): *Non iusta faciendo iustus fit, sed factus iustus facit iusta.*

30 Cf. W. A. 18; 719, 34ff.: *Ecclesia est abscondita, latent sancti.* (The church is hidden and the saints are not apparent.)

31 In the Larger Catechism, he wrote (W. A. 30, I; 188, 23): . . . he has a special community (*gemeyne*) in the world which is the mother, bearing and nurturing every Christian by the word.

32 Cf. Kurt Matthes, *Das Corpus Christianum bei Luther im Lichte seiner Erforschung* (= *Studien zur Geschichte der Wirtschaft und Geisteskultur,* ed. by Rudolf Häpke, vol. V), Berlin: Curtius, 1929.

33 He was often sorely beset by the thought that he as a single individual had dared to stand against the authority of the Roman Church. Indeed, he asked himself the question: "Do you think that all earlier teachers knew nothing? Why should you regard all our fathers as fools? Have you alone been preserved as the seed of the Holy Spirit in our time? Should it be possible that God should have left his people in error for so many years?" (W. A. 23; 421, 26ff.: "Meinest du, dass alle vorigen Lehrer nichts gewusst haben? Müssen dir alle unsere Väter Narren sein? Bistu allein des heiligen Geistes Nestei blieben auf diese letzte Zeit? Sollt Gott so viele jahrelang sein Volk haben irren lassen?" The concern which he expressed in this question was, not whether he had *discovered* something new but whether he could really claim to have *rediscovered* the word, the *old* Christian truth. Certain that the word was on his side, he therefore regarded the question as irrelevant. "I do not claim to be a prophet," he wrote on another occasion, ". . . but though I am not a prophet, I am nevertheless certain in my own mind that the word of God is with me and not with them, for I have the Scripture on my side."

(W. A. 7; 313, 17ff.: *ich sage nit, dasz ich eyn prophet sei, . . . bin ich nit ein prophet, szo bynn ich yhe doch gewisz fur mich selbs, das das Wort gotis bei mir und nit bei yhnen ist, dennich yhe die schrifft fur mich habe."* Cf. Holl, *op. cit.,* p. 382.

NOTES TO CHAPTER FOUR

1 The following books may prove helpful in further study: Benjamin B. Warfield, "On the Literary History of Calvin's Institutes," in *Calvin and Calvinism* (New York: Oxford University Press, 1931), 373-478; Albert Autin, *L'Institution Chrétienne* (Paris: Société d'Editions Littéraires, 1929); Julius Köstlin, "Calvin's Institutio nach Form und Inhalt," in *Theologische Studien und Kritiken,* 41 (1868), 7-62, 410-486; A. Mitchell Hunter, *The Teaching of Calvin* (Glasgow: Maclehose, 1920); Paul Wernle, *Der evangelische Glaube nach den Hauptschriften der Reformatoren,* Vol. III: *Calvin* (Tübingen: Mohr, 1919); Wilhelm Niesel, *Die Theologie Calvins* (München: Kaiser, 1938). In his book *Books of Faith and Power* (New York: Harpers, 1947, p. 29-57), John T. McNeill gives a summary of the last edition of the *Institutes.*

The best critical edition of Calvin's *Institutes* has been furnished by Peter Barth and Wilhelm Niesel under the title: *Joannis Calvini Opera Selecta* (Munich: Kaiser, 1926-1936). The 1536 edition of the *Institutes* is printed in Vol. I; the 1559 edition appears in Vols. III-V. The text is so printed that the changes made in the several editions by Calvin are clearly indicated.

2 John Calvin, *The Institutes of the Christian Religion,* translated by John Allen. 6th American edition. (Philadelphia: Presbyterian Board of Education, 1928), I, 21f.

3 *Institutes,* III; 7, 1. Allen translation, I, 618f.

NOTES TO CHAPTER FIVE

1 *The Judgment of Martin Bucer Concerning Divorce,* translated by John Milton. London, 1644.

2 Cf. Wilhelm Pauck, *Das Reich Gottes auf Erden. Eine Untersuchung zu Butzers "De regno Christi" und zur englischen Staatskirche des sechzehnten Jahrht.* (Berlin and Leipzig, 1928), p. 111. The ideas of Butzer, to which this article refers, are fully represented in this book. Cf. now the to date fullest treatment of Butzer's work in England by Constantin Hopf, *Martin Bucer and the English Reformation* (Oxford: Blackwall, 1946).

3 Cf. "De regno Christi" in *Scripta anglicana,* pp. 1-170; "De vera cura animarum," *ibid.,* pp. 260-356; Dialogi oder Gesprech von der gemainsame [=res publica; commonwealth!], und der kirchenübungen der Christen, Und was yeder Oberkait von ampts wegen aus Göttlichem befelch an denselbigen zu versehen und zu besseren gebüre. Augsburg, 1535.

4 W. A., xi, 271, 20.

5 *Ibid.,* xi, 249,26ff.

6 Emanuel Hirsch, *Die Reich-Gottesbegriffe des modernen Denkens* (Göttingen, 1922), p. 7.

7 *WA,* lii, 266. 16.

8 *Script. angl.,* p. 20.

9 *Ibid.,* p. 55. Butzer defines faith as *persuasio* (e.g., *Enarrationes in quatuor Evangelia* [1536], pp. 219 ff.); Luther speaks exclusively of *fiducia.* Cf. on this point the remarks by Hans Emil Weber, *Reformation, Orthodoxie and Rationalismus,* Gütersloh: Bertelsmann, 1937, p. 212.

10 *Dialogi,* p. O3v. Cf. Pauck, *Reich Gottes,* pp. 60 ff.

11 *Script, angl.,* p. 11. The same point is emphasized by Henri Strohl in his

article "Bucer Interprète de Luther" in *Rev. d'Histoire et de Phil. Rel.*, vol. *xix* (1939), pp. 223 ff. He claims that Butzer was a better interpreter of Luther than Melanchthon was. But this book should not be read without reference to Robert Stupperich, Die Kirche in Martin Bucer's theologischer Entwicklung, *Archiv für Reformationsgeschichte,* vol. 35 (1938), p. 81 ff.

[12] *Ibid.*, p. 157.

[13] *Ibid.*, p. 31. The fullest discussion on Butzer's ecclesiology now available is that by Jacques Courvoisier, *La Nation d'Eglise chez Bucer,* Paris: Alcan 1933. He too compares Luther and Butzer, but he inclines to judge Luther from a prejudiced Reformed point of view.

[14] Cf. Gustav Anrich, *Martin Bucer* (Strassburg, 1914), p. 83.

[15] Cf. Pauck, *Das Reich Gottes,* pp. 19 ff. Butzer says expressly in *De regno Christi (Script. angl.,* p. 149) that no law deserves the name of law unless it contains the fundamental law of love as it is given in the Bible.

[16] Cf. Ferdinand Kattenbusch, *Die Doppetschichtigkeit in Luthers Kirchenbegriff* (Gotha, 1928).

[17] Cf. Henri Strohl, *L'épanouissement de la pensée religieuse de Luther* (Paris and Strassburg, 1924), pp. 322 ff.

[18] Karl Holl, *Gesammelte Aufsätze,* Vol. I, Luther (Tübingen, 1923), p. 186. The interpretation of Luther's theology as it is given in this article depends largely upon Holl's work.

[19] *Script. angl.,* pp. 32 ff., 136.

[20] Karl Holl, *Luther,* p. 347.

[21] *Dialogi,* p. U4b.

[22] Cf. Karl Müller, *Kirche, Gemeinde und Obrigkeit nach Luther* (Tübingen, 1910); Hermann Jordan, *Luthers Staatsauffassung* (1917); Julius Binder, *Luthers Staatsauffassung* (Erfurt, 1924). The remarks of John A. W. Haas, *The Problem of the Christian State* (Boston, 1928), are not quite adequate. The point of view of R. H. Murray in *Erasmus and Luther* (London, 1920), pp. 320 ff., and in *The Political Consequences of the Reformation* (Boston, 1926), is not always convincing, though stimulating.

[23] *WA,* vi, 258, 31 ff.

[24] *Ibid.*, xi, 257, 39.

[25] *Ibid.*, p. 258, 3.

[26] *Ibid.*, p. 248, 29. Butzer's views of the Christian magistrate are instructively, if incompletely, discussed in the Freiburger dissertation by Rudolph Schultz, *Martin Butzer's Anschauung von der christlichen Oberkeit. Zella-Meklis* (Thür.): Nordheim, 1932.

[27] *Script. angl.,* p. 5.

[28] *Dialogi,* p. N4v: "Die regierung sollen sehen, dass ihre unterthonen recht und wol leben. Das mag nun nit sein, wa sie nicht vor allem zum waren Gotsdienst gezogen werden. An dem hangen alle tugenten, auch alles glück und heyl. Denn die das reych und die gerechtigkeit Gottes suchen, wirdt alles gutes selb zufallen, sagt Christus der Herr. Darum müssen die gottsäligen obren die Religion nit als ein mittel zum eusserlichen friden brauchen, wie die gottlosen tyrannen thund, sondern die Religion selb lassen jr end sein, darumb sy alles thun und anrichten, das bei den jren durch jr ampt der regierung der nam Gottes als mehr gehailigt, und sein reych mehr ausgepreytet und bass erbowen werde."

[29] *WA,* xi, 262, 7.

[30] *Ibid.*, xii, 330, 30.

[30a] Butzer preferred to speak of the state as *respublica.* This is due to the fact that his political thinking was formed primarily by his experience in the city state of Strassburg. Cf. Hans Baron's important study on "Calvinist Republicanism" in *Church History,* vol. VIII (1939), p. 30 ff.

[31] *Script. angl.,* p. 158.

[31a] *WA,* xi, 251, 34.

[23] *Ibid.*, xxxii, 307, 19; 440, 9, 23.

[33] *Ibid.*, li, 242, 6.

34 *WA*, xvi, 377, 6.

35 *Ibid.*, li, 242, I.

36 *Ibid.*, li, 239, 21.

37 *Ibid.*, vi, 457, 28 ff., 467, 17 ff., 450, 21 ff., 466, 13 ff., 465, 25 ff.

38 When Butzer met Luther for the first time he was an enthusiastic Erasmian (cf. Anrich, pp. 4 ff.). He heard Luther in a disputation on the *theologia crucis* at an Augustinian convent in Heidelberg, 1518 (*WA*, I, 353 ff.). Butzer wrote his impressions to his friend, the Humanist Beatus Rhenanus (cf. Daniel Gerdesius, *Introductio in Hist. Ev. Seculo xvi* [Groningen, 1774], pp. 175 ff.). His comparison of Luther with Erasmus is interesting: "Cum Erasmo illi conveniunt ommia, quin uno hoc praestare videtur quod quae ille duntaxat, innovat. hic experte docet et libere" (1). Even at Butzer's funeral, his friendship with Erasmus is mentioned (*Script. angl.*, p. 885). The following references on Butzer's Erasmian character are worth remembering: Erasmian influence upon Butzer's method of exegesis (A. Lang, *Evangelienkommentar Mart. Butzers,* pp. 20 f., 30, 54 f., 58); humanistic influence upon Butzer's attitude in the controversy about the Lord's Supper (Cf. W. Koehler, *Zwingli und Luther,* Vol. I, Leipzig, 1924). The same influence governed Butzer in his political efforts to bring about a religious union (cf. P. Vetter, *Die Religions-verhandlungen auf dem Reichstage zu Regensburg* [Jena, 1889], pp. 79 ff.; M .Lenz, *Briefwechsel Philipps des Grossmütigen mit Butzer* [Leipzig, 1880 ff.], I, 271 ff., III, 31 ff.; Robert Stupperich *Der Humanismus und die Wiedervereinigung der Konfessionen,* Leipzig: Heinsius, 1936). The moralistic concept of religion and the plan to bring about a moral reformation of the world was common to all Humanists (cf. W. Sohm, *Die Schule Joh. Sturms und die Kirche Strassburgs* [München, 1912], p. 112; R. Seeberg, *Dogmengeschichte* [Leipzig, 1920], IV, 2, 629; Otto Ritschl, *Die reformierte Theologie des 16. und des 17. Jahrh.* [*Dogmengeschichte des Protestantismus,* Vol. III, Göttingen, 1926], pp. 123 ff.).) Hans Emil Weber (*op. cit.,* p. 203-217), interprets Butzer's thought in terms of a "*christozentrische ethische Geistesmystik.*"

NOTES TO CHAPTER SIX

1 *Studien und Kritiken* (1884), p. 417.

2 *Die calvinische und die altstrassburgische Gottesdienstordnung* (Strassburg, 1894).

3 *Calvins Prädestinationslehre* (1897), pp. 17 ff.; 69 ff.

4 *Dogmengeschichte* (Leipzig, 1898), II, 254; now IV, 2, 556.

5 *Der Evangelienkommentar Martin Butzers* (1901), p. 373.

6 A. Lang, *Calvin* (Tübingen, 1909); *Reformation und Gegenwart* (Gütersloh, 1918), p. 176; cf. E. Doumergue, *Calvin,* IV, 401 f., V, 23 f.

7 G. Anrich, *M. Bucer* (1914), p. 144.

8 *Dogmengeschichte des Protestantismus* (Göttingen, 1926), III, 122 ff. In respect to the theological relationship between Butzer and Calvin cf. also Joh. Adam, *Evangelische Kirchengeschichte der Stadt* Strassburg (1922), pp. 217 ff., and the remarks of H. Strohl in his interesting study on "Martin Butzer, précurseur du Christianisme social en Alsace du XVIe siècle" in *Le Christianisme social* (1922), pp. 993-1011. Professor Strohl has often emphasized the influence of Butzer upon Calvin; see particularly his detailed study "La Notion d'Eglise chez les Reformateurs" in *Rev. d'hist. et de phil. relg.,* vol. XVI (1936), pp. 265 ff.

9 *Ibid.,* p. 125.

10 *De ontwikkeling van Bucers praedestinatie-gedachten* (Amsterdam, 1922).

11 Scheibe takes a similarly careful attitude; p. 73.

12 *Op. cit.,* p. 146.

13 *Calvin* (Tübingen, 1909), p .47, n. 15. Cf. E. Doumergue, *Calvin,* IV, 424.

14 A. Lang, *Calvin,* pp. 78 ff.

15 Cf. his discussion in *Metaphras. et Enarrat. in Epistolam ad Romanos* (Strassburg, 1536), pp. 358 ff.

16 Cf. Richard H. Grützmacher, *Wort unt Geist* (Leipzig, 1902), pp. 116-122; O. Ritschl, *op. cit.,* pp. 129 ff.; W. Pauck, *Das Reich Gottes auf Erden* (Berlin, 1928), pp. 5 ff.; 13 ff.

17 *Calv. opp.,* 10, p. 404. Published in Strassburg, 1539. Cf. Scheibe, *op. cit.,* pp. 69 ff.

18 *Calv. opp.,* 31 (1557), p. 13.

19 *Ibid.,* 45 (1555), p. 4. *Bucerum praesertim sanctae memoriae virum et eximium ecclesiae doctorem sum imitatus..* Cf. Paul Wernle, *Calvin* (Tübingen, 1919), pp. 34, 81. Lang mentions an influence of Butzer's book: *De vera cura animarum.* Cf. *Ref. und Gegenwart,* p. 183. Opposing view: Doumergue, *Calvin,* IV, 39.

20 *Calvin,* p. 21.

21 Paul Pannier, *Calvin à Strassbourg* (Paris, 1925), pp. 11, 13.

22 This assumption is based on a letter of Butzer to Farel, dated May (most probably 1528), which Kampschulte used for his theory that Calvin was a student of Butzer. Herminjard refuted this theory, suggesting that Butzer speaks of Olivétan. Cf. H. Eells, "Martin Butzer and the conversion of John Calvin," *Princeton Theol. Rev.* (1924), p. 402.

23 Herminjard, III, 202 ff.

24 *Ibid.,* p. 204. Cf. the discussion by Eells, *op. cit.,* pp. 407 ff.

25 Herminjard, IV, pp. 117 ff.; cf. the correction of the date (not *Dec.* 1) by Eells, pp. 412 ff.

26 *Ibid.,* p. 119.

27 *Ibid.,* p. 119, n. 7, 9, 10.

28 Cf. Eells, pp. 415 ff.

29 *Calv. opp.,* 10, pp. 137 ff.

30 *Ibid.,* p. 142 f.

31 See Calvin's own account in *Opp.,* 31, pp. 25 ff. Cf. Doumergue, II, 225 ff.

32 *Calf. opp.,* 10, pp. 341; 344 ff.; 348.

33 Pannier, *op. cit.,* pp. 9, 54 f. Cf. also the fascinating accounts of Doumergue in *Calvin* (1902), II, 203 ff., and of Hastings Eells, *Martin Bucer,* New Haven: Yale University Press, 1931, p. 229 ff. This detailed biography of Butzer unfortunately lacks attention to theology.

34 Cf. Bohatec in *Calvin-Studien* (Tübingen, 1909), p. 440; Lang, *Calvin,* pp. 78, 192. Compare also John T. McNeill, *Unitive Protestantism,* New York: Abingdon, 1930, pp. 68 ff. and 178 ff.

35 *Op. cit.,* p. 55.

35a This is also the judgment of Courvoisier, *op. cit.,* p. 147.

36 *Strassburg un die calvinische Kirchenverfassung* (Tübingen, 1928). See also Francois Wendel, *L'Eglise de Strasbourg sa constitution et son organisation* (Paris, 1942).

36a See the full discussion of this relationship in Joseph Bohatec, *Calvin's Lebre von Staat und Kirche,* Breslau: Marcus, 1937, p. 460 ff.

37 The old Butzer seemingly wanted to exclude the congregation in this respect. According to *De regno Christi,* the ministers elect the elders, in contrast to the order of Strassburg, where he had the presbyters elected by the congregation, which led to the formation of conventicles. (Cf. W. Sohm, *Die Schule Joh. Sturms und die Kirche Strassburgs* [München, 1912], p. 163.)

38 *Calvin* (Tübingen, 1909), pp. 13 f.

39 Georg Klingenburg, *Das Verhältnis Calvins zu Butzer auf Grund der wirtschaftsethischen Bedeutung beider Reformatoren* (Bonn, 1906). Cf. Doumergne, *Calvin,* V, 688 f., compare also R. H. Tawney, *Religion and the Rise of Capitalism* (New York, 1926), pp. 105 ff. and Bohatec, *op. cit.,* pp. 719 ff.

39a Cf. Hans Baron, *op. cit.*, p. 38 ff., who proves Calvin's dependence on Butzer's *Lectures on the Book of Judges.*

40 *Op. cit.*, p. 12.

41 Herminjard, VI, 242 f.

42 Doumergue, II, 701.

43 *Calv. opp.*, 11, p. 299: *Et si qua in re spei vestrae non respondeam, scis me sub tua protestate esse. Admoneas, castiges, omnia facias quae patri licent in filium.*

44 Herminjard, VI, 235 (letter to O. Myconius of Basel [Sept., 1541]: *Datis ergo operam ut juvete virum certe eximium, et cujus perfecto parem, excepto Philippo, nullum habemus, ardore, eloquentia et judicio).*

45 To A. Blaurer; T. Schiess, *Briefwechsel der Gebrüder Blaurer* (Freiburg, 1910), II, 133.

46 Herminjard, VIII, 150 f.

47 E.g., *Calv. opp.*, 10, pp. 414 ff. (July 7, 1542); pp. 456. (Oct. 28, 1942); pp. 634 f. (Oct. 28, 1543); *ibid.*, 12, pp. 152 ff. (Aug. 29, 1545); pp. 162 f. (Sept. 8, 1545).

48 Cf. *Calv. opp.*, 12, pp. 507; 520 f., 555 f.

49 *Ibid.*, 13, p. 5.

50 *Ibid.*, pp. 147 ff.; 181 f.; 197 ff.

51 *Ibid.*, p. 56: *Tum forsan dabit, ut quod expetii toties, videam vestras ecclesias.*

52 *Ibid.*, p. 199.

53 *Ibid.*, pp. 350, 358, 574.

54 Schiess, II, 442 f.

55 August 11, 1549 to A. Blarer; Schiess, III, 56. Note the following verses to a satirical poem on Butzer (communicated by A. Erichson in his little book *Martin Butzer, der elsässische Reformator* [Strassburg, 1891], p. 33); *Butzer der butzt auch am Rhein, Nimmt zuletzt ganz England ein.*

56 *Calv. opp.* 13, p. 489. To Farel he wrote (August 18, 1550, *ibid.*, pp. 624 f.) that he would not mention the Zurichers again in his letters to Butzer, in order not to hurt his feelings.

57 *Ibid.*, 12, p. 729: *Sed obsecro te, mi Bullingere, quo iure nos a Bucero alienaremus quum huic nostrae confessioni quam posui subscribat? Ego virtutes et raras et permultas, quibus vir ille excellit, in praesentia non praedicabo. Tantum dicam me ecclesiae Dei gravem iniuriam facturum, si hunc vel oderim vel contemnam. Taceo ut de me privatim sit meritus.*

58 *Ibid.*, 13, p. 165.

59 To Seymour: *ibid.*, 13, pp. 16 f., 18 f., 64 ff., 528 ff. To Edward VI: *ibid.*, 13, pp. 669 ff.; 14, pp. 30 ff., 38 ff., 341 ff.

60 *Calv. opp.*, 20, pp. 401 f. This letter was written a few days before Butzer's death. Butzer never read it.

61 *Ibid.*, pp. 393 f.

62 *Ibid.*, 13, pp. 424, 457, 534 f.

63 *Ibid.*, 14, p. 106: *Nuncius de Anglia nondum rediit. Sed interea de Buceri morte certior factus magnum accepi dolorem. Quod nollem, brevi sentiemus quantam ecclesia Dei iacturam fecerit. Satis dum vivebat reputabam quam praeclaris dotibus excellerit: quam utilis adhuc nobis foret, melius nunc demum ex orbitate ipsa agnosco.* To Viret he writes a few weeks later (*ibid.*, pp. 121 f.): *Moeror quem ex Buceri morte concepi sollicitudinem ac metum auget. . . . Quam multiplicem in Bucero iacturam fecerit, quoties in mentem venit, cor meum prope larcerari sentio.* And still a few weeks later to Farel (*ibid.*, p. 133): *De Buceri obitu nihil attigeram, ne vulnus meum scinderem.*

64 Schiess, II, 308.

65 *Ibid.*, I, 721.

66 *Ibid.*, I, 742.

57 *Ibid.*, I, 648: *In vera theologia tantum quisque rite novit quantum vita exprimit.*

68 *Enarr. in quat. Ev.* (Basel, 1536): *Vera theologia non theoretica et*

speculativa, sed activa et practica est. Finis siquidem ejus agere est, hoc est
vitam vivere deiformem.
69 Schiess, I, 774: *Religio nititur fide efficiente communionem sanctorum.*
70 *Ibid.,* II, 131 f.
71 Schiess, II, 119.
72 It is most interesting to observe how often the judgments of Gierke, Maitland, Figgis apply also to Butzer. Cf. O. Gierke, *Genossenschaftsrecht,* III (Berlin, 1887). English translation by F. W. Maitland, *Political theories of the M.A.* (Cambridge, 1900); F. N. Figgis, "Respublica Christiana," in *Transactions of the Royal Hist. Soc.,* 3d series (London, 1911), V, 63 ff.
73 "Fides et caritas" is another slogan in Butzer's theology. Note how F. W. L. Baum (*Capito and Butzer* [Elberfeld, 1860]) emphasizes it in his representation of B.
74 Herminjard, VI, 20. This is the theme of his last work, *De regno Christi.*
75 Schiess, I, 773.
76 *Ibid.,* I, 772 f.
77 *Ibid.,* I, 641.
78 G. O. Ritschl, *op. cit.,* p. 129, n. 26.

NOTES TO CHAPTER SEVEN

1 Ludwig Pastor, *Die kirchlichen Reunionsbestrebungen während der Regierung Karls V.* Freiburg: Herder, 1879. See particularly the excellent discussion of Robert Stupperich, *Der Humanismus und die Wiedervereinigung der Konfessionen.* Leipzig: Heinsius, 1936.
2 Cf. John T. McNeill, *Unitive Protestantism.* New York: Abingdon Press-1930, p. 100. Cf. also Alfred Adam, Die Nationalkirche bei Luther in *Archiv für Reformationsgeschichte,* vol. 35 (1938), p. 40 ff.
3 A good discussion of the history of the negotiations of the Curia about the council is to be found in Stephan Ehses' introduction to his edition of The *Acta* of the Council of Trent. (*Concilium Tridentinum,* vol. IV. Freiburg: Herder, 1904, p. XV-CXXXVIII). A survey of the Roman Catholic and Protestant literature about the council is offered by Vincent Schweitzer in his edition of the Tridentine *Tracts* in the same collection. (*Conc. Trid.,* vol. XII, (1930, p. XLVI-LXXX).
4 Cf. the discussion of this issue by Paul Joachimsen, *Das Zeitalter der Reformation* (Propyläen-Weltgeschichte (ed. W. Goetz), vol. III, Berlin: Propyläen Verlag, 1930, p. 175 ff.
5 E. A. (Erlanger edition of Luther's works) 57, 31 f.
6 Karl Brandi, *Kaiser Karl V.* München: Bruckmann, 1937 (English translation, New York.)
7 Cf. Ludwig Pastor, *History of the Popes.* Second ed., vols. IX-XIV. London: Kegan Paul, 1923.
8 Cf. Walter Friedensburg, *Kaiser Karl V und Papst Paul III,* 1534-1549 (=Schriften des Vereins für Reformationsgeschichte, Nr. 153). Leipzig: Heinsius, 1932. Joachim Müller, *Die Politik Kaiser Karls V am Trienter Konzil. Zeitschr* für Kirchengeschichte XLIV (1925), p. 225-275; 338-427.
9 Cf. *Conc. Trid.,* vol. IV (Ehses), p. LXXXIX ff.
10 Cf. *Corpus Reformatorum* (ed. Schulthess), Braunschweig, Schwetschke, 1834-60, vol. II, p. 655. W. A. (Weimar ed. of Luther's works), 50, p. 164.
11 *Conc. Trid.,* vol. IV (Ehses), p. CXI ff.
12 W. A. 50, p. 192-253. Cf. Hans Volz, *Luther's Schmalkaldische Artikel und Melanchthon's Tractatus de potestate papae. Theol. Studien und Kritiken,* vol. 103 (1931), p. 1-70.
13 The official text is printed in *Conc. Trid.,* vol. XII (Schweitzer), p. 208-215.
14 W. A. 50, p. 288-308.

[15] W. A. 50, p. 509-653. The excellent introduction to this edition by F. Cohrs (*ibid.*, p. 488-506) contains a full analysis of Luther's attitude toward the conciliar question.

[16] The first draft and the official text of this Breve are printed in *Conc. Trid.*, vol. IV (Ehses), p. 364-379.

[17] W. A., 54, p. 206-299. See also the introduction by O. Clemen, p. 195-204.

[18] *Admonitio Paterna Pauli III Romani Pontificis in invictissimum Caesarem Carolum V, cum scholiis.* Calvin opera (ed. Baum, Cunitz, Reuss), Braunschweig: Schwetschke, 1868, vol. VII (=Corp. Ref. vol. XXXV), 258-287. There is an English translation by Henry Beveridge in *Tracts Relating to the Reformation by John Calvin,* Edinburgh, Calvin Translation Society, 1844, vol. I, p. 237-286.

[19] *Ibid.*, p. 257 (Tracts, I, p. 257).

[20] *Ibid.*, p. 263 (Tracts I, p. 263).

[21] *Ibid.*, p. 279 ff. (Tracts I, p. 278 f.).

[22] *Acta Synodi Tridentinae cum Antidoto. Calvini Opera,* vol. VII (=*Corpus Ref.*, vol. XXXV), p. 373-506. (Translated in *Tracts,* vol. III. Edinburgh: Calvin Translation Society, 1851).

[23] *Ibid.*, p. 382 f.

[24] *Ibid.*, p. 386 ff.

[25] *Ibid.*, p. 412 (Tracts III, p. 68).

[26] *Corpus Ref.*, vol. VII, p. 637.

[27] *Ibid.*, p. 736.

[28] *Corpus Ref.*, vol. XXVIII, p. 380-468.

[29] I have had access only to a German translation ed. by R. Bendixen (Leipzig: Dörffling, 1884).

[30] Cf. the article by Johannes Kunze in *Realencyclopaedie für prot. Theologie und Kirche.* 3rd. ed., vol. III, p. 796-804.

[31] See the studies by Kurt Dietrich Schmidt, *Studien zur Geschichte des Konzils von Trient.* Tübingen: Mohr, 1925; Hanns Rückert, *Die Rechtfertigungslehre auf dem Konzil von Trient.* Berlin: de Gruyter, 1926.

NOTES TO CHAPTER EIGHT

[1] Cf. Johannes Kühn, *Die Geschichte des Speyer Reichstags,* 1529 (Schriften des Vereins für Reformationsgeschichte, No. 146.) Leipzig, 1929, pp. 257 ff.

[2] Works (Weimar edition), Vol. 39, I, p. 47, 19.

[3] *WA.,* I, pp. 557 f. (Resolutiones disputationum de indulgentiarum virtute, 1518). The passage which is here translated follows upon a reference to Tauler's description of the tortures (*poenae*) of despair in his German sermons.

[4] *WA.,* XVIII, p. 633.

[5] *WA.,* VIII, p. 379. Written at Wartburg castle in 1521!

[6] See the interesting symposium edited by Paul Tillich under the title *Protestantismus als Kritik und Gestaltung,* Darmstadt, 1929; therein especially Tillich's article on "Der Protestantismus als kritisches und gestaltendes Prinzip." In this connection, I should like to refer also to Tillich's book, *Religiöse Verwirklichung,* Berlin, 1930, especially the chapter on "Protestantische Gestaltung." These essays have been incorporated in Tillich's book *The Protestant Era.* Chicago: University of Chicago Press, 1948.

[7] The Luther biography by Rudolph Thiel (2 vols., 2nd ed., Berlin 1936), which depicts the Reformer as a theonomous prophet, makes much of these difficulties.

[8] See for example: Jacques Maritain, *Trois réformateurs (Luther, Descartes, Rousseau),* Paris, 1925; (critically reviewed by Karl Holl in *Revue de Theol.*

et Philos., XV, 1927, pp. 260-70). E. Katzer, *Luther und Kant,* Leipzig, 1910; H. Ostertag, "Luther und Kant," *Neue Kirchliche Zeitschrift,* XXXVI, 1925, pp. 765-807.

⁹ Hort Stephan, *Luther in den Wandlungen seiner Kirche, Giessen,* 1907. See also the discriminating discussion of the problem by Adolf von Harnack, *Dogmengeschichte,* 4th ed., Tübingen, 1909, III, pp. 808 ff.

¹⁰ "Beantwortung der Frage: was ist Aufklärung?" in *Berlinische Monatsschrift,* III, 1784, pp. 481-94.

¹¹ F. Schleiermacher, *The Christian Faith.* English translation by H. R. Mackintosh and J. S. Stewart. Edinburgh, 1928, I, p. 63.

¹² Cf. Ernst Troeltsch, *Protestantisches Christentum und Kirche,* pp. 624 ff. The changes of the Protestant church concept are well described by Carl Damour, *Die Epochen des Protestantismus,* Bern, 1935.

¹³ *Works,* V, p. 9, quoted by John M. Mecklin in his important book, *The Story of American Dissent,* New York, 1934, p. 342.

NOTES TO CHAPTER NINE

¹ E. Bevan, *Symbolism and Belief,* London, 1938, p. 174.

NOTES TO CHAPTER ELEVEN

¹ This concept which Harnack made popular as a description of the nature of Roman Catholicism is used by *Friedrich Heiler* as the key to the understanding of the Roman Church in his monumental work *Der Katholizismus. Seine Idee und seine Erscheinung* (München: Reinhardt, 1923). He interprets Roman Catholicism by viewing it as a complex of seven different types of religion: It is a religion of primitive superstition; a legalistic religion; a political-social religion; a rationalistic religion of theological doctrines; an esoteric mystery-religion; an evangelical religion of salvation; and a mystical religion.

² Karl Adam, The Spirit of Catholicism. New York: Macmillan, 1930, p. 18.

³ Adam, *op. cit.,* p. 19.

⁴ Adam, *op. cit.,* p. 124.

⁵ Pastoral Letter of Cardinal Katschthaler, Archbishop of Salzburg (2. Feb. 1905). Cf. Karl Mirbt, Quellen zur Geschichte des Papsttums. 4th ed. Tübingen: Mohr, 1924, p. 498 f.

⁶ Adam, *op. cit.,* p. 186.

⁷ Thomas Aquinas, *In Symbol.,* a. 9, *Comp. theol.,* c. 147.

⁸ Thomas Aquinas, *Summa th.* III, q. 64, a. 2, ad 3.

⁹ Abbot Ansgar Vonier, *Das Christliche Menschenbild in der Liturgie und seine übernaturliche Verwirklichung im Sakrament* in Otto Iserland, *Die Kirche Christi.* Einsiedeln-Köln: Benzinger, n.d., (probably 1938/39), p. 81.

¹⁰ Dom Anselme Robeyns, O.S.B., *Der Kult der Kirche in seiner Bedeutung und Gestaltungskraft für das soziale Leben,* in Iserland, *op. cit.,* p. 102.

¹¹ *Ibid.,* p. 107.

¹² Theodore Wedel, *The Coming Great Church.* New York: Macmillan, 1946, p. 90.

¹³ I am aware of the fact that the classical Protestant Confessions (those of Lutheranism, Calvinism, Anglicanism and Methodism) state the phrase I am referring to as follows: "Where the Word is rightly preached *and the sacraments are rightly administered,* there is the church." It may therefore be expected that I treat also the Protestant interpretation of the sacraments. Such a discussion might be regarded as particularly desirable, because it would illuminate the nature of Protestantism in special contrast to Roman Catholic sacramentalism. It is my conviction that there is no characteristically Protestant sacramentalism that can be regarded as the *"pendant"* of the Roman Catholic

teaching and practice. The signs of the sacraments celebrated in Protestant churches, Baptism and the Lord's Supper, are effective only because of the Word and it is the Word that constitutes the true nature of the sacrament. In the sacrament, Christ is therefore present in no way different from his presence in the Word. Only the manner in which his presence is realized or apprehended is of a special nature. The celebration of the sacraments is designed to show that Christ is present to each individual only in so far as he enters into the community of the church (Baptism) and in so far as he lives in spiritual communion with his fellow members (the Lord's Supper). The Lutheran and the Anglican conceptions of the sacraments do not contradict this interpretation but they imply something additional due to the fact that they have preserved certain features of Catholic sacramentalism.

In order to explain the nature of Protestantism in contradistinction to the spirit of Roman Catholicism, it is therefore sufficient to emphasize the central significance of the Word and it is not necessary to deal with the sacraments in a special way.

[14] The words *"and heard"* are not mentioned in the creeds, but the specific teachings of the Reformers demand that they should be implied. The writings of Luther and Calvin abound in expositions of the right hearing of the Word.

[15] W. A. 40, I; 589, 8.

[16] W. A. 10, III; 329.

[17] W. A. 10, I; 335.

NOTES TO CHAPTER TWELVE

[1] Adam, *op. cit.,* p. 8.

[2] Professor Adam writes very bluntly (*op. cit.,* p. 163: "There is only one answer to the question whether other communions have not also a vocation and a power to save men, and the Church is quite intolerant about it. For the very reason that these communions have set themselves up against the original unity of the brethren in faith and love, they appear to Catholic consciousness as institutions which have not arisen out of the spirit of Jesus, and therefore as purely human and even anti-Christian creations. The Church cannot but anathematize them and she will continue to do so until the Lord comes." Professor Adam is able to reconcile with this statement a willingness to regard non-Roman churches as Christian. In the general context of the quotation just cited he writes also (p. 159 f): "The Church would belie her own deepest essence . . ., if she ever were to recognize some collateral and antagonistic Christian church as her sister and as possessing equal rights with herself. She can recognize the historical importance of such churches. She can designate them as Christian communions, yes, even as Christian churches, but never as the Church of Christ." I suppose that what is here meant is that non-Roman churches can be regarded as "Christian" only in the sense that they are "heretically Christian". This implies that a conversation between Protestants and Catholics about Christianity is possible only on the condition that the truth of Roman Catholicism is taken for granted. Roman Catholics must under all circumstances refuse to admit that any other form of Christianity but their own can be true. It is therefore quite hopeless to engage them in mutual search for the proper understanding of the Christian faith. Their dogmatism permits no debate. There, in this unrelenting arbitrary pride, the Protestant sees the root of the dividedness of the Christian church. For he regards it as impossible that any human understanding of the Christian gospel can ever be absolutely final.

[3] Mirbt, *op. cit.,* p. 465 f.

[4] Cf. Adam, *op. cit.,* p. 39.

[5] Cf. the discussion of the question in Joseph Lortz, *Die Reformation in Deutschland* (Freiburg: Herder, 1939-1940) vol. I, p. 173-177. (He states [p. 173]): *"Das System des Okhamismus ist wurzelhaft unkatholisch".* This is a modern dogmatic but not an historical judgment. This holds true also for the very interesting opinion, which opens strange vistas into the mind of modern Roman Catholicism, that "Luther overcame in his own thinking a Catholicism which was not Catholic" (p. 176).

[6] Lortz, *op. cit.,* vol. I, p. 120. (All quotations from this work are translated from the original German.) The sentences here quoted are rendered in a rather free translation. At this particular point Professor Lortz does not express himself very clearly, perhaps because he found it rather difficult to give adequate recognition to the significance of personal religiousness. In order to avoid misunderstandings, I therefore quote also the German text: "Das Problem der christlichen Gesamthaltung wird nur gelöst im Ineinander von objektivem Heilsgeschehen und subjektiver Gesinnung. Das ganze Christentum ist nur im Zusammenhang beider Elemente gesichert jedoch dergestalt, dass das Gesinnungsmässige des Menschen nicht so schwer ins Gewicht fallen kann wie die objektive Kraft und das objektive Geschehen des corpus Christi mysticum. Andererseits ist es doch, gemäss der Predigt Jesu vom ersten Bussruf an, die bessere, innere Gerechtigkeit der Menschen die ausschlaggebend ist. Je nachdem diese letztere Verpflichtung für sich allein genommen wird oder nicht, entsteht die protestantische Haltung. Die Übersteigerung des persönlich—religiösen Ernstes bedeutet häretische Gefahr."

[7] *Ibid.,* p. 10.

[8] *Ibid.,* p. 229.

[9] *Ibid.,* p. 162.

[10] *Ibid.,* p. 164.

[11] *Ibid.,* p. 402.

[12] *Ibid.,* p. 190 f.

[13] *Ibid.,* p. 394.

[14] *Ibid.,* p. 231.

[15] *Ibid.,* p. 184 f.

[16] *Ibid.,* p. 436

[17] Robert William Dale, Protestantism. London: Milton Publishing League, 1877, p. 38.

[18] *Ibid.,* p. 34 f.

[19] Adam, *op. cit.,* p. 98 ff.

[20] Encyclical *Vehementer,* February 11, 1906.

[21] Dale, *op. cit.,* p. 91.

[22] Daniel T. Jenkins, *The Nature of Catholicity.* London: Faber and Faber, 1942, p. 112.

NOTES TO CHAPTER THIRTEEN

[1] *Works* V, 19. See the chapter on "The Nature of Protestantism", also the article by Robert H. Nichols on "The Influence of the American Environment on the Conception of the Church," *Church History,* vol. XI (1942), 181 ff.

NOTES TO CHAPTER FOURTEEN

[1] Cf. E. E. Aubrey in John Knox (ed.), *Religion and the Present Crisis.* Chicago: University of Chicago Press, 1942, p. 16.

[2] Cf. Ralph H. Gabriel, *The Course of American Democratic Thought.* New York: Ronald Press, 1940, p. 18.

[3] Cf. Gabriel, *op. cit.*, p. 36.
[4] Cf. Gabriel, *op. cit.*, p. 149 f.
[5] Cf. Gabriel, *op. cit.*, p. 330.

NOTES TO CHAPTER SEVENTEEN

[1] Shailer Mathews, *The Faith of Modernism* (New York: Macmillan, 1925), p. 23.

[2] See the article by W. W. Fenn on "Liberalism" in the *American Journal of Theology* (1913), pp. 509 ff.

[3] See Karl Barth's essay on "Das Wort in der Theologie von Schleiermacher bis Ritschl" in his book *Die Theologie und die Kirche* (München: Kaiser, 1928), pp. 190 ff.

NOTES TO CHAPTER NINETEEN

[1] E.g., H. N. Wieman, and J. S. Bixler, whom I consider as "radical theological liberals" differ profoundly from each other. And Emil Brunner, Reinhold Niebuhr, and Anders Nygren, whom I regard as furtherers of the program of the "new evangelicalism" (they themselves may not think so), can certainly not be said to hold the same views. The difference of the individual opinions of "ecumenical theologians" is so obvious that it hardly needs to be mentioned.

[2] I do not mean to suggest that this task is the *exclusive* privilege of American theologians, for I recognize that it is presented also to the theologians of the churches of other lands; I am addressing myself here particularly to Americans.

Index

309

15535